Dastardly Discourse

Dastardly Discourse

Rescuing Rhetorical Capital
from Indecency and Incivility

MEG GORZYCKI

RESOURCE *Publications* · Eugene, Oregon

DASTARDLY DISCOURSE
Rescuing Rhetorical Capital from Indecency and Incivility

Resource Publications
An Imprint of Wipf and Stock Publishers
199 W. 8th Ave., Suite 3
Eugene, OR 97401

www.wipfandstock.com

PAPERBACK ISBN: 978-1-7252-6223-2
HARDCOVER ISBN: 978-1-7252-6224-9
EBOOK ISBN: 978-1-7252-6225-6

Manufactured in the U.S.A.   03/09/20

Contents

Preface

Scratch the surface of current events and history and you will always find a good story—in fact, you will find several stories for the same episode, each recited by people who believe they know what is going on, even though their accounts are very different. Very little about us has changed over thousands of years of civilization. We have always had a good story to tell about who we are, why we are here, and what we ought to feel, think, and do. Our stories consistently concern power and wealth, and we have always told ourselves stories to justify why some have it and some do not. Our words announce what we believe and feel, even if these things are untrue. We tell ourselves stories to rationalize all things. We are creatures with existential concerns, and we have used language for thousands of years to understand the cosmos and our place in it. We are also creatures with material concerns who have used language to justify our ambitions and destroy those who interfere with them. We have used language to inspire, discover, develop, and imagine. History teaches us that the stories we tell and the words we use profoundly affect the world we create and the mind we inhabit.

I began this essay as a response to research that my colleagues and I conducted at a four-year public university.[1] We investigated the reading proficiency of undergraduates, administered a survey of their reading habits and attitudes towards reading and reading instruction, and also administered a survey of faculty habits and attitudes towards reading and reading instruction. The research produced alarming data. Not only does the average college undergraduate read at a level far less than what the National Assessment of Adult Literacy calls "proficient," but many students and faculty do not seem to care very much about that. Apparently, for the sake of removing barriers to students' persistence to degree, some colleges and universities are not asking students to read much, read critically, or to develop and fortify their rhetorical capital.

---

1. See: Gorzycki, et al., 2016; Howard et al., 2018; and Gorzycki, et al., 2020.

The findings of the study led me to imagine a world wherein reading and rhetorical skills atrophied as a result of indifference and accommodation. I thought about what would happen if the gatekeepers of literacy and rhetorical capital—the skills of listening carefully, focusing patiently, critiquing information fairly and thoroughly, crafting erudite and logical arguments, and so forth—stopped holding people to high standards of communication and critical consumption of propaganda. What would happen to scholarship? What would happen to democracy? What would happen in the market? What would happen to our professions? What would happen to our civility? What would happen to our souls?

I do not have to imagine anything. Our rhetorical capital is being depleted all the time. Our communication often leaves us ill-informed, distracted from serious issues by sensation, and unsympathetic to people whose voices do not echo our own. Our narratives and discourse encourage an infantile and dualistic view of ourselves and the world. They coax judgement before intelligent questions are asked and sound evidence is presented.

Communication and our standards for rhetorical proficiency have changed over the last 60 years. Digital shorthand replaces whole sentences. Letters that once were rich in complex and sophisticated discourse are replaced by abbreviations peppered with emogis. Elementary schools have relaxed expectations for students' mastery of writing, grammar, spelling, and penmanship. Electronic media is a stream of endless commercials that tells us we can purchase our way out of mediocrity, boredom, misery, and low self-esteem. Colleges and universities award diplomas to students who can barely read at the 10th grade level. Corporate news media are long on spectacle but short on substance. Elected officials, who, in theory represent people worthy of representing us, fill the airwaves with hate speech and distortions of truth so regularly that people feel like they have been left to the wolves.

The technology of communication has improved over the last 60 years, but our humanity has not changed anywhere near as radically. Cellular devices and satellites have made it easier to stay in touch with others, and digital platforms and software have made it easier to access information, data, and research. Technology has also increased our appetite for speedy communication and immediate answers and feedback. It has made it possible for people who lack education and expertise to represent themselves on the Internet as if they were authorities on the issues. It has also made it possible for images to be altered to give the appearance that people were in certain places doing certain things, when in fact they were never in that place doing those things. In addition, technology has facilitated the expansion of media outlets that all compete for audiences and commercial sponsorship. As audience interests tend to lean towards the sensational and unsophisticated, programming, including that for news shows and commentary, makes the adjustment to make a buck.

My interest in rhetorical capital is more than academic. Whether we go to college or not, our values, attitudes, and behavior are all influenced by the things we hear and see. Much of what our senses absorb is propaganda in the form of advertising, entertainment, and political rhetoric. We live in a world where others want to persuade us all the time. I am concerned about whether we have enough rhetorical capital to recognize dastardly discourse when we hear it. I am concerned about whether we have control of the narratives that make us who we are, and have the skills and will to resist and confront propaganda that infects our spirituality and humanity with hate, fear, greed, vengeance, and indifference to those who are poor and vulnerable.

We are creatures of stories, and we use myths and narratives to explain our origins, our purpose, what we should value, who and what we should love, glorify, fear, despise, trust, and obey. Narratives from the lips of demagogues can create prejudices against people whom we have never met, and confidence in things that are patently false. I am concerned that our national narratives, which tend to put the United States on a pedestal above all others, may sabotage our spirituality and humanity. I am concerned that in the name of pragmatism, our narratives become deaf to the spiritual needs of society. I am concerned that in the name of God, we will become beasts utterly devoured by our own nationalism, militarism and materialism.

As an educator, it is in my DNA to believe that we can make the world a better place by learning the truth about ourselves and each other, and how to play nice in the sand box. As a spiritual person raised in the Catholic faith, I understand the power of ritual, pastoral instruction, and prophetic missives to arouse the conscience, and encourage a life lived for causes higher than oneself. As a person who sees the failures of education, news media, church sermons, and politics to fortify our rhetorical capital, I feel the tug of cynicism. There are no miracle cures for impoverished rhetoric and dastardly discourse. There are only individuals and their commitment to critique their own narratives, hold their children to high standards of discourse, and speak truth to power. It would be grand if such individuals outnumbered the people who are careless in their discourse, unconcerned about their narratives, and do little to teach their children to read, think, and live for causes higher than themselves. It would be grand to live in a society where denial of our shortcomings was not epidemic.

Acknowledgements

The gumption to write so critically about the way Americans talk to each other and their global neighbors comes from childhood experiences, wherein most adults were on the same page when it came to teaching kids to speak honestly and respectfully. In that world, parents openly corrected children who were vulgar or verbally abusive, even the children were not their own. The gumption comes also from early-in-life encounters with the prophetic tradition, wherein there is no deference to color, creed, class, or gender; there is only reverence for the dignity of life, the commitment to serve causes greater than ourselves, and the truth. Thank you Mrs. Meyer, Mrs. Owens, Sr. Vincent, Sr. Bernadette, Sr. Methodius, Sr. Virgene, Sr. Lea, Fr. McCarthy, Mr. Skinner, Mr. Bender, Mrs. Savage, Mrs. Hoffman, Ms. Blum, Mr. Falor, Mr. Sylvester, and Ms. Koopmans for taking child development seriously, and for holding students in your care to high standards of discourse and respect for causes greater than ourselves.

Chapter 1

An Introduction to Dastardly Discourse

WORDS MATTER

What do Jesus of Nazareth, Jon Stewart, Howard Beale, and my mom have in common? Need a hint? OK, let's explore who is who. Jesus of Nazareth was a Jewish teacher of spiritual wisdom who lived in Roman-occupied Palestine, ruled by Tiberius Caesar. His life and death have for millions of people become a source of moral guidance and salvation. Jon Stewart is an American comedian, writer, actor, and former host of the *Daily Show* on Comedy Central. His life and activism may have become a source of spiritual wisdom for some, but he is more widely known for his humor and commentary on the hypocrisy and irony of American politics and culture. Howard Beale is a fictional news anchorman who is a central character in the film, *Network*.[1] Beale is the angry prophetic voice against television's manipulation of public opinion who screams, "I'm as mad as hell and I'm not going to take it anymore!" He's the guy who directs viewers to throw their TVs out the window. My mom is the woman who gave birth to me and my five siblings. She worships Jesus, chuckled at some of Jon Stewart's sarcasm, and thought Beale was too crazy to watch.

Still cannot see the common thread? Alright, let's try some quotations. Jesus said to his disciples, "A man is not defiled by what enters his mouth, but by what comes out of it" (Matt. 15:11). In a discussion with CNN's Tucker Carlson (host of *Crossfire*), Jon Stewart criticized CNN's news programs for being too friendly to corporate interests. Stewart pleaded with Tucker,

---

1. *Network*, directed by Sidney Lumet (1976; USA: MGM).

"Stop, stop, stop, stop hurting America." He continued, "You know. . . you have a responsibility to the public discourse, and you fail miserably."[2] Howard Beale cried out to his audience:

> Listen to me: Television is not the truth! Television is a God-damned amusement park! Television is a circus, a carnival, a traveling troupe of acrobats, storytellers, dancers, singers, jugglers, side-show freaks, lion tamers, and football players. We're in the boredom-killing business! So if you want the truth. . . Go to God! Go to your gurus! Go to yourselves! Because that's the only place you're ever going to find any real truth.

My mom? Well, she warned her kids, "If you use that kind of language again, I'm going to wash your mouth out with soap!" And she did.

Each of these individuals is telling us that words matter. They are telling us that it is not right to cause pain and suffering with our stories and comments, and that it is wrong to lie. They are telling us that our words are used all too often to anesthetize our minds, and to distract us from what really matters. Jesus, Jon, Howard, and mom all understood that we can create a hell on Earth by what we say to each other, or we can create communities in which truth and benevolence prevail.

Much of our lives passes before we realize that what was in front of our eyes was a projection of what we wanted to see. Further, many of us have lived with illusions instead of truth, and believed that we were in possession of our thoughts and personal narratives when in fact we were not. Some have argued that illusions are social necessities. They give people a sense of well-being, and they neutralize their desire to rebel and disrupt the peace. Many of us live according internal narratives that contradict the faith we espouse. The stories we tell ourselves about who we are and how we should live are powerful in the sense that they determine the quality of our lives and the lives of others. The scenarios of our lives are often shaped by social norms and persuasive discourse without our awareness. Because narratives and myths are so powerful, they will get substantial attention in this book.

Rhetoric and how our lives are shaped by public discourse matters very much to people who take their spirituality, faith in a sacred purpose for life, and moral excellence seriously. In the U.S., faith and spirituality are no small matter. A 2018 study found that 80 percent of Americans say that they believe in God or a higher power that is a spiritual force.[3] In addition, approximately two thirds of those who believe in God talk to God and believe that God determines what happens to them at least some of the time. The

2. Willis, "Jon Stewart on Crossfire," para. 1–10.
3. Pew Research Center, "When Americans Say," para. 3–6.

study also reveals that 53 percent of those who claim no religion believe in a higher power or spiritual force. Americans are, however, divided on the matter of whether a belief in God is necessary in order for a person to be moral, with roughly one half of Americans on either side of the question.[4]

For many, religion plays an important role in the narratives that provide people with a purpose in life and a moral compass to get through a world of deception and vice. Spiritually grounded individuals understand that words play a profound role in how they interpret the world, and blaze their moral pathways. Some of the most eloquent and charismatic individuals who speak "in the name of God," or with executive or expert authority on matters, speak not for the sake of advancing respect, empathy, and justice, but for the sake of replacing our own spirituality and conscience with their agendas and world views.

Being in possession of our own conscience requires us to objectively examine our beliefs and where they come from. It demands honest inventories of what influences our thinking, and the extent to which we adjust our hearts and minds so that we fit neatly into the social groups we love and revere. It means acknowledging that just because we go to church does not mean that we are not hypnotized by commercial and political propaganda. It requires a clear understanding of what theologian Paul Tillich called the "ultimate concern," or the thing that answers our most profound existential questions about life, purpose, and destiny—the thing that brings all other considerations in our lives into its orbit.[5] Everyone, regardless of creed or spirituality, benefits from knowing that lots of people would very much like to manage our beliefs and define our "ultimate concern" in ways that may hurt us.

Propaganda has been around for hundreds of years, and has been transformed into a deadly science. At the turn of the twentieth century, Edward Bernays, the nephew of Sigmund Freud, used his uncle's ideas to refine and create new strategies sway voters and consumers. He asserted that people must be manipulated for their own good. Bernays argued that democracy depended the success of an invisible elite to shape public opinion and habits, so that people would be compliant and still feel like they were thinking for themselves.[6]

Bernays held that most people are unaware of their own motivations, and that businesses could improve their profits by understanding and exploiting these motives. He made a fortune showing corporations including

4. Pew Research Center, "Worldwide, Many See Belief," para. 1–2.

5. Tillich, *Dynamics of Faith*, pp. 1–34.

6. Bernays, *Propaganda*, p. 9.

General Electric, American Tobacco Company, Proctor and Gamble, and CBS, how to do this. He added to his treasure by consulting with government officials who created political propaganda that targeted foreign countries. Their goal was to convince the masses that unions and reformers were all communist dupes. Bernays helped orchestrate campaigns that allowed United Fruit and other US companies to exploit and oppress our neighbors south of the border for decades.[7]

Bernays once stated that, "The public is not cognizant of the real value of education, and does not realize that education as a social force is not receiving the kind of attention it has the right to expect in a democracy."[8] Bernays held that schools and universities should be highly responsive to social evolution, and craft instruction that imparted society's highest ideals and values. At present, the public still does not realize the real value of education. The half-hearted effort to cultivate rhetorical capital and critical discourse in our schools and universities suggests that education in the U.S. is largely vocational in its mission. As colleges and universities reduce general education requirements in the liberal arts and as majors in the arts and humanities has waned, it seems that educators themselves are retreating from the idea that studies in ourselves, the human condition, virtue, and the individual's moral obligations are expendable in the academy's rush to produce the next generation of scientists, engineers, and entrepreneurs.

RHETORICAL CAPITAL

When we think of the word "rhetoric" many of us have negative feelings. The word is associated with unproductive rambling or the blathering of intellectuals who like to hear their own voices. We may think of politicians who are asked a question in a debate or press conference, and who dodge the question by taking up a different topic. Getting past the negative connotations of rhetoric is important, because when used wisely, it can do a great deal of good.

In the classical sense, rhetoric is persuasive oratory. It includes public testimonies, debates, and speeches. In ancient Greece, it was generally understood that the function of rhetoric was to convince audiences that certain assertions were true and virtuous. In their use of syntax, tone, cadence, and semantics, speakers took care to make choices that maximized audiences' receptivity to the message.[9] Not everyone in the ancient world

---

7. See Tye's *The Father of Spin* for a synopsis of Bernays and his enterprise.

8. Bernays, *Propaganda*, p. 121.

9. Olmstead, *Rhetoric*, p. 10–11.

thought that the art of rhetoric was a good thing. Aristotle only tolerated it, as it often whipped up the public's emotions and left listeners vulnerable to the eloquent deception of scoundrels. Plato thought it best that the masses refrain from debate and consult with experts when confronted with moral and legal quandaries, and Socrates, who detested the demagogues' abuse of rhetoric, cherished it as a means of knowing and improving oneself.[10]

Hundreds of years ago, grammar, logic, and rhetoric were the heart of liberal arts education in the medieval trivium. It was essentially a study of the mind, because words represented the quality of thought, reason, logic, and values; and, it exposed private beliefs about the world and morality.[11] American schools and universities borrowed heavily from medieval education, as can be detected in their commitment to teach the liberal arts throughout the existence of the American university.

Rhetoric is frequently used to perpetuate our national narrative. National narratives are typically a blend of legends, myths, and facts that teach members of society about who they are, where they came from, what they must be, and what legitimizes their ambitions. National narratives are often filled with sanitized versions of the nation's past, and heroes who personify the virtues and ideals that the nation values the most. National narratives are in some ways persuasive speech, because they often have the effect of convincing people that their nation is exceptional and deserves to have greater wealth, privilege, and power than others around the globe. National narratives and myths have several functions. They reinforce a sense of national identity in the face of immigration and diversification of the nation's population. They arouse consensus for national actions, such as war or radical changes in the law, and they transmit ideas about what it means to be a responsible citizen.[12] National narratives and myths may or may not be grounded in accurate accounts of the past, yet, they are for many people a source of pride and justification for their attitudes and prejudices.

Experts in rhetoric recognize social narratives and propaganda in art, architecture, and literature.[13] Rhetoric can be literal and subjected to criticism based on the logic of its assertions, or it can be literary and figurative, and subject to criticism based on interpretations and subjective associations.[14] Rhetoric is a product of circumstance and context. It responds to

---

10. See Wardy, *Birth of Rhetoric* for an introduction to rhetoric.

11. Joseph, *Trivium: The Liberal Arts*, p. viii.

12. Bouchard, "National Myths," pp. 276–297.

13. Meyer, *What is Rhetoric*, pp. xiv–xv.

14. Flecha, et al., "Theory of Communicative Action," pp. 109–127, and see: Habermas, *The Theory of Communicative Action*.

what exists, what is *perceived* to exit, and it often frames the perimeters of what is possible.[15]

"Capital" connotes something of worth. It is associated with assets and resources that can be augmented, diminished, invested, squandered, or devalued. Rhetorical capital is essentially a construct that regards many aspects of communication. It has been defined as, "the aggregate persuasive resources inherent in entities."[16] In this sense, rhetorical capital refers to the particulars of the spoken words, text, or images that influence people's thoughts and motivate their behavior. This kind of capital might be the startling jolt we get when we see a photograph of children shot dead by a crazed gunman, as the image arouses the will to punish or extend compassion. It might be a catchy jingle giving us permission to indulge our cravings for pizza. Rhetorical capital may refer to the artifacts that are placed around a public speaker, such as flags, or statues, as they may stir sentiments that open us to the speaker's message.

In this book, rhetorical capital includes more than elements of text and imagery. It here refers to the cognitive tools, metacognitive skills, and epistemological beliefs that readers, viewers, and listeners bring to the table of reading, viewing, and listening. It is the sum total of the mental strategies, intellectual habits, principles, values, and self-discipline we use to interpret information and to determine its significance. Thus rhetorical capital is not just stimuli in the environment, it is the set of tools or "capital" we use to decode and evaluate the stimuli.

Cognition pertains to thinking. It regards our capacity to synthesize, evaluate, analyze, make inferences, identify implications, judge the quality of evidence offered for assertions, detect assumptions, assess relevance, spot biases, and apprehend the significance of information.[17] Metacognition refers to our ability to monitor our own thinking as we are thinking.[18] It is concerned with sensitivity to our own attention span, the awareness of our own visceral responses to what we read, see, and hear, and with the level of our comprehension as we read and listen.

Epistemology refers to what we believe about the nature of knowing and knowledge. In general, those who believe that knowledge is a matter of clear "rights and wrongs," or clear "true" and "false," represent

15. See Poulakos, "Toward a Sophistic Definition of Rhetoric." Also see Toye's *Rhetoric*, pp. 7–30.

16. Ish-Shalom, "The Rhetorical Capital of Theories," p. 281.

17. For a substantial discussion on the roles of thinking in reading see Forrest-Pressley and Walker' *Cognition, Metacognition, and Reading.*

18. See Garner's *Metacognition and Reading Comprehension* for an introduction to the subject.

an unsophisticated level of epistemological thinking. They tend to believe knowledge is easy to obtain, and rely heavily on authoritative sources, such as teachers, textbooks, and officials to tell them the facts.[19] Those who represent high levels tend to believe that knowledge, right, wrong, true, and false are sometimes ambiguous, complex, and nuanced, and that it takes a great deal of effort to know something with absolute certainty. Those at the higher level of epistemological beliefs tend to see that knowledge is constructed over time and sometimes changes with new insight and evidence.[20] As will be explored in this text, there is reason to be concerned that educators, journalists, politicians, and religious leaders are not doing enough to help people grow beyond lower levels of epistemological development.

The rationale for expanding the definition of rhetorical capital is that the skills that are used to decode, analyze, and critique rhetoric are often the same tools required to develop and disseminate rhetoric. The logic is simple: If you want to catch a thief, think like a thief. Effective rhetorical design is sensitive, for example, to the audience's needs, the implications of words, potential emotional hooks that might influence listeners, and when to omit certain facts to win somebody's trust. In short, an expansive definition of rhetoric capital gives us the ability to see rhetoric from the author's or speaker's point of view, and thus to anticipate potential efforts to influence or manipulate us.

THE NEUROLOGICAL LENS

Building rhetorical capital is more than a psychological endeavor. Like all development of language skills, it has important neurological components. Reading proficiency, for example, relies upon the coordinated operations of several regions of the brain. These regions orchestrate attention, visual processing, coordination of eye movements, memory, mental associations, de-coding, and imagination that, when combined, produce meaning.[21] Even in grade school, we understood that people read things in order to learn things. What is not so transparent is that the act of reading itself *creates* neurological pathways that improve our capacity to store vocabulary, think analytically, empathize, associate ideas and experiences stored in our

---

19. Perry's *Forms of Ethical and Intellectual Development in the College Years* laid the foundation for modern theories about how epistemology develops. As with many developmental models of behavior, change is predicated by cognitive dissonance that can be leveraged by formal education to provoke growth and sophistication.

20. See Kitchener and King, "The Reflective Judgment Model."

21. See both Wolf, *Reader Come Home* and Dehaene *Reading in the Brain*.

memories, and create new knowledge. In other words, reading builds the individual's knowledge base while constructing anatomical networks that enable additional learning and word processing.

With voluminous reading comes the acquisition of new vocabulary. A new word acts like a multisided puzzle piece that has many options for connecting itself to new and old experiences, ideas, concepts, and words. Children who have never seen or ridden in a subway, for example, are likely to understand the concept of "subway" if their memory of "train" and "underground" can be accessed. Vocabulary growth is associated with knowledge building and discerning how the meaning of words is shaped by the context in which the words appear.[22] Reading is also associated with the capacity to imagine things from other people's perspective, and so contributes substantially to the development of empathy.[23]

Reading is also positively correlated with the maturation of the frontal lobe of the cerebrum, which is involved in executive brain functions including impulse control, judgement, memory, problem-solving, and communication.[24] Functional imaging of brain activity illustrates that children who are unskilled readers have less of the neurological networking between regions of the brain that children with highly developed reading skills possess.[25] This neurological networking is essential in cognition. Developing literacy and improving our reading skills has a powerful impact on the structure of our brains. Even as adults, the development of reading skills causes changes in brain structure, whereby new neurological networks are created, and new possibilities for rhetorical processing are forged.[26] Is it any wonder, then, that one of the best things parents can do for their children is to get them to read at a very early age, and that one of the best things to do to help the aging brain stay sharp is to read?

OBEDIENT EYES AND EARS

The neurological, cognitive, metacognitive, and epistemological aspects of rhetoric are not the only factors that affect the way individuals understand public discourse and rhetoric. The milieu in which public discourse takes place also impacts us. Cultural norms and peer pressure often play powerful roles in what we are willing to believe, how we think about something,

22. Cunningham and Stanovich, "What Reading does for the Mind," pp. 138–139.
23. Wolf, *Reader, Come Home*, pp. 42–53.
24. Houston, et al., "Reading Skill and Structure," pp. 5–6.
25. Keller and Just, "Altering Cortical Connectivity."
26. Skeide, "Learning to Read."

and what we value. The pressure that society exerts on individuals to be politically correct, or to think and feel in ways to validate one's identity in a given group is very real. Sometimes without being conscious of it, people say things that they have never thought about just to "fit in."

Rhetoric functions in many ways. It frames the way we define problems and influences our receptivity to new ideas and perspectives. It impacts the way we judge alternative solutions and our perception of the urgency to act. Rhetoric influences the way we decide who has a legitimate voice in matters, and who does not. It colors our view of which facts are relevant to our lives and decisions and which are not. The rhetoric we absorb from teachers' lessons, priestly sermons, political speeches, advertising, newscasts, social media, news commentary, literature, and entertainment delivers more than information. It tells who us deserves our attention and empathy and who does not. It shapes our understanding of "good guys" and "bad guys." It presses into our psyches attitudes about what is real and true and what is illusionary and false. It has the potential to convince us that black is white and white is black.

To illustrate the point that we are conditioned to think in certain ways, consider the rhetoric of Adolph Hitler and George W. Bush.[27]

Readers who have just experienced a visceral reaction—either towards these two men, or to the fact that the author placed these two names in the same sentence—may do well to pause and consider whether their reaction was one of piqued intellectual curiosity, or displeasure about the author's potential bias. That simple exercise may be helpful to understand the extent to which one is open to new ideas. In any event, both Hitler and Bush were powerful men who were interested in creating the world in the image of what they thought world ought to be. Both used rhetoric that was pragmatic in the sense that it defined national problems in material ways that made sense to people, and offered material solutions to these material problems. Both used rhetoric that was romantic in the sense that they used imagery that portrayed their nations as heroic and noble, and both used rhetoric filled with promises of prosperity.

Some people get upset when others compare Hitler with American presidents. In the case of Hitler and Bush, readers may argue that since the worlds these two men created were very different, any comparison is automatically unfair and ridiculous. Bush did not build death camps and murder six million Jews, nor exterminate hundreds of thousands of others based on their ethnicity, sexuality, disability, or political affiliations. Bush did not invade countries on all sides of the US with the intention of

27. Thompson, "Magic for a People," 350–71.

creating "lebensraum" (living space) for US citizens in which conquered people would become U.S. slaves. By putting rhetorical capital to work, and by putting aside our assumptions about who should be compared and who should not be compared, however, one may see that Hitler and Bush did have several things in common. To understand this is to better understand that throughout history, ambitious men have routinely behaved in similar ways, and thus, history is a picture of the human condition that remains relatively fixed regardless of time and place.

Both Hitler and Bush believed that their nations were superior to all others, and both held that their cultural way of life represented the pinnacle of human civilization. Both men defined the source of their nation's problems as a certain group of people.[28] Both used rhetoric to demonize the enemy, and rendered the humanity of enemies irrelevant. Both men saw their nations as global saviors, and both used pre-emptive strikes to accomplish their goals. Both were determined to kill in order to secure natural resources they believed were vital to their nations, and for both, oil was a cardinal resource of interest.[29] Both Hitler and Bush claimed to have divine or supernatural support for their causes.[30]

Why does this comparison matter? What matters is that many of us have been conditioned to believe that one of these men in the comparison is evil incarnate, while the other is not. What matters is that in our history lessons and public discourse, many of us have never been invited to think about the universal characteristics of the abuse of power. What matters is that, whenever we exempt someone from critical analysis, we essentially hold those individuals to lower standards of morality than the ones we demonize the most.

Our schools do not teach certain things; our ministers do not preach about certain things; our journalists do not report certain things; and, our civic leaders do not investigate or speak about certain things. With each missing fact, and each unrepresented perspective comes the temptation to think that we have the full picture. In the case of Hitler and Bush, an honest inventory of their behavior illuminates the reality that "good guys" and "bad

28. Hitler blamed the Jews, Bolsheviks, Jehovah's Witnesses, and homosexuals, for Germany's crisis (*Mein Kampf*), while Bush blamed Islamic Fundamentalists, terrorists, and "un-American" Americans for the U.S. crisis.

29. Hitler's campaign at Stalingrad (winter 1942) aimed to knock out Soviet defense in the oil-rich region of the Caspian Sea. Bush's war against Iraq (2003) is a chapter in U.S. oil interests in the Middle East; see: Muttitt, *Fuel on the Fire*.

30. Colorful and well-documented discussions of these two men's world view and rhetoric are found in: Draper's *Dead Certain*, Fritz, Keefer, and Nyhan's *All the President's Spin*, Haas' *George W. Bush, War Criminal*, Weikart's *Hitler's Religion*, and Bullock's *A Study in Tyranny*.

guys" often have a lot in common. It suggests that, regardless of time, place, and form of government, people with power often share prejudices and assumptions about their entitlement to kill. It also underscores the reality that those who proclaim that they will bring peace and civility often bring war and inhumanity.

SUBJECT, PURPOSE AND ORGANIZATION

This book is essentially about improving our awareness of the rhetoric that shapes our values, beliefs, and attitudes. It is about building resistance to narratives that estrange us from our spiritual and humanitarian "ultimate concerns," our own love of neighbor, and commitment to self-improvement. It is also about how we can build and sustain our own rhetorical capital for the sake of communicating with fairness, compassion, and respect for the truth. This discussion presumes that we live in a world that is frequently hostile to an honest, compassionate, respectful, and patient exchanges of ideas. It presumes that, we are conditioned to expect instant answers, win debates by bullying our adversaries, and to twist the facts to suit our objectives.

The following chapters respond to several threats to the quality of our rhetoric and public discourse. These threats include our egos and our determination to silence conversation that dissents from our own convictions and points of view. They include our insatiable appetites for media content that is shrill with sensation and spectacle, and void of analysis and thorough reporting. They include our abuse of technology, and how we, including our government leaders, have turned the Internet into a venue for hate speech, and narcissistic posturing. The threat to the quality of our rhetoric and public discourse also includes the dilapidated state of academic reading in college, and religious idolatry of nationalism, and materialism.

The intended audience of this book is the general public, who may be disgusted by the quality of our national discourse and who may be interested in remedies. The intended audience includes academics and the students they teach, religious pastors and the people they counsel, and parents whose children will inevitably be raised in part by social media and advertising.

This book has four core purposes. First, it is to help readers understand the properties of rhetorical capital and its impact on our civic and spiritual lives. Second, it is to present readers with a look at our national narrative and its impact on our civic and spiritual lives. Third, it aims to clarify why college professors, news media pundits and journalists, government leaders, and clerics cannot be wholly or automatically relied upon to revitalize rhetorical capital. Fourth, this book presents readers with some resources with which to explore their own narratives, their own receptivity to propaganda, and their potential to improve their own communication skills.

As this book will explain, higher education, the news media, government officials, and religious leaders are limited in their ability to restore, build, refine, and sustain the quality of our rhetorical capital. In some instances, these entities do not always want Americans to see through the balderdash of political rhetoric, nor to recognize our own exploitation and disempowerment when we see it. In some instances, these entities have agendas that are in conflict with doing their part to ensure fair, honest, and compassionate civil discourse.

Chapter two takes a hard look at why we should be concerned about rhetoric and public discourse, and addresses matters such as hate speech and fake news. Chapter three introduces the findings of experts relative to reading proficiency, and explores what research tells us about reading and the development of rhetorical capital in higher education. Chapters four and five continue the discussion about higher education with a look at curriculum and political correctness. Chapter six examines the news media, while chapters seven and eight address the American narrative, nationalism, and special interests in governance. Chapter nine discusses the alliance between religion, materialism, and nationalism, and chapter ten invites readers to think about empowerment. After a brief conclusion in chapter eleven, readers will find in chapter twelve, inventories, reflection tools, and activities that facilitate self-reflection and pathways for improving one's own discourse and rhetorical capital.

References to biblical passages in this book are from the *New Oxford Annotated Bible: With Apocrypha* (RSV), unless otherwise noted. Some terms in this book have very specific meanings, as so the following list of lexiconic use may be helpful.

- **Academic reading** refers to critical reading skills, such as those that the National Assessment of Adult Literacy associates with reading proficiency. It also regards reading that relies on a sound understanding of disciplinary discourse.

- **Cognitive tasks** refer to discrete thinking activities. In this discussion, they are largely willed activities that can be monitored by the individuals who are engaged in the task. Cognitive tasks that are central to reading proficiency include: identifying biases; detecting the author's purpose; discerning main ideas from peripheral and tangential ideas; identifying implications, inferences, lacunae, and meaning of text; synthesizing information in multiple texts; and, assessing the strength of evidence offered for assertions.

- **Critical reading** is intense and highly analytical reading to achieve superior comprehension, interpretation, and evaluation of assertions.

- **Disciplinary discourse** is comprised of conversations among scholars and researchers in a specialized field of study. Expertise in disciplinary discourse is characterized not only by abundant knowledge of subjects in the discipline, but a deep understanding of research methods, applicability of data, and the way the discipline informs other disciplines.

- **Humanism** has roots in the philosophical movements of the Renaissance that retreated from religious doctrines asserting that God was the only source of knowledge, wisdom, beauty, and goodness. In this text, it generally refers to a secular philosophical world view wherein human beings can know truth and achieve goodness by using reason, being self-disciplined, and genuinely committed to the well-being of others.

- **Prophetic voices** appear on occasion in this text, and refer to those that speak truth to power. The prophetic voice is often a dissenter, and one who calls attention to the gap between the ideals and values people espouse, and their actual behavior.

- **Public discourse** includes speeches, debates, news programs, televised entertainment, advertising, Internet content, published manuscripts, research, and casual conversation.

- **Spirituality** refers to a sacred force that binds creation together, and that that endows it with a divine purpose that transcends and often stands in opposition to material and profane endeavors. The spiritual experience is sometimes intuitive. It persistently calls individuals to love others as brothers and sisters, and to honor the sacred force of life in nature. Spirituality in this text refers to an aspect of the human experience that is associated with God, a higher power, or sacred mystery that is the source of life and eternity. In this text, it is not the sole property of a particular religion, nor contained by a specific institutional doctrine.

Chapter 2

Why Get in a Rhetorical Twist?

HARM'S WAY

The business of getting inside our heads and influencing the way we think and behave is big business. Our attention is itself a commodity to be bought and sold. Pop-ups and "Cookies" invade the pages of websites at a furious pace. Political parties spend millions of dollars researching public attitudes and values before spending even more millions to produce and distribute ads designed to influence our votes.[1] Common sense tells us that we are better equipped to resist commercial and political propaganda if we are able to tell the difference between horse sense and hokum, and that good judgement requires the ability to fully digest information we consume.

Propaganda is effective when it modifies our thinking and behavior and when it neutralizes our conscience. It is especially effective when it is so subtle—so implicit in the sights and sounds of daily life—that it is invisible. Propaganda can steer attention towards things that are of little consequence, and convince us not to scrutinize the things that are of great consequence. It can leave audiences with the notion that there are no conflicts of interest where they do exist, and make us feel proud, entitled, and self-indulgent when we ought to be humble, gracious, and self-sacrificing. Perhaps the most insidious propaganda is that which tells us that there are no causes greater than ourselves, and that the ultimate meaning of life is material in nature. Such propaganda is toxic to spirituality and the transcendent and tangible dimensions of humanitarianism.

1. Issenberg's *The Victory Lab* explores how this works with historical examples.

We are all vulnerable to the stories we tell. We all have incentives to be dishonest, and we all have the capacity to be bamboozled by charismatic celebrities and authorities with esoteric titles and credentials. We all have the potential to place ourselves in harm's way because we do not question what we were being told and because we reject facts in evidence. Our vulnerability and our current state of social discord are good reasons to get into a rhetorical twist—these sound the alarm to pay attention to how words are used.

The late Senator Patrick Moynihan (D-NY) once quipped that, "those who control the dictionary control the debate."[2] He was right. A brief exploration of the term "middle class" reveals the mischief interpretations enable. According to federal economic experts, the "middle class" includes people who earn between $40,000.00 and $240,000.00, and some definitions stretch the spectrum of incomes even further.[3] The merits of a "middle class tax cut" depends on which point along the spectrum one's income falls. The "middle class tax cut" might be a cut only for those earning over $180,000 a year, and so offers no cut for those who earn $60,000 a year. By bragging about a "middle class tax cut," a candidate may earn lots of points with middle class voters who do not grasp that they were never part of the deal.

The term "collateral damage," puts an interesting spin on death, as it is a popular euphemism for civilians that were killed or wounded in war. The term cushions the blow of images of mangled and burnt bodies of men, women, and children from the mind. The term "collateral" suggests that the carnage was justified, because it was an "acceptable" or "equitable" exchange of one thing for another. The word "damage" conjures the notion that something can be repaired. It is the word we use to describe the adverse effects of a tornado or flood from which we might recover. Whoever controls the dictionary is often also the same one that controls the interpretation of a speakers intentions, what matters about the context in which things are said, and what standards of credibility assertions must meet.[4]

Presidential rhetoric plays many roles in the republic, including that of defining the country's political reality. The definition of reality, of course, is always subject to the analysis and fact-checking of journalists and scholars. Normally, however, these people are at a disadvantage because they do not always have open access to government documents and the files of private

2. Daniels, *Keeping the Republic*, p. 71.

3. Gleckman, "Who is Middle Class," para. 4–15. Gleckman notes that by some measurements, "middle class" can represent incomes between $13,000 and $230,000 or more.

4. See Bagdikian's *New Media Monopoly*; Herman and Chomsky's *Manufacturing Consent*, and Attkisson's *The Smear* for documentation of and commentary about corporate news and its impact on our values and democracy.

corporations. Presidents may alter political realities by adjusting how issues and ideas are framed, using misleading euphemisms and vocabulary, and describing things in ways that conjure strong associations where there are either no associations, or very weak associations.

It was no small matter when President George W. Bush (R-TX) declared that the U.S. would fight the war against terrorism by way of covert operations, law enforcement, financial influence, diplomacy, and military strikes, and announced to the world's nations that, "Either you are with us, or you are with the terrorists."[5] Bush framed the 9/11 attacks as an expression of religiously motivated hatred for America's democracy and freedoms. He exclaimed, "We are not deceived by their pretenses to piety. . .They are the heirs of all the murderous ideologies of the 20th century" who kill to amass power.[6]

Arguably, the speech did what it was supposed to do. It rallied an angry citizenry to support the president's will to hold the nation's assailants accountable by *any means necessary*. Bush also issued an ultimatum to Americans and foreigners alike. By claiming that "you are either with us or with the terrorists," Bush not only articulated his expectations for international support, but conveyed to attentive American ears that any rhetoric that contested his political reality was false, hostile, and unpatriotic. As a result, many with questions held their tongues and are still silent. Lingering questions pertaining to 9/11 include why the Saudis were treated with deference in America's quest for accountability. The Bush family's business ties with Saudi royals has lasted for generations, and so having Saudi nationals flying hijacked planes into American civilian targets is mystery with special intrigue.[7]

Public narrative plays an important role in society. The way our national agenda, civil conduct, business behavior, crime, achievements, foreign relations, and ambitions are portrayed can have a profound impact on whether we trust and care about each other, or whether we fear and hate each other. Our narratives can ignite or quell activism. They can incite mass confidence in demagogues. They can inspire healing introspection and teach us to respect the prophet voice in worldly affairs.

DAVID AND THE KINGDOM OF HAPPY

David Brooks, a conservative journalist who has written for the *New York Times*, appears regularly on the *PBS News Hour* and is author of several books. He was a protégé of William F. Buckley, Jr., a cold warrior who was

5. Bush, "Address to Joint Session," para. 13.
6. Ibid, para. 12.
7. See Unger's *House of Bush, House of Saud* for a history of the cozy collaboration.

renowned for supporting covert interventions and aggression abroad on the basis of his conservative Catholic morality.[8] Brooks' erudite commentary and keen surveys of the social and political landscape of the U.S. have been praised by liberals and conservatives alike, in part because he consistently plays nice with his antagonists, and is genuinely open to alternative explanations for things.

Recently, Brooks got himself into trouble. His latest two books, *The Road to Character* (2015, Random House) and *The Second Mountain: The Quest for a Moral Life* (2019, Random House) are a departure from the typical pundit's rhetoric about economic trends, foreign policy, and presidential approval ratings. Rather than stick to prose that translates data into coherent insights, or illuminates the pros and cons of a particular aspect of the legislative process, he is wandering into the rhetorical gardens of philosophy and theology. He is exploring the meaning of life, the profundity of human connections, and using words like "sin" to describe social behavior. Brooks admonishes American culture for driving so much of our spirituality into no man's land with endless commodification of our person and endless want. His editorial perspective is offensive to some not because it is subjective, but because it scolds us.

In response to *The Second Mountain*, columnist Robert Samuelson of the *Washington Post* wrote a letter to Brooks in which he invited Brooks, to "lighten up."[9] Samuelson's patience with Brooks' assertions that we have created a "culture of lies," and that we have focused on the wrong things when seeking a source to happiness was apparently worn thin by many of society's strolls around the utopian block. "You seem disappointed that we haven't arrived in some Garden of Eden paradise," writes Samuelson, "I yearn for this as well, but I have reconciled myself to the inevitability of imperfection." Samuelson then adds:

> There is no virtue in feeding this frenzy of pessimism, just because it fits the temper of the times. We need to recognize the limits of our condition. Many legitimate problems can't be solved, and some problems aren't worth solving. . .
> It is also worth noting that things could be worse.[10]

Brooks "violated" one of America's cardinal unspoken rules: "Thou shalt not be a downer." As journalist Barbara Ehrenreich has explained,

---

8. See Funt's "The Transformation of David Brooks," and Hendershot's "Open to Debate," which explores Buckley's pugnacious defense of conservatism and how it shaped political debate.

9. Samuelson, "David Brooks, Let Me Respectfully Suggest," para. 1–6.

10. Ibid, para. 7–8.

Americans insist on perpetual optimism, and are compulsively positive about our national identity and our personal lives, regardless of the odious mess that lies beneath the veneer.[11] Brooks attacked the Kingdom of Happy. He used his prophetic voice and violated the unwritten mandate that all must be cheerleaders of the "best country in the world."

In the end, Brooks may doing little more than exercising his prophetic voice. In the Kingdom of Happy, one can either be a cheerleader and be loved, or be prophetic and be scorned. Brooks is challenging what Samuelson calls "the limits of our condition." He believes that many of the existential problems that we might find "unsolvable" are actually solvable when we are willing to change our values and perspective. Samuelson's remarks imply that he sees greater limitation to—and perhaps greater futility in—public discourse about our moral character. He seems to be saying, "This is as good as it gets, kid. . .relax. . . we're doin' the best we can." He reminds Brooks that it is the job of journalists to point out our shortcomings, yes, but also to be "realistic." Ahh, to be "realistic!" That is where the one holding the dictionary prevails. Brooks' message is that we should all think very seriously about what is real, because we have been in denial about our condition for so long, we may not know.

Our appetite for happiness and its twin, our tendency to deny reality, are reasons to refine our rhetorical capital. The ability to hear the prophetic message embedded in social critiques, pundits' analyses, and scholarly essays, is one that helps individuals view issues through the prism of spirituality, humanism, and moral principles. Prophetic rhetoric in American culture is often cast as the malcontent's doom and gloom, yet, it is so often full of hope that we *can be better than we think we can be.*

Despite the potential wisdom they may offer, many do not want prophetic voices to have a platform in public discourse. They are irritating. They are frequently associated with raving charlatans who extort the faithful's bank accounts in exchange for God's blessing. They are sometimes seen as angry people who want others to be as miserable as they are. Prophets are not very good cheerleaders. They reminded people about the gap between their publically espoused values and the way the actually live. A society that cannot respect the place of the prophetic voice in its own process of becoming civil and humane, however, is profoundly limited in the way it can quell dastardly discourse and restore its rhetorical capital, as it will not mind the gaps between espoused values and reality.

11. Ehrenreich's *Bright-Sided* reveals how a relentless appetite for happy endings and sliver-lined clouds can get us into trouble, hurt us, and make us vulnerable to people who do not care about our well-being.

FAKIN' IT

Arguably, we should be upset about our public discourse because so much of it is false. Fake news is not a novelty. It is an American tradition. From propaganda circulated in the colonial era about the "savage" nature of Native Americans,[12] to the mythology that slaves enjoyed their captivity,[13] to the narrative that the U.S. invaded Iraq in 2003 because Saddam Hussein possessed weapons of mass destruction and was planning on using them against the U.S. and its allies[14]—we Americans fancy a spin. Fake news presents three threats to spirituality, humanism, and our commitment to civility. First, it is difficult to detect. Second, it can make us ignorant of things that are tearing us apart and rotting our character from the inside out. Third, it often incites the will to destroy and kill.[15]

Fake news often has the look and feel of legitimate journalism. Janet Cook, a writer for the *Washington Post*, won a Pulitzer Prize in 1981 for her story about "Jimmy," an eight-year old heroin addict. The tale was so horrifying that it moved public officials to find "Jimmy" and do something to save him and others like him. After an unsuccessful attempt to find the boy, Cook admitted that she invented the story, and returned her prize.[16] In 1998, executives at *The New Republic* found that one if its star journalists, Stephen Glass, had fabricated dozens of stories that often depicted the "debauchery" of public officials. Glass, along with editors who had failed to rigorously check the facts, were dismissed.[17] Public apologies and termination restored some of the integrity of news agencies, but full faith and confidence in news media is elusive. By 2018, only 45 percent of Americans trusted mass media.[18]

Journalists are not the only ones who take liberties with the truth. Politicians on both sides of the aisle also dabble in the dark arts. One study found that in the fall of the 2016 presidential election, Trump averaged 20

---

12. Merrell's "Second Thoughts" explores how American historians have treated Native Americans over time.

13. Campbell's *The Celluloid South* addresses the role of Hollywood films' in perpetuating the myth of happy slaves.

14. Hoeffel's *The Iraq Lie* is told from the perspective of a former U.S. Congressman. It traces the Bush administration's plans to remove Hussein from office and its success in deceiving millions of Americans

15. Lazer, et al. "The Science of Fake News," p. 1095.

16. McNair, *Fake News*, p. 28.

17. Ibid, pp. 28–29.

18. Jones, "U.S. Media Trust," para. 1–3.

false claims per day.[19] Another inquiry of statements made by politicians in
2016 found that Hilary Clinton and Barack Obama made publically false
statements between 17 and 14 percent of the time.[20]

Dishonesty is legendary in modern American history. President
Franklin Roosevelt lied about negotiations with the Soviets at the Yalta
Conference, President Kennedy lied about the Cuban Missile Crisis, President Lyndon Johnson lied about the Gulf of Tonkin assault, and President
Reagan lied about trading arms for hostages in the Iran-Contra Affair.[21] The
press and members of the pentagon lied to Americans about the "missile
gap," which spurred support for mass increases in nuclear weapons production.[22] Kennedy suffered from Addison's disease and chronic venereal
infections, but routinely lied to the public about his health.[23] Secretary of
Defense Robert McNamara and Pentagon officials lied to President Johnson
about progress in Vietnam.[24] President Nixon lied about his knowledge of
the Watergate burglary.[25] President Bill Clinton lied about his extra-marital
sexual liaisons.[26]

What is different now in the 21st century is that fake news is jet-pro-
pelled by digital technology that makes it possible for anyone to post editorials and information, and reach millions of people instantly. The average
person cannot manage the scale of information available, and is ill-equipped
to analyze the credibility of sources. The phenomenon of fake news, writes
Professor of Journalism, Brian McNair, has created "a crisis of trust in elites,
including political and mainstream media elites, whose members are struggling to maintain their traditional roles in our liberal democracies."[27] The
crisis is immediate to the republic, because the judgement of its people is
predicated on what they know and do not know.

19. Dale and Talaga, "Donald Trump," para. 4–5.

20. McGranahan, "An Anthropology of Lying," p. 245.

21. Altman's When Presidents Lie takes readers through the details of each of these
episodes.

22. Preble, "'Whoever Believed,'" pp. 801–826.

23. Reeves, President Kennedy, p. 43–44.

24. McMaster's Dereliction of Duty is an excruciating look at the arrogance that
dragged the U.S. into war.

25. Dean's Nixon Defense is an insider's chronology of events that led to Nixon's
resignation.

26. Hitchens' No One Left to Lie To exposes the history of Clinton's dishonesty about
many issues.

27. McNair, Fake News, pp. x–xi.

The digital revolution has compounded the problem of fake news. By 2017, roughly 47 percent of Americans got their news from social media.[28] By 2018, college students represented one third of social media users who got their news from entities such as Facebook and Twitter.[29] Anyone—including the amateur and poorly educated— may post a blog, create a website, and use social media to disseminate information and opinion.[30]

The incentive to write fiction and present it as truth is real. Some merchants of misinformation earn tens of thousands of dollars a month for their creations, as advertisers are eager to exploit audiences that graze the gossip.[31] Excited by the number of "likes" posted in social media, readers join the bandwagon of approval which is rich in subjective and un-researched assertions.[32] Posting a "like" in social media is readily translated into "I agree," and thus provides a sense of reasoned consensus. A "like" can also be misread as "this is true."

The ability to manipulate images digitally is robust and widely used for entertainment. The problem is that the lines between what is real and what has been manufactured for laughs is not clear. In May, 2019, House Speaker Nancy Pelosi (D-CA) criticized Facebook for posting a doctored video clip that depicted her as intoxicated and inarticulate, and requested that Facebook remove the post. Though Facebook said the Pelosi video was a "satire," many viewers thought that the video was legitimate. Facebook refused to remove the clip, asserting that the altered imagery was acceptable to its "community standards."[33] Facebook is in a position to norm community standards because its viewership is so wide. It has an incentive to set low standards because the bizarre and the sensational attracts readers, and thus, ad dollars. Arguably, Facebook's "community standards" do not reflect love of neighbor.

The digital revolution has also revolutionized the communication between elected officials and the public. Using social media, executives can reach millions of people without having to go through a journalist and editorial staff to be heard. Without the journalist "middle man," people are able to choose the subjects that they want to discuss, and are not compelled to answer questions they may not want to answer. This development places

28. Shearer and Masta, "News Use across Social Media," para. 1.

29. Ibid, para. 6.

30. Tandoc, Lim, and Ling, "Defining 'Fake News,'" pp. 139–140.

31. Michael Miller's *Fake News: Separating Truth from Fiction* explores this murky business in detail.

32. Sundar, "The MAIN Model," p. 84.

33. Halpern, "Facebook's False Standards," para. 1–8.

immense responsibility on social media users to use the platforms with integrity and respect for public well-being, and social media consumers to be especially critical.

HATIN' IT

It is estimated that at least half of those who use social media in the U.S. are exposed to hate material.[34] Much of the hate speech in social media aims to recruit people to political associations and to sell merchandise, while reinforcing stereotypes and promoting the idea that some groups are superior to others.[35] The adverse effects of hate speech on those who are the targets of hate include lowered self-esteem and self-imposed restrictions of movement and social engagement.[36] Research also finds that hate-speech contributes to an increase in discrimination, and that prejudice desensitizes people to the humanity of others.[37] Hate speech has also been linked to difficulties with learning and non-persistence to degree in post-secondary education.[38]

Legally, hate speech pertains to language that advocates discrimination, violence, and hostility towards others.[39] Hate speech serves a psychological and social purpose, which is to reinforce the hierarchy of power in a society, and to communicate to individuals the terms of their membership. More than a means of "blowing off steam," hate speech is rhetoric designed to strip others of their dignity, and declares to targeted groups that their presence in the community alone justifies their abuse and victimization.[40] Hate speech is protected by the First Amendment. In public attempts to limit it, the Supreme Court has refrained from making hate speech a crime, and opined that Americans are best served by a wide scope of free speech. They posit that, in a democratic society, it is easier to bear hate speech than it is to bear censorship and state regulated rhetoric and discourse.[41]

People can go a long time hiding their hatred behind polite conversation. It is often when they are confronted with anger and fear that is beyond their psychological and spiritual capacity to manage their feelings that their hatred is unmasked. In the digital world, people may enjoy the "secret

34. Hawdon, Oksanen, and Räsänen, "Exposure to Online Hate," p. 7.

35. Gerstenfeld, Grant, and Chiang, "Hate Online," pp. 30–31.

36. Gelber and McNamara, "Evidencing the Harm in Hate Speech," pp. 2–4.

37. Soral, et al., "Exposure to Hate Speech," p. 137.

38. Saha, "Prevalence and Psychological Effects," pp. 4–8.

39. Fisch, "Hate Speech," pp. 464–468.

40. Waldron, *Harm in Hate Speech*, pp. 2–5.

41. Abrams, *Friend of the Court*, pp. 116–118.

company" of those who hate as they hate, and indulge their appetites for rhetoric that they would not publically consume. Most people, for example, report that they are not racist, yet survey data from Internet searches reveal that people are ravenous consumers of white supremacist rhetoric and racist blogs and websites.[42] It is very difficult to know with absolute accuracy how many people are committed to their hatred as a way of life, and the extent to which individuals are ready to turn their hatred into violent acts.

Rhetoric can have lethal consequences. In societies where frightened and angry people are overwhelmed by uncertainty and disruptions to the status quo, demagogues whose rhetoric radiates strength, confidence, and knowledge of the absolute truth, tend to attract a following. Demagogues from both the right and the left frequently scapegoat certain groups, and encourage the belief that these groups are not worthy of a fair hearing. The rhetoric of demagogues and their minions in the media tell society who has a legitimate place in the public conversation about national policies and who does not. It tells us which issues matter, which causes for our problems are authentic, and which ones are fake or unimportant. It tells us which way is the right way to see things, and ridicules the alternatives.

Hate speech is often a prelude to assault and genocide. Excited by propaganda that warned of Tutsis' intention to take control of Rwanda, Hutu peasants shot, beat, and butchered with machetes over 800,000 Tutsis in 1994.[43] The "Butcher of Bosnia," Radovan Karadzic, brought death to over 200,000 Muslim civilians during the Bosnia War (1992 to 1995), announcing that he was restoring the glorious and heroic Serbia of medieval lore by way of ethnic cleansing.[44] Nazi propaganda remains iconic for its villainy, as it transformed ordinary citizens into a killing machine that methodically went about genocide as if it were the day shift at a car factory.[45] These episodes and many more like them bear witness to the reality that when people are faced with crises that are difficult to overcome, they are vulnerable to strongmen who assure them that if society were purged of certain "malignant elements"—the Jews, the blacks, the immigrants, the liberals, the gays, the infidels—all will be well.

---

42. Stephens-Davidowitz, *Everybody Lies*, pp. 1–14.

43. Schabas, "Hate Speech in Rwanda," pp. 141–143.

44. Donia, *Radovan Karadzic*, pp. 1–7. Note: The fall of communism in the Soviet Union in 1991 opened the question of how former communist East European nations would be defined and governed. Ethnic groups once bound together by the communist state found themselves competing for power and territory. Also see Cohen's *Serbia's Secret War* for a history of conflict among ethnicities in Balkan Peninsula.

45. Murray, "Constructing the Ordinary," pp. 52–54.

THE LEADER'S RHETORIC

The rhetoric of national leaders can have lethal consequences, even if they are not personally mobilizing death squads or bombing villages. In a republic, where the state does not strictly control what people think or say, the standards of responsible thought and speech are defined and reinforced by cultural norms. Many look to leaders as examples of what is decent and fair. Ray Price, speech-writer for Presidents Nixon and Ford, observed that the American public measures their executives against an ideal that combines the qualities of kings, heroes, and gods. He noted, "They want him [their president] to be larger than life, a living legend. . .someone to be held up to their children as a model. . .in somewhat the same way which peasant families pray to the icon in the corner. Reverence goes where power is."[46]

Price's remarks remind us that people have a deep psychological need for leadership that radiates security and power. They remind us that people hunger for living icons that provide them with a sense of national pride and moral superiority. They also suggest that, since worldly power arouses reverence, it may compete with other things in our lives that prompt our reverence, such as the Kingdom of God or sacred teachings about love and humanity. Price's statements underscore the reality that when leaders speak, they create a template for thinking and rhetoric that is acceptable in society. We have heard the eloquence of leaders call us to be better than we thought we could be, and conversely, we have heard the coarseness of leaders urge us to cling to fear and hatred for the sake of our egos and partisan prowess. Thanks to the digital revolution, we may read and hear discourse that was presented long before our birth, and we can be inspired and instructed by people from times and places different form our own. We can compare and contrast the thinking of our leaders, and decide for ourselves which discourse resonates with inspiration to live for great causes, or with discourse that stirs cynicism and incivility.

In 1967, Senator Eugene McCarthy (D-MN) denounced the war in Vietnam. McCarthy who nearly became a Benedictine monk, found his way to sociology, economics, and law. He ran for president in 1968, but was nudged aside by Democrats who favored fellow Minnesotan, Senator Hubert Humphrey. Humphrey was willing to take up Johnson's war in Vietnam; McCarthy was not. He wrote words about the impact of the Vietnam War that are meaningful today, as war drags on in Afghanistan and the Middle East, and as the "old men" warn of terrorism they helped to create:

---

46. Price quoted in Mercieca and Vaughn, "Barack Obama and the Rhetoric," p. 3.

The scriptural promise of the good life is one in which the old men see visions and the young men dream dreams. In the context of this war and all of its implications, the young men of America do not dream dreams, but many live in the nightmare of moral anxiety, of concern and great apprehension; and the old men, instead of visions which they can offer to the young, are projecting, in the language of the secretary of state, a specter of one billion Chinese threatening the peace and safety of the world—a frightening and intimidating future.

The message from the administration today is a message of apprehension a message of fear, yes—even a message of fear of fear.

This is not the real spirit of America. I do not believe that it is. This is a time to test the mood and spirit:

To offer in place of doubt—trust.

In place of expediency—right judgment.

In place of ghettos, let us have neighborhoods and communities.

In place of incredibility—integrity.

In place of murmuring, let us have clear speech; let us again hear America singing.

In place of disunity, let us have dedication of purpose.

In place of near despair let us have hope.

This is the promise of greatness which was seated for us by Adlai Stevenson and which was brought to form and positive action in the words and actions of John Kennedy

Let us pick up again these lost strands and weave them again into the fabric of America.

Let us sort out the music from the sounds and again respond to the trumpet and the steady drum.[47]

In 1974, when the U.S. economy was in recession, the price of oil was soaring to new heights, and Americans were increasingly irritated by Arab attitudes towards the West, Senator William Fulbright (D-AK) discussed a crisis that he thought was far greater than the price of oil.

We cannot blame the oil producers for the irresponsible, rapacious extravagance of our vaunted "way of life." We Americans are not only living beyond our economic means; we are damaging the world's ecology by depleting irreplaceable raw materials, by consuming renewable resources such as forests and fish faster than the earth's natural processes can replace them, and by

47. McCarthy, "Denouncing the Vietnam War," para. 23–35.

fouling the rivers and oceans beyond their natural capacity for
cleansing themselves.

Even if we could afford our extravagant life style—the over-
powered automobiles, the beefsteak diet — for dogs and cats as
well as for humans—the throwaway boxes and bottles, the gadgets and whimsies that clutter our surroundings from the kitchen
to the Pentagon and even the moon—it would still be important
to conserve and cut back, to go back to living more simply. Over
and above the material waste, our high living is also wasteful
and destructive in the psychological sense. We have long passed
the point of diminishing returns as between our gadgets and
luxuries and the human satisfactions that they yield. Like spoiled
children who have had too many toys, we are always looking for
new playthings—and encouraged to do so by the massive advertising industry—but the gadgets only amuse us for a moment or
two, and then we are off in search of something else.

Living affluently is not the same thing as living well. Living well requires a certain harmony with nature, a sense of pace
about time, the taking of pleasure in simple things—the view
of a mountain or the sea, a fine day, the company of family and
friends. I recently visited the People's Republic of China, where
I saw a great deal that I admired. . . In China nothing is wasted
because there is nothing to waste. I thought as I visited the
Chinese cities and countryside that the American people must
be fifty or a hundred times more affluent than the Chinese, but
not—surely not—fifty or a hundred times happier.[48]

In 1976, Representative Barbara Jordan (D-TX) addressed the Democratic National Convention. At a time when the Watergate scandal was fresh
in our minds, recession nipped at our heels, and an energy crisis was under-
way, she spoke with confidence about us.

In this election year, we must define the "common good" and
begin again to shape a common future. Let each person do his
or her part. If one citizen is unwilling to participate, all of us are
going to suffer. For the American idea, though it is shared by all
of us, is realized in each one of us.

And now, what are those of us who are elected public officials
supposed to do? We call ourselves "public servants" but I'll tell you
this: We as public servants must set an example for the rest of the
nation. It is hypocritical for the public official to admonish and
exhort the people to uphold the common good if we are derelict in
upholding the common good. More is required—more is required

48. Fulbright, "Clear and Present Danger," para. 16–18.

of public officials than slogans and handshakes and press releases. More is required. We must hold ourselves strictly accountable. We must provide the people with a vision of the future.[49]

These are prophetic voices from the past. They are hopeful and proud. They are the words of a generation that faced hardship and crises that were not brought about by their personal conduct, but that undertook the task of healing and restoring none-the-less. In our finest moments, many leaders have called attention not only to our mistakes and character flaws, but pointed to a clear way forward that was aligned with our highest ideals for peace, justice, and good will. America's leaders have helped people think through extremely difficult situations, including those in which the breakdown of law was caused by law-makers, and the breakdown of peace was caused by peacemakers. In their honesty about the source of our suffering and crisis, they helped us retain our faith in democracy and our willingness to help make the world a better place.

Our leaders' rhetoric has the potential to chart a course either for civility and cooperation, or for combativeness and incivility. Actions bear witness to the power of words. In counties where Donald Trump held rallies in his 2016 bid for the presidency, hate crimes rose by 226 percent in just over a year.[50]

Less than two months prior to the El Paso and Dayton massacres (August, 2019), Trump said to his followers at a campaign rally that the caravan of immigrants coming from Central America was "an invasion." He ranted, "How do you stop these people. . .You can't. . ." At that point, a member of the crowd shouted, "Shoot them!" Trump grinned as the audience laughed and cheered. Then the President chuckled, "That's only in the panhandle you can get away with that stuff."[51] He has repeatedly insulted people of color, Muslims, women, and anyone who disagrees with his world view and public conduct, and has called developing nations "shit-hole" countries.[52] Faced with criticism from four junior congressional representatives who condemned the conditions of border detention facilities, Trump tweeted that the group of women, Alexandria Ocasio-Cortez (D-NY), Rashida Tlaib (D-MI), Ilhan Omar (D-MN), and Ayanna Pressley (D-MA) "go back and help fix the totally broken and crime infested places from which they

---

49. Jordan, "1976 Democratic National Convention," para. 19–20.

50. Choi, "Hate Crimes Increased," para. 1–5; also see Connolly, "House to Probe Rise in Hate Crimes," para. 1–5.

51. Reuters, "Trump Calls Caravan," see video.

52. Silva, "Trump's Full List," para. 1–3.

came."[53] That was not "locker room talk." That was rhetoric posted for the nation to behold. On July 16, 2019, the House of Representatives voted to condemn Trump's racist comments about the Congresswomen of color.[54] It was an act of decency in the tradition of Barbara Jordan, William Fulbright, and Eugene McCarthy. It was an act that declared, "Words matter."

The executive's comments have not only been offensive to people, but are sometimes inconsistent and confusing. On July 28, 2019, three people were killed and 15 were injured in Gilroy, California by a gunman who later shot himself. On August 3, a gunman killed 22 people and injured 20 others in El Paso, Texas. A day later nine people were killed and 27 were injured as a man opened fire in Dayton, Ohio. The shooters were all white males under the age of 25. On August 5, 2019, Trump addressed the nation:

> In one voice, our nation must condemn racism, bigotry, and white supremacy. These sinister ideologies must be defeated. Hate has no place in America. Hatred warps the mind, ravages the heart, and devours the soul. . .
>
> We must recognize that the Internet has provided a dangerous avenue to radicalize disturbed minds, and to perform demented acts. We must shine light on the dark recesses of the Internet, and stop mass murders before they start. The Internet is likewise used for human trafficking, illegal drug distribution, and so many other heinous crimes. The perils of the social media cannot be ignored, and they will not be ignored.[55]

The president stated that more attention ought to be given to "early warning signs." He also charged that, "We must stop the glorification of violence," including that found in "grizzly and gruesome video games" that are too accessible to "troubled youth." He called for the nation to "better identify mentally disturbed individuals who may commit acts of violence and make sure those people not only get treatment, but when necessary, involuntary confinement." To this he added, "Today I am directing the Department of Justice to propose legislation ensuring that those who commit hate crimes and mass murders face the death penalty, and that this capital punishment be delivered quickly, decisively, and without years of needless delay."[56] This rhetoric is confusing. Should we treat shooters as "mentally disturbed" people who are conditioned by the Internet to kill and need to be

53. Cole, "Trump Tweets," para. 4.

54. Smith, et al., "House Votes," para. 1–6.

55. Trump, "President Trump Address," para. 11–12.

56. Ibid, para. 16–20.

cured, or treat them as criminals beyond redemption who should receive an expeditious execution?

Ultimately, Trump's address following the mass shootings did what all good political rhetoric should do: it framed the problem and set a perimeter around "legitimate discourse" on the matter. While Trump acknowledged the reality that the US has a culture of violence, the rhetoric directed audiences' attention to the shooters and not the culture of making money from violent media and the accessibility of guns. Shooters have "disturbed minds," and are "troubled youth;" they are the "mentally disturbed," who were "radicalized" by "grizzly and gruesome video games." The party line was simple: mass shootings are the result of an individual's pathology that is exacerbated by technology. Here was an opportunity to say something insightful and useful about what we can do to decrease our appetite for violent entertainment and direct our children's interests to more humane subjects. The ideas were not forthcoming.

THEM WHAT'S GOT THE DICTIONARY

Less than three weeks following the shootings in El Paso and Dayton, Trump gave an interview to journalists on the topic of trade with China. He listed his grievances against the Chinese, and asserted that by way of underhanded means, they have taken billions of dollars out of the United States. He then stated, "I am the chosen one; somebody had to do it; so I'm taking on China—I'm taking on China and trade."[57] Naturally, in a society grounded in Judeo-Christian teachings, the remark sent convulsions through the media. By evoking the image of a messiah, Trump elevated himself above all others and suggested that God had divinely ordained him to slay the treacherous red dragon.

The president may feel like trade with China is a problem that others should have solved. His rhetoric might have been sarcastic. However, in the context of Trump's larger narrative about the world, in which he often places himself on a pedestal at the center, the unfortunate remark resonated like an infatuation with power.[58] The reference to divine election is troublesome in light of the executive's occasional remarks in which he asserts that he is the only one who can fix our problems and make America great again.[59] From a spiritual perspective, some might say that these assertions are idolatrous. From a humanistic perspective, some might say that such remarks smack of

57. Campisi, "Trump on 'Chosen One' Remark," para. 8.
58. Malkin, "Pathological Narcissism," pp. 51–68.
59. See: Applebaum, "I Alone can Fix It;" and Jackson, "Donald Trump Accepts."

demagoguery. Others might argue that Trump's assertions prop up his own self-esteem, as his public approval rating rested between 35 and 46 percent from January, 2017 to August, 2019.[60]

Many Christians have fueled the perception that the president represents the will of God. The executive received 81 percent of the evangelical votes cast in the 2016 election, and many of the faithful believe God has given Trump special moral authority to fight evil as it is manifest in abortion, gay marriage, opposition to prayer in school, and tyranny abroad.[61] The President has a personal pastor and spiritual advisor, Paula White, whose guidance is aimed at keeping him on his Christian path.[62] Others have stoked the President's confidence in his alignment with the Almighty Creator, by announcing that Jewish people love Trump like he is the "Second coming of God."[63] Projecting omnipotence onto mere mortals is dangerous business. It is both idolatrous and toxic to democracy.

We are a violent society. Shoot 'em up video games and presidential platitudes about destroying our enemies are only part of the bloody mosaic. We are a pre-emptive strike kind of town. Our police shoot first and ask questions later, and, we entertain our children a steady diet of monsters, mayhem, and murder. We are quick on the draw when it comes to justifying these things, and frequently get angry with people who question whether these things are aligned with our spirituality and humanitarianism. Some Americans are proud of the fact that our president hates certain people and brags about sexually harassing women.[64] In our country, apologies for assaulting the dignity of the human being are slow and selective.

Sometimes, we make violence invisible by the way we define and perceive violence. The Recession of 2008 is a good example of what dictionary twisting can do. Though not framed in the language of violence against innocent people, the banks and law-makers who engineered the Recession of 2008 committed acts of violence against millions of people around the world as pensions evaporated, families lost their homes, businesses closed, trade was disrupted, and public employees were forced to take furloughs and wage cuts.[65]

---

60. Statistia Research Team, "Do You Approve," see interactive chart.

61. See: Green, "On Praying for Presidents" and "One Way to Push Back."

62. Glenza, "Paula White," para. 9.

63. Barnes, "President Praises Conservative Radio," para. 1–3.

64. Oh. "Trump, Who Once Said," para. 4.

65. Reich's, *Economics in Wonderland* is a clear and well-illustrated explanation of how economic policies and regulation work to shift wealth to the rich at the expense of everyone else.

Why does rhetoric about violence stick to some subjects and slide off others? Perhaps the answer is that when we use the word "violent" to describe our actions and their results, we expect that accountability will follow. Perhaps we are selective in our sense of accountability. In the case of the Recession of 2008, to fully expose the real people, who made real decisions that caused real calamity, would come too close to an indictment of our government and capitalism itself. The fact that people generally did not describe the events that led to the Recession of 2008 as acts of violence soothes us, and makes us more receptive to the assertion that the architects of the disaster had the right to take radical risks in the market, despite warnings not to do so, because they were "acting for the best interests of all."[66] In short, "noble" motives justified the high risk behavior, deregulation, and fraud, and so the repercussions do not fall into the same category as violent crimes, such as murder, arson, rape, or assault with a deadly weapon. Take the politically correct spin off the activities of bankers who caused the Recession of 2008, and we may perceive that institutionalized greed *is* a deadly weapon.

We are challenged today to navigate our way to truth through relentless tides of news, commentary, and opinion. The rhetorical capital needed for such a mission includes some understanding of how media functions in society and how secular and religious leaders design persuasive discourse. In theory, formal education is supposed to develop our rhetorical capital. It is supposed to teach us how to read deeply and proficiently, think critically, and judge wisely. It is also, in theory, supposed to keep pace with innovations in society, so that we may intelligently respond to information and/or the lack of it. The college experience is arguably fertile soil in which to cultivate sophisticated and robust rhetorical capital. Post-secondary studies represent the occasion to refine the intellect and form discernment. Yet in many instances, explicit and systematic cultivation of rhetorical capital is marginal at best because rhetorical capital is not profitable cash crop.

---

66. MacPhee, *Structured to Fail*, pp. 255–327. President Clinton appointed Brooksley Born to chair the Commodities Futures Trading Commission. She warned that fraud and lack of regulation in derivatives trading put the economy on track for disaster, and was ridiculed by Federal Reserve Chairman Alan Greenspan and by Treasury Secretaries Robert Ruben and Lawrence Summers. Born predicted the meltdown of 2008 ten years before it occurred.

Chapter 3

Crusades and Crucibles

BLAZING SANDALS

Once upon a time, college professors were supposed to be solemn sages, who floated above the politics and prejudices of the era as to remain objective conduits of knowledge and truth. The best of them became great fountains of wisdom, renowned for their constant gardening of virtue and reasoned thinking. In the ideal, they held high standards of academic proficiency and chided students for sophomoric and sloppy thinking. Colleges and universities in the U.S. have produced some of the world's most outstanding professionals across all disciplines, and have astonished the world with their research. They have made it possible for millions of people to enter the middle class and to provide lives for their families that are better than what they might have had without higher education. In the ideal, higher education was and is about becoming worldly and humbled by the opportunity to gain knowledge to be used for society's good.

Once upon a time, I believed that education would save humanity from itself. I assumed that any teacher worth his or her salt would be on board with that noble mission. Those were the days of blind idealism and the crusading knights of the pedagogical roundtable. As a faculty consultant at a state university, I was confident that when presented with evidence, college professors would have epiphanies about the developmental aspects of post-secondary education, and devote less energy to the didactic recitations declarative knowledge, and more to pedagogies that explicitly cultivated cognition, literacy, epistemological development, and rhetorical capital. I was so sure. Now, I am not so sure.

Today, there is tremendous pressure on college professors to be unconditional cheerleaders of their institution, and to ensure that the rates of persistence to degree are high. Students themselves tend to be more interested in college as a stepping stone towards upward mobility, and less interested in studying subjects and developing skills that are not immediately related to their majors. My doubts about higher education's capacity to restore and build rhetorical capital springs from the reality that no institution—not even the best universities—can force individuals to hunger for the refinement of their minds that comes of immersion in courses targeting reading proficiency, critical thinking, epistemological development, ethics, understanding the human condition, and rhetorical capital. Schools and universities can create conditions where individuals may be inspired to immerse themselves in such studies, but they must also attend the reality that if students do not see an expedient pathway to a career, they may not reach targeted numbers of enrollment.

My doubts are also a reaction to the reality that many colleges and universities have priorities that pull resources away from deep and meaningful curriculum and instruction. Having been an educator for 35 years, I have witnessed changes in social norms relative to education, and changes in what state officials, tax-payers, parents, students, university administrators, and faculty expect from post-secondary education. Some of my peers describe the changes as the "corporatization of higher education." Others say that higher education on their campus has become that of a "third world," meaning that expectations for excellence are very low. Many assert that for the sake of "keeping the doors open," and for the sake of ensuring that everyone—including those who are poorly prepared, unmotivated, and low-achieving—has an overwhelmingly favorable opportunity to acquire a college diploma, institutions have adjusted requirements, lowered standards, inflated grades, and become more "consumer friendly" by emphasizing vocational learning and relaxing strident requirements in the liberal arts.

Higher education may toss a few coins in the direction of our rhetorical capital, but it is not wholly up to the task of building and refining it. Though many instructors do a great deal to improve their students' critical thinking, academic reading, and civic discourse, the development of rhetorical capital is a priority that in many cases cannot compete with other institutional priorities. While experts have published a great deal about reading proficiency, epistemological development, critical thinking, and literacy, much of their work slides past college instructors and the administrators who do not want to address the possibility that low persistence rates may be due in part to a lack of reading proficiency. In some institutions, professors are chastised for calling attention to students' poor reading and writing skills. They are sometimes told that such rhetoric is a "deficit-based" approach to teaching and learning, and therefore offensive and unjust when compared to the "asset-based" approach.

Rhetorical capital is impoverished in part because those who have the ability to do something about it are sometimes ignorant about it or unwilling to design curriculum and instruction that will radically reverse the course of bankruptcy. In fairness to the professoriate, they themselves are often prevented from being exemplary teachers who invest a great deal of time, thoughtfulness, and energy into cultivating rhetorical capital and the cognitive and epistemological development that accompany it. They frequently face institutional obstacles, including the misalignment between the institution's espoused values and their pedagogical practices, burdensome committee obligations, and tenure requirements that only superficially consider teaching. Many colleges and universities that boast a commitment to producing students who are critical thinkers, highly proficient in rhetorical skills, culturally competent, and globally aware, but who do not conduct institutional studies to assess the extent to which graduating seniors demonstrate high levels of achievement in these things.

Colleges and universities are not always populated with idealists buoyantly addressing students' academic deficiencies and exerting endless energy to improve reading proficiency and rhetorical capital. They are not always populated by competent instructors. In some institutions, there are rules that prevent instructors from suggesting that those who have remedial needs take advantage of special services, because it is perceived as discouraging and humiliating. Instructors seeking tenure know that they must earn high scores in student evaluations, and that student satisfaction typically receives greater weight in the "evaluation" of instructors than peer observation and student achievement.

In consultations with instructors, I have learned that our students are frequently taught by individuals who have no teaching experience and no formal pedagogical training. Many instructors are part-time lecturers who dash between campuses to cobble together income sufficient to their needs. They have no duties relative to committee service or student advising, and so they are not an integral part of the campus leadership that has the potential to set policies and pursue reforms. Many instructors design courses in ways that minimize their workload. Instead of assigning essays and research papers that are designed to improve rhetorical skills, research, and reading and writing proficiency through re-writes and formative critiques, they assign poster projects and open-book exams focused on declarative knowledge. Some instructors have dispensed with evaluation altogether, and award grades abased on attendance and "effort." Some simply leave the matter of grading to graduate assistants who have no expertise in composition, critical thinking, or disciplinary discourse.

Professors have astounded me with what they say about teaching and learning. Professor "Alpha" sought my counsel because many of his students were not reading and not even buying the assigned textbook. When I cheerfully told the professor that I had some ideas and resources that might be integrated into course work to improve reading compliance and reading skills, he slammed his hand on the table in front of me and barked, "I did not come to you so that you could tell me how to teach reading; I came here so that you could tell me how to teach without assigning reading!"

Professor "Beta" asked me for insights about how to improve his student evaluations. An expert in his field, Beta had no training in teaching or course design, and was fearful that poor student evaluations would sink his chances for tenure. Beta did not know the difference between course outcomes and program objectives, nor did he have a sense of how to create an effective scope and sequence of course work, nor how to craft exercises and assessments. When I asked him how he determined content of each lesson, he replied, "I just go into the classroom and start talking about what is on my mind or something that was on television recently."

Professor "Delta" had been assigned a writing-intensive course that nobody in her department wanted to teach. She had never studied or taught composition. She requested my assistance in developing writing exercises, grading rubrics, and class activities that would help students advance their information literacy and writing skills. Though she held a doctorate, she was unable to conceptualize the discrete steps involved in writing a research paper, and imagining what kind of activities and resources might be appropriate for instruction aimed at improving discrete tasks. Delta was anxious about the options I presented, and complained that she was "not very good at grammar" and did not know anything about syntax. She said, "I'm just going to read the papers and see if they [students] have a general idea about the subject. . .I don't have time to grade writing, and their writing I so bad, it's hard enough just to read it."

There is still a crusade to wage. The crusade is to improve the curriculum and instruction of post-secondary education, so that students possess a great store of rhetorical capital. The crusade is to make proficient reading, critical consumption of information, and cognitive and epistemological development explicit learning outcomes in every program. The goal of the crusade is to integrate instruction targeting critical reading, information literacy, and critical thinking into courses at all levels of the undergraduate studies in ways that are systematic, consistent, explicit, and assessed in

meaningful ways. At present, these things are largely integrated on an episodic basis, if they are integrated at all.

The revolution to build rhetorical capital does not begin with the composition of fresh pedagogy. It begins with an unflinching interrogation of
conscience. It starts with the administrators' and faculty's honest analysis of
the disparity between the glowing ceremonial rhetoric of convocations and
commencements, and tarnished mediocrity of practice. It begins with an
honest assessment of the integrity of everything the institution does. It begins by admitting the folly of assuming that when professors dish out high
percentages of "As" and "Bs," the institution has solid evidence of exemplary
student achievement. It begins with a re-dedication of time, talent, and resources to build a citizenry that is intellectually equipped to respond wisely
to the deluge of political and commercial propaganda energized by digital
media. It continues with the courage to to make changes in curriculum,
faculty development, and tenure processes.

Rather than building a national beacon that stands for one monolithic
strategy to improve students' academic and critical reading in higher education, I think campfire will suffice. I have traded my silver spurs for sandals, and am ready to stoke a hearth around which instructors can discuss
their experiences, consider their students' vulnerability in a world awash
in propaganda, and explore the possibilities of pedagogical reform in their
own institutions. The campfire that is fueled by its own local timber burns
the brightest. Pedagogical reforms that are generated locally tend to be the
most effective, because locally developed reforms specifically target the
community's needs and are crafted with regard to the local availability of
resources. Institutions that pretend to be something that they are not, or try
to be all things to all constituents will find a few candles burning brightly
somewhere on campus, but it will probably not be the kind of bonfire that
draws everyone into a single, collegial sing-along.

WHAT EXPERTS SAY ABOUT READING PROFICIENCY

The remainder of this chapter is devoted to what research tells us about
reading and higher education, which will illuminate why colleges and universities are limited in their ability to be the salvation of rhetorical capital.
Colleges and universities do many things very well, yet, as they are human
institutions, they are capable of human error and hubris. Their leaders are
also tempted to serve many masters, even when those masters treat teaching
and learning like the last thing for which the university was established.

The definition of reading proficiency and literacy are controversial, as experts have diverse opinions based on data from cognitive, neurological, psychological, pedagogical, and sociological studies. There is consensus, however, on four assertions about reading proficiency and literacy: 1) Learning to read is a life-long, developmental process; 2) There is a link between language proficiency and critical thinking; 3) Academic reading proficiency plays an important role in disciplinary mastery and discourse; and, 4) Reading proficiency and rhetorical skills can improve with systematic and explicit instruction at all levels.

Reading is Developmental. Literacy experts understand that reading is developmental by nature, and thus reading can be improved and made more sophisticated over one's lifetime.[1] The developmental nature of reading is both neurological and psychological. This means that when individuals cultivate their reading skills, it changes neurological structures in the brain, whereby new connections between neurons fortify networks of information that enable memory encoding and retrieval, mental associations, articulation, analysis, and discerning. Reading is also developmental in the psychological sense, which means that reading can change people's thinking, perceptions, understanding, and attitudes.[2]

As we acquire more vocabulary, we build their store of "mental adhesives," which consists of facts, concepts, and impressions that stick to our memories and enhance the capacity of our memories to hold onto new information, including words, images, and ideas. Learning can take place in the act of reading because readers can decode symbols denoting letters, turn them into words, and turn words into meaningful syntax. Learning the rules of grammar and syntactic construction opens the reader to nuances and subtle aspects of interpreting information. Then, the brain does something really magical; it allows readers to conjure abstract pictures of the text, to link new information with prior knowledge, to imagine the significance of newly acquired information, and to envision what it must be like to see the world from someone else's (the author's or a fictional character's) point of view.[3]

Researchers find that many educators at all levels harbor the notion that there is a point at which individuals have learned how to read well enough to begin reading to learn, and so, no further reading instruction is necessary. Laboring under this misunderstanding of reading as a developmental phenomenon, many college instructors assume that, because their

---

1. See Alexander, "The Path to Competence."

2. A substantial discussion of this is found in Dehaene's *Reading in the Brain.*

3. Maryanne Wolf's *Reader, Come Home* offers a wonderful discussion of why this is so amazing.

students finished high school, their students read proficiently enough to comprehend college level text.[4] This approach to the development of reading in post-secondary education ignores the reality that reading instruction may do much to improve students' capacity to engage in disciplinary discourse and improve the quality of critical thinking. Instructors generally do not see that when they separate literacy, critical reading, and rhetorical skills from "course content"—which is usually defined as the declarative knowledge and/or core skills of a given subject—they create a false dichotomy that severs knowledge from the means of knowing.[5]

Reading and Critical Thinking. Reading is essentially about building meaning from text.[6] Not all reading taxes the brain in the same way. It is possible for people to read without exerting much intellectual energy, and to know all they need to know. Scanning a grocery list, for example, points us in the right direction at the supermarket, but is not the same as distilling the salient ramifications of a political speech. Reading is a very sophisticated behavior. Even when children are learning to read, they are experiencing the phenomenon that words can have more than one meaning, and be clear to the speaker, but not the listener. By way of example, I recall an experience from second grade in which I was humiliated in front of the whole class. Via television, our class studied Spanish with "Don Miguel," who one day visited our class to speak with students.[7] He paused beside me, placed a toy elephant on my desk, and asked in Spanish "is the elephant large or small?" My brain short-circuited as I did not know enough Spanish to ask Don Miguel if he meant the puny little figurine on my desk or the real elephant found in Africa. Paralyzed by anxiety to say the right thing, I said nothing. It was an eight-year old's rhetorical nightmare.

Reading builds rhetorical capital by adding vocabulary to our memories. Vocabulary is rhetorical capital. One of the reasons why many students struggle in school at all levels is because their store of vocabulary is impoverished. Studies find that individuals are more likely to encounter a richer vocabulary when they read than when they engage in conversation, and that avid readers have greater language skills than those who do not read much.[8]

The cognitive consequences of reading go beyond the reader's ability to associate new knowledge with old knowledge, experiences, and abstract

4. Holshuh and Paulson, "The Terrain of College," p. 7.

5. Draper, "Every Teacher," pp. 376–380.

6. Haas and Flowers, "Rhetorical Reading Strategies," pp. 167–168.

7. Howard Hathaway played Don Miguel on public television's "Ya Hablamos Español," which aired on Minneapolis station KTCA during the 1960s.

8. Cunningham and Stanovich, "What Reading Does for the Mind," pp. 143–146.

images and concepts. Reading challenges readers to correctly interpret text. It challenges them to assess the relevance, purpose, accuracy, significance, fairness, and credibility of assertions.[9] To a large extent, reading is reasoning. Edward Thorndike, a pioneer of Educational Psychology at the turn of the 20th century, postulated this in 1917, as he observed that reading involved many discrete mental procedures. He noted that readers made judgements on how to give proper weight to different words or groups of words to extract meaning, and that readers had to detect the right relationship between words and phrases in order to apprehend a cogent idea or accurately describe a scenario.[10]

The idea that reading comprehension tests provided a window to critical thinking and reasoning was pivotal in the development of intelligence tests and college admissions exams such as the SAT. Many of these initial exams were riddled with questions that fell short of representing the individual's true capacity to reason, as they relied on the individual's familiarity with certain cultural artifacts and attitudes.[11] In addition, these tests were often used to justify racism and to further the cause of eugenics and forced sterilization.[12]

Despite the controversies surrounding the SAT, it provided a framework for assessing reading proficiency. The verbal portion of the ACT, SAT, and the instruments used to by the National Survey of College Students to measure the literacy of undergraduates consistently use test items that target the same cognitive and critical thinking tasks. At the level of proficiency, these tasks include the reader's ability to: compare and contrast ideas and assertions; detect author's purpose and/or bias; identify implications; make inferences; assess the strength and sufficiency of evidence offered for claims; summarize main ideas; synthesize information from disparate texts and sources; and determine cause-effect relationships.[13]

Disciplinary Discourse. Masters of a given subject are expected to possess more than a great store of declarative knowledge, such as facts and the ability to define concepts. Experts in a disciplines are immersed in the culture of that discipline, and so they have a unique way of seeing subjects

9. Paul and Elder's, *How to Read a Paragraph* introduces readers to their set of cognitive tasks in reading.

10. Thorndike, "Reading as Reasoning." The entire article is a fascinating look at some of the first modern scientific scholars viewed cognition in the reading process.

11. Lehmann's *The Big Test* traces the chronology of the SAT, its use, misuse, strengths and limitations.

12. White's *Intelligence, Destiny, and Education* explores the disturbing history of American education's flirtations with social Darwinism, eugenics, and racial hygiene.

13. Baer, Cook and Baldi, "The Literacy of America's College Students," p. 13. Also see: Barry, "The Evolution of Reading Tests."

that is different from the way the average person sees subjects. The expert is familiar with an esoteric lexicon, specialized research methods, the standard thresholds of credibility and significance when analyzing data, and has greater sensitivity to the discrete variables and conditions that influence how knowledge is created and applied in the discipline.[14] To achieve a high level of proficiency in a discipline, individuals are required to think, read, and write as do the experts in that discipline.[15]

Experts observe that highly proficient academic readers use diverse reading strategies to comprehend material and know when to adjust their strategies to apprehend information. Experts also read with a clear purpose in mind. They are thinking as they read about the meaning of words, the implications of assertions, the merits and veracity of what is written, how the assertions relate to concurring and competing assertions, and about how to summarize cardinal points in the text.[16] Highly proficient readers routinely engage metacognitive habits, which include self-monitoring of comprehension and awareness of their own biases and visceral reactions to the text.[17]

Typically, college instructors do not target these discrete behaviors, nor do they help students formally explore the differences between novice and expert reading.[18] Students are generally left to "catch as catch can" when it comes to cultivating their rhetorical capital and academic reading skills. The advancement and refinement of literacy in higher education is largely a "hidden curriculum."[19]

Teaching Matters. Research confirms that reading instruction at the college level improves rhetorical capital. Students who engage in reading communities (groups that meet to review and discuss articles and books) that are facilitated by instructors show improvement in both reading and critical thinking.[20] Instructional strategies that place reading comprehension at the forefront of lessons, and use activities such as journal writing, critiquing, comparing and contrasting, and summarizing also improve students' engagement in reading.[21] Studies demonstrate that when vocabulary is explicitly cultivated, student learning across all disciplines is enhanced,

14. See: Erickson, Peters, & Strommer, *Teaching the First year College Students*, p. 122; Porter, "Constructing an Understanding;" and, Shanahan and Shanahan, "What is Disciplinary Literacy?"

15. See: Hermida, "The Importance of Teaching Academic Reading Skills."

16. Mulcahy-Ernt and Caverly, "Strategic Study Reading," pp. 191–193.

17. Isakson and Isakson, "Preparing College Students," p. 156.

18. Bosley, "I Don't Teach Reading," p.290–296.

19. Isakson and Isakson, "Preparing College Students," p. 156.

20. Weiss, Visher, and Wathington, "Learning Communities," pp. 37–47.

21. Hermida, "The Importance of Teaching," pp. 23–28.

and students are better able to participate in disciplinary discourse.[22] In addition, direct instruction that teaches students how to preview reading, highlight, annotate readings, elaborate on readings, and interrogate readings, improves students' comprehension, especially when those practices are routinely modeled and exemplified.[23]

In studies of college students' attitudes towards and perceptions of academic reading, undergraduates consistently remind educators that they want reading instruction.[24] While some desire only tips and hints about how to pluck key information from the text, others want to learn how to be more critical readers.[25] Many also want instructors to illuminate the relevance of reading assignments and integrate them more substantially into course work.[26]

ALL QUIET ON THE PEDAGOGICAL FRONT

Reading instruction matters to organizations that represent higher education's ideals. The Association of American Colleges and Universities [AACU] asserted that, "Even the strongest, most experienced readers making the transition from high school to college have not learned what they need to know and do to make sense of texts in the context of professional and academic scholarship—to say nothing about readers who are either not as strong or as experienced."[27] The Intersegmental Committee of the Academic Senates of the California Community Colleges, the California State University, and the University of California (ICAS) agreed that reading instruction ought to follow students into the undergraduate experience.[28]

Instructors find that reading is important because it contributes to academic success.[29] They assert that reading improves students' ability to engage in disciplinary discourse.[30] Many instructors also believe that

22. Francis and Simpson, "Vocabulary Development," pp. 100–106.

23. Holschuh and Aultman, "Comprehension Development," pp. 28–136.

24. Howard, et al. "Academic Reading," pp. 198–199.

25. Gorzycki, et al. "Reading is Important," p. 14.

26. Vafeas, "Attitudes Towards and Use of Textbooks," pp. 253–255.

27. Association of American Colleges and Universities, "Value Rubric; Reading," para. 1–2.

28. Intersegmental Committee of the Academic Senates of the California Community Colleges, the California State University, and the University of California, "Academic Literacy."

29. See: Cox, Friesner, and Khayum, "Do Reading Skills Courses Help;" Cherif, et al., "Why do Students Fail?"

30. See: Hermida, "The Importance of Teaching;" Lei, et al., "Resistance to Reading;" Manarin, "Reading Value."

reading is a cardinal way to acquire declarative knowledge.[31] College courses typically rely on textbooks and articles to support instruction. Faculty have reported that the benefits of reading go beyond the act of obtaining declarative knowledge. ICAS, for example, notes that reading should stimulate imaginations, critical thinking, and the capacity to argue and own ideas.[32] The AACU asserts that, "The command of language is crucial to finding out what others think and what one thinks or wishes to think.[33]

Despite affirmation from educational policy-makers that fostering growth and development in the area of reading and literacy is important, reading instruction in colleges and universities is slim pickings.[34] Reading instruction is often a superficial undertaking in post-secondary education partly because there are many ways to conceptualize reading instruction, and partly because instructors generally have the freedom to determine whether such instruction is vital or not.

Those who believe that students ought to have reading instruction in college generally fall into three categories. The first group believes that reading instruction is necessitated by low levels of student reading proficiency, and not by the fact that reading is a set of skills developed over a life-time. These folks tend to advocate remedial reading programs.[35] The second dislikes remedial programs, but believes that alternatives, including first-year course work, is a good place to augment and improve students' reading and rhetorical skills.[36] These two approaches regard college level reading instruction as something that is done to ensure that students are ready for undergraduate work, and so once students reach that level, no further reading instruction is necessary. The most radical option is to systematically integrate explicit reading and rhetorical instruction across the curriculum at all levels, with an eye to assessment, proficient disciplinary discourse, and fostering the development of rhetorical capital. This takes the life-long developmental approach to reading. At present, college students receive little, if any, explicit and systemic reading instruction. In general,

31. Bosley, "I Don't Teach Reading," p. 290.

32. Intersegmental Committee of Academic Senates, *a Statement of Competencies*, pp. 2–4.

33. Botstein, "Redeeming the Liberal Arts," p. 76.

34. Holschuh and Paulson's, "Terrain of College Developmental Reading" provides an overview of the point.

35. See: Boatman and Long, "Does Remediation work?" Merisotis & Phipps, "College Remediation;" Merisotis and Phipps, "Remedial Education in Colleges;" Attewell, et al., "New Evidence."

36. See: Boylan, "Exploring Alternatives;" Soliday and Gleason, "From Remediation to Enrichment."

reading instruction in college is episodic, and most likely to be administered in remedial, writing, or research courses.

Remarkably, investigations into why students drop out of college normally do not shine a light on students' reading proficiency. Instead, it lands on issues such as campus life, interactions with faculty, student support services, motivation, and mindsets.[37] Since the 1970s, researchers and college administrators have emphasized the importance of institutional behaviors that impact student retention. This emphasis represents a shift away from the traditional view that students' retention and academic success was largely a matter of students' ability and motivation. While institutional behaviors are vital factors in student success, the attention they have received over the last few decades has dwarfed attention given to student literacy, academic reading, disciplinary discourse, and rhetorical capital. Studies that shifted the responsibility of retention and persistence away from the student and onto the institution paved the way for a shift away from didactic and teacher-centered instruction to pedagogy of student-centered strategies and engagement. Despite the links between critical thinking and epistemological development to academic reading, the idea that immersing students in critical reading and rhetorical analysis was never well received as "hands-on" learning and student engagement in and of itself.

Professor of Speech Communication and author, Maryellen Weimer, summarizes five key practices of learner-centered teaching: 1) Administering abundant student engagement and hands-on exercises; 2) Providing explicit instruction that targets skills such as problem-solving, critical thinking, and generating hypotheses; 3) Encouraging reflection; 4) Giving students some control over the learning process; and, 5) Encouraging and facilitate collaboration.[38]

Weimer, one of the nation's leading scholars on learner-centered teaching, recognizes the false dichotomy of teaching course content separately from skills. She notes that traditionally, students have been expected to pick up the skills necessary to complete academic tasks, as instructors assumed that by completing assigned work, they would organically acquire the knowledge and skills needed to do a good job. She argues that by coupling course content with explicit skills instruction, students may apprehend the way experts in the field think about knowledge, and immediately apply new skills to their own learning.[39]

37. Tinto, "Leaving College;" Astin, "Making Sense;" Chickering and Gamson, "Development and Adaptations."

38. Weimer's, *Learner-Centered Teaching* addresses these with examples.

39. Ibid, pp. 121–126.

Weimer's assertions have terrific implications for teaching academic reading and developing rhetorical skills, but, like so many other scholars of learner-centered teaching, she offers relatively little discussion and guidance on the matter of systemic and scaffolded reading instruction in the college experience. While citing the benefits of exercises in which instructors and students discuss how to identify and why to highlight salient information in a text, for example, she leaves readers with the impression that reading is largely undertaken for the purpose of acquiring declarative knowledge and interesting ideas.[40]

Weimer is not the only educational expert who contributes to the invisibility of reading instruction in the college experience. George Kuh's "High-Impact Practices," a seminal presentation of pedagogy that is aimed at increasing student persistence to degree, does not typically place academic reading skills at the top of the practices. The list generally includes: Frist Year Seminars; Common Intellectual Experiences; Learning Communities; Writing-Intensive Courses; Collaborative Assignments and Projects; Undergraduate Research; Diversity/Global Learning; ePortfolios; Service-Learning/Community-Based Learning; Internships; and, Capstone Courses and Projects.[41] It is possible that reading is implicit in some of these practices, and that Kuh simply subsumed reading and rhetorical skills into his high-impact practices, but if so, why remain silent on the matter when unpacking the discrete elements of each practice? Kuh says little about academic reading as a developmental phenomenon and its vital role in epistemological development and disciplinary expertise.

A 2014 national study of factors leading to college drop-out rates notes that the need for remedial reading courses is a factor in retention, but does not speak to the students' ability to grow in disciplinary literacy and discourse as they complete upper division courses.[42] Even when researchers acknowledge the role of underpreparedness, remedial course work, and academic performance in students' persistence, students' reading proficiency is wholly marginalized, as if it is not a factor at all.[43] Moreover, some of the founders of the movement for student-centered teaching as a means of increasing persistence to degree, students' reading proficiency remains a ghost in the machine.[44]

---

40. Ibid, pp. 134–136.

41. Kuh, *High-Impact Practices*, pp. 13–17.

42. Therriault and Krivoshey, *College Persistence Indicators*, pp. 4–5.

43. Stewart, Lim, and Kim, "Factors Influencing."

44. Tinto, a pioneer in grasping the link between campus culture and persistence, wrote "Reflections on Student Persistence," which notes the importance of "self-efficacy," but says nothing about students' reading skills.

WHAT RESEARCH TELLS US ABOUT STUDENTS

Students consistently report that they value reading in college.[45] They do not, however, always value reading for the same reasons that experts in literacy and rhetoric value reading. Students confess that their compliance with reading is dismal. Research shows that only 30 to 50 percent of students routinely complete reading assignments before they attend class.[46] Students do not comply with reading assignments for many reasons. Some say that they have no time to complete their readings and that their readings are boring or irrelevant.[47] Many have asserted that it is not essential to read assignments in order to do well in the class and get passing grades.[48] Students find that they get what they want out of courses by taking good notes in class, or getting information from alternative sources, such as classmates or digital items that instructors post on course management systems. Students often read at the surface of text, and find that kind of reading is sufficient for how instructors assess learning.[49] Students also decide whether reading is vital based on the course subject, and hold that it is not important in certain subjects such as art, engineering, or general education courses outside one's major.[50]

The reality that many undergraduates earn good grades and degrees without reading suggests that academic reading is largely concerned with acquiring declarative knowledge, and not with engaging the text for the purpose of analyzing scholarly research, evaluating or contextualizing assertions, or critically thinking about implications, evidence, the author's purpose, and meaning of assertions. Reading to collect a few main ideas or to define something is very different from reading that is aimed at sharpening students' ability to analyze and critique discourse. In short, mining the text for declarative knowledge is an activity that dwells at the shallow end of the cognitive task pool—the bottom of Bloom's taxonomy.[51] Students who

45. See Howard, et al, "Academic Reading;" Pecorari, et al., "Reading in Tertiary Education."

46. See Brost and Bradley, "Student Compliance; "Clump, Bauer and Bradley, "The Extent;" Del Principe, "I Bought the Book;" "Ryan, "Motivating Novice Students;" Sappington, Kinsey, and Munsayac, "Two Studies of Reading;" Hoeft, "Why University Students Don't Read."

47. See Howard, et al., "Academic Reading;" Vafeas, "Attitudes Toward and Use of Textbooks;" St. Clair-Thompson, Graham, and Marsham, "Exploring the Reading Practices."

48. See Howard, et al., "Academic Reading;" Brost and Bradley, "Student Compliance;" Baier, et al., "College Students Textbook Reading."

49. See Linderholm, "Reading with Purpose;" Manarin, et al., "Critical Reading;" Gorzycki, et al., "Reading is Important."

50. See Gorzycki, et al., "Reading is Important."

51. Bloom's "taxonomy for educational objectives scaffolded cognitive tasks

are successful at recalling the declarative knowledge (key facts, main ideas) from the text, and who rewarded for doing so with outstanding grades, may get the impression that they are highly proficient, critical, and sophisticated readers when they are not.

College students are remarkably confident in their reading skills. They declare that they are proficient with reading scholarly articles, while their own professors express far less confidence in their skills.[52] Some may rate themselves generously because they lack the awareness of what differentiates the novice from the expert.[53] Their confidence, however, is betrayed by their performance on reading tests. Research shows us that many college students graduate with only basic to intermediate reading skills, which, together with their high self-ratings of reading skills, raises the question of whether they understand the difference between various levels of reading proficiency.[54] In one study, 848 undergraduates, mostly juniors and seniors, earned an average grade of 60 percent on a reading test using 11th grade reading material, and 13 percent of the students got three or less questions on the test correct.[55]

In 2018, the SAT benchmark score for "Evidence-Based Reading and Writing" (sometimes referred to as the "verbal" portion of the test) was 480.[56] The national average score for the verbal component in 2018 was 536, and 70 percent of test-takers that year met the college-readiness benchmark.[57] The disparities among scores for Evidence-Based Reading and Writing disaggregated by race/ethnicity were dramatic. While over 80 percent of Asians and whites achieved college-readiness, 58 percent of Hispanics/Latino, 50 percent of blacks, and 48 percent of Native Americans achieved college-readiness.[58]

The SAT and other similar exams to determine the readiness of students for post-secondary studies regard rhetorical capital as an important criteria for college admissions. The SAT and its equivalents test assess writing samples. The quality of writing is directly related to critical thinking, a large

---

according to the complexity and sophistication of the thinking required to complete the task with identifying at the bottom of the pyramid and analysis, synthesis, and evaluation at the top. See Anderson and Krathwohl *A Taxonomy for Learning.*

52. Howard, et al., "Academic Reading." Manarin, "Reading Value."

53. See Dunning, "Dunning-Kruger Effect," pp. 247.

54. See Baldi, "A New Study of the Literacy;" Baer et al., "The Literacy of College Students."

55. Gorzycki, et al., "An Exploration of Academic Reading," p. 151.

56. College Board, "Understanding Scores," see tables.

57. College Board, "SAT Suite Results, 2018."

58. Ibid.

store of knowledge, a sound grasp of the rhetorical problem, and the ability to synthesize ideas and information, determine the credibility of assertions, the clarity and logic embedded in one's articulation, and the ability to criticize one's own composition.[59] Writing is thus an aspect of rhetorical capital, and its proficiency relies on well-developed rhetorical capital.

The nexus between reading proficiency and writing proficiency goes beyond the pragmatic reality that students often need to gather information before they report or develop a thesis. Deep and critical reading develops in writers an acute sensitivity to the logic of discourse, and contributes to the writer's ability to suspend judgement, empathize with others, and recognize the meaning and value of ambiguity.[60] Writing proficiency bolsters students' ability to develop a cohesive and cogent thesis and to muster counter-arguments.[61] These counter-arguments may provoke empathy, as they are often laden with interests that compete with their own, and that differ from their own perspectives.

WHAT RESEARCH TELLS US ABOUT FACULTY AND ADMINISTRATION

Faculty almost always agree that reading is very important in the college experience. They claim that it is vital to academic success.[62] They state that it improves disciplinary discourse and class discussion.[63] Despite the sound endorsement for academic reading, reading instruction tends to live in the margins of the college experience. One meta-analysis of 50 studies that probed what faculty believe is important in college teaching and learning concluded that faculty hold that the development of expertise, negotiating meaning, and encouraging the creation of knowledge, are vital, yet, nothing explicit was said about reading and rhetorical proficiencies.[64]

---

59. Flower and Hayes, "A Cognitive Process," pp. 367–375.

60. Flower and Hayes, "The Cognition of Discovery" for an interesting discussion of ambiguity and nuances in creative writing process. Intersegmental Committee of the Academic Senates of the California Community Colleges, the California State University, and the University of California, "Academic Literacy," p. 3.

61. Nussbaum and Kardash, "The Effects of Goals Instructions," pp. 163–166.

62. See: Cox, Friesner, and Khayum, "Do Reading Skills Courses Help." Cherif, et al., "Why do Students Fail?" Intersegmental Committee of the Academic Senates of the California Community Colleges, the California State University, and the University of California, "Academic Literacy."

63. See Lei, et al., "Resistance to Reading;" Hermida, "The Importance of Teaching."

64. See Kane, Sandrettto, and Heath, "Telling Half the Story."

Research indicates that faculty do not provide reading instruction to college students for several reasons, including their belief that reading is a subject entirely distinct and separate from course content.[65] From this perspective, reading instruction does not enhance learning about subjects, nor improve students disciplinary mastery; it merely takes time away from "real" course material. Some faculty believe that reading is a simple matter of decoding text, and that students learn how to do this years before they enter college.[66] Faculty do not teach reading instruction because they often teach as they were taught, and lack pedagogical training to integrate reading instruction into their curriculum and instruction.[67]

Not all faculty assign robust and numerous reading and writing assignments. In one study, a third of the students indicated that they had not taken a college course that required more than 40 pages of reading in a week.[68] Students report that writing assignments vary by course discipline. In general, students in humanities courses are far more likely to be required to write 20 pages for courses than are students in engineering, math, and technology courses.[69] In consultations, many faculty have confided that they no longer assign essays or research papers because "students do not know how to write," and "it is painful to read their writing." This practice has aroused some discord among faculty. As one colleague said, "Teachers complaining that reading students' writing is painful because students don't know how to write is like saying that they don't want to teach because students need to be taught."

Faculty take many of their cues about teaching and assessing student work from administration. Administrators at the state level sometimes set goals that compromise the quality of teaching and learning in general, and the development of rhetorical capital in particular. In 2017, the Chancellor of the California State University system (CSU)—the largest state university system in the nation—with about 440,000 students—announced that the CSU was eliminating remedial courses.[70] The measure was part of the CSU's "Graduate Initiative," which called for significant increases in the graduation rates of all 23 campuses in the CSU.

---

65. See Tagg, "Teachers as Students."

66. See Bosley, "I Don't Teach" and Huber, "Disciplines."

67. See Halpern and Hakel, "Applying the Science."

68. Arum and Roska, *Academically Adrift*, p. 71.

69. Ibid, p. 80.

70. Jackson, "CSU Ends Remedial Courses." Also see: Assembly Bill 705 for insights to the rationale.

The elimination of remedial courses made students happy. It meant no more paying for courses that did not generate college credit, and no delays in enrolling in regular college courses. The new policy made some faculty members happy too, as they believed the remedial courses stigmatized students, and frustrated their persistence to degree. Other faculty members were troubled. For several years running up to the 2017 decision, roughly one third of CSU first-year, first-time students required remedial English and Math. Many were dismayed that the mandate left each university in the system responsible for figuring out how it would respond to students' needs in the wake of zero remediation.

Each university in the system essentially had three choices. First, they could require all students with an SAT verbal score to take a specially designed general education course that would teaching reading skills and generate college credit. Second, universities could forget about creating special courses, let the students proceed through their undergraduate courses, take reading courses if they wanted to, and let the dust settle where it settled. Third, the universities could create a program whereby explicit reading instruction was integrated across all disciplines and all levels along a scope and sequence that inched students toward reading proficiency, epistemological growth, and rhetorical competence. In choosing any of these options, universities could also have created special reading centers, reading tutoring programs, and an institutional means of assessing the efficacy of their response to students' reading needs.

To date none of the 23 universities in the CSU has chosen the third option, the one that most closely represents teaching aligned with the developmental nature of reading. Admittedly, in order to implement the third option and do that well, faculty would have to be trained in reading instruction, and develop skills necessary to create effective learning activities and assessments related to academic and critical reading. For some professors, the very suggestion that this something college instructors ought to do provokes hisssing red-faced rage.

The CSU is not the only system impacted by large numbers of underprepared students. The demand for remedial courses over the last five decades has been as relentless as it has been controversial. In 2006, over half of those enrolled in two-year colleges and nearly 20 percent of freshmen enrolled in four-year colleges required remediation. Of those who completed remedial courses, less than 10 percent in two-year colleges and about 35 percent in four-year colleges persisted to degree.[71] Remediation is a politically volatile subject. Ethnic minorities typically do not score as highly on

---

71. Complete College America, *Bridge to Nowhere*, pp. 6–10.

standardized reading exams as do whites, and so critics assert that the tests are a means of slowing the academic progress of vulnerable populations.[72]

In 2011, states, students, and their families spent $3 billion for remedial classes.[73] Investigations of the effects of college remedial reading courses have produced mixed results. Measuring the benefits is complicated by the fact that not everyone agrees on what constitutes "college level reading."[74] Some find that most students who complete remedial courses complete their degrees, while others find the opposite is true and blame remediation for discouraging talented and smart individuals from finishing their degrees.[75]

The great kerfuffle over reading remediation at the college level is due in part to the refusal of educators at the college level to accept the reality that learning to read is a life-long process. It is exacerbated by a sense of urgency imposed on the academy to push students through undergraduate programs as quickly as possible. Since experts do not categorize reading according to age or grade, but according to competency with a given skill set, there is no external pressure imposed upon the academy to have students read "at their appropriate grade level." The National Assessment of Adult Literacy (NAAL) uses an instrument to measure reading skills that assess readers' ability to perform certain cognitive tasks, such as detecting implications and distinguishing main ideas from peripheral statements. Test-takers represent four categories of reading skill ranging from "Below Basic" (able to read only short simple text, such as traffic signs and recipes), to "Proficient" (able to read dense and complex test, synthesize sources, and analyze rhetoric).[76] Colleges and universities, however, normally do not use the NAAL nor any other instrument to measure their graduates' reading skills.

The question of whether the university cares about the development of rhetorical capital looms large. In some ways, the question is being answered every day by what students learn and do not learn in their college courses. The question is answered every time colleges and universities set admission standards, determine course requirements, hire instructors, create curriculum, decide which is the best way to measure student achievement, decide the content of faculty development workshops, determine what data should be included in institutional self- studies, and decide whether to invest in academic support services or not.

72. Perez, "Different Tests, Same Flaws," pp. 23–25.

73. Complete College America, p. 2.

74. Merisotis and Phipps, "Remedial Education," pp. 71–74.

75. Attewell, et al., "New Evidence," pp. 886–892.

76. Hauser, et al., *Measuring Literacy*, 87–107.

WHY PICK ON HIGHER EDUCATION?

Historian Jacques Barzun wrote that in the U.S., education is "a passion and a paradox," because while millions want it, they are also degrading it by wanting it "free of charge and free of work."[77] His observation is as true today as it was 60 years ago when he made the point. There are at least four arguments for higher education to be more serious and proactive about developing rhetorical capital. First, the academy is one of the few institutions in society that is specifically charged with improving cognition and intellectual skills and habits. The unique purpose of higher education is to overcome ignorance and encourage individuals to be skeptical towards assertions and claims. In their mission statements, colleges and universities routinely announce their commitment to the liberal arts traditions of building creative problem-solvers, compassionate professionals, and critical thinkers.[78] In theory, we expect college graduates to possess certain traits, including slowness to judgment, an analytical and inquisitive mind, respect for diverse perspectives, and a commitment to consider the common good when deliberating.

Second, the university is in a unique position to conduct research about the consequences of public discourse gone wild. It has the resources to undertake studies of local and national leadership with an eye to what is happening to the quality of public discourse, why that is happening, and what is jeopardized under the circumstances. Arguably, findings of such research may be useful in educational partnerships between schools, universities, and community organizations that are dedicated to adult education seeking to improve people's understanding of propaganda, hate speech, and fake news, and aiming to improve people's communication skills.

Third, evidence tells us that many adults, including college graduates, are not proficient with literacy skills. A national study in 2009 revealed that 10 percent of adults in the U.S. read below the basic level of proficiency—a total of 30 million.[79] In addition, roughly 12 percent of students in two-year colleges and 7 percent of students in four-year colleges and universities read at only the basic or below basic level.[80] In other words, many college students who are able to read and comprehend directions for a cake mix are not able to read and comprehend a government report about the consequences of producing and consuming genetically engineered butter and eggs. The national study also noted that, "The average literacy of the U.S.

77. Barzun, *House of Intellect*, p. 89.
78. Delucchi, "Liberal Arts Colleges," pp. 415–416.
79. See: National Center for Education Statistics, *Basic Reading Skills*.
80. Baer, Cook, and Baldi, The Literacy of America's college students, p. 13.

college students was generally the same regardless of how long students had been in college, their enrollment status, or the number of post-secondary institutions they attended."[81] In other words, many students graduate from college with the same level of reading skills that they had when they first enrolled.

Finally, research indicates that employers are not very pleased with the rhetorical skills of college graduates. In a recent study of over 1,000 managers and corporate executives, researchers found that just 57 percent believed college graduates had the skills to enter their professions, and only 34 percent believed these graduates had the knowledge and skills needed for advancement.[82] Executives and managers agree that colleges and universities should do a better job of grooming written and oral communication, problem-solving, critical and ethical thinking, collaboration, and real-world application of knowledge and skills.[83]

Colleges and universities are products of culture. They walk the line between being the gatekeeper of the highest ideals relative to intellectual and personal development, and being diploma mills that cater to the lowest common demands of their "customers." Colleges and universities are highly attentive to what motivates enrollment and persistence to degree. They are also very attentive to the quality of their curriculum and instruction when they are held accountable to external accrediting agencies and associations. A nursing program, for example, might receive much more support and resources to develop top tier education than programs in history, art, or literature, because the passing rate of nursing students who take state board exams matters to those who promote the institution as a great place to learn, and students of history, art, and literature typically do not take state board exams.

Further exploration of higher education sheds light on why college educated individuals do not always have great stores of rhetorical capital, and what keeps colleges and universities from asking more from their students in the way of intellectual achievement. As is explained in the next chapter, the democratization of our institutions that was undertaken with great pride and promise has lead us to troubled waters. Subsequent discussion will also reveal how faith that the market will eventually and justly sort out the well-educated individuals from the poorly educated has contributed to mediocre instruction in our colleges and universities.

81. Ibid, p. 6.

82. Hart and Associates, *Fulfilling the American Dream*, p. 8.

83. Ibid, p. 11.

Chapter 4

Democratizing the University and the Bumpy Road of Liberal Arts

A MOVING TARGET

Though generally not known by the name "rhetorical capital," reading proficiency, logic, oration, composition, and critical thinking have always been cultivated in liberal arts education. Their place and meaning, however, have not remained stagnate. Rather than being a monolithic entity, liberal arts has had and continues to have many incarnations. Liberal arts education takes its meaning, value, and content from the context in which it is administered. As society's perception of needs change, so too does the perception of what it means to be educated in the liberal arts tradition. Social, economic, and political agendas leave their mark on liberal arts education as they frequently determine the perimeters of legitimate and essential inquiry.[1]

As the American higher education evolved, pluralism and secularism displaced the centrality of Christianity in education, and replaced it with science, reason, and humanism. Reverence for traditional liberal arts curriculum that was rich in classical studies and piety waned as the U.S. industrialized, and society questioned the practicality of liberal arts. In 1828, the *Yale Report* sounded the academic alarm that liberal arts and humanities

---

1. Schrecker's *No Ivory Tower* richly details the experience of McCarthyism in higher education and it impact on education, culture, and public discourse. Hartman's *A War* unpacks the thesis that culture is power and offers searing insights on public debate over art, education, literature, history, and science.

education were in peril.[2] It sought to preserve studies in the classics, arguing that they disciplined the mind and cultivated a taste for reason and wise judgment. While some dismissed the manifesto as an elitist missive against egalitarian ideals, others saw it as a legitimate warning that material priorities were creeping into the sanctuary of the academy with ruinous implications.[3]

Some claim that liberal arts education died in 1862, the year that the Morrill Land-Grant Act provided incentives for states to purchase federal land for the construction of state colleges.[4] The legislation envisioned a new generation of colleges dedicated to agricultural, vocational, and technological studies. The Morrill Act boosted college enrollment, and was perceived as a means of settling and developing the West. In 1870, just 63,000 students attended post-secondary institutions in the U.S., and by 1900, that number had nearly tripled.[5] Though greater numbers of Americans went to a college, there was still no mass conviction that college was a better path to success than hard work and apprenticeship.

Fourteen years after the Morrill Act, Johns Hopkins University opened its doors as America's first research university. The research university added another ripple to the tempestuous debates over the purpose of higher education and liberal arts. The research university favored specialization in undergraduate studies, and by the end of the 20th century, demonstrated special zeal for STEM programs (science, technology, engineering and math). Research universities sought professors who were dedicated researchers. They would be awarded plum resources and their teaching loads would be minimized. Reaction against this new paradigm for higher education was immediate. Professors at Harvard and Columbia University developed the Great Books program in the early 1900s with the goals of sustaining a liberal arts education that prepared individuals for responsible and virtuous citizenship in a republic based on Western ideals.[6] The program quickly spread to other universities.[7]

During the Gilded Age, popular rhetoric glistened with narratives about building character.[8] Fiction, advertising, sermons, essays on civility

2. See: Herbst, "The Yale Report of 1828."

3. See: Lane, "The Yale Report of 1828."

4. Axtell, "The Death of the Liberal Arts College," pp. 339–52.

5. Snyder, *120 Years of American Education*, pp. 64–65.

6. Graff's *Professing Literature* and Lacy's *Dream of a Democratic Culture* trace the origins and aims of the Great Books Movement of the early 20th century. See: Stevens, "Philosophy of General Education," pp. 166–183.

7. Stevens, "Philosophy of General Education," pp. 184–188.

8. Salazar' *Bodies of Reform* and Hilkey's *Character is Capital* discuss the creation and function of character literature in the Gilded Age. The literature placed responsibility

and manliness, manuals on fitness, pamphlets on child-rearing, and pedagogical discourse were filled with references to character-building and the
virtues of a sound moral character. Americans unabashedly placed the individual's virtue and vice front and center in public discourse about social
morality. In the decades to come, this centrality would be displaced by new
sciences and new attitudes about the individual in society. Sigmund Freud's
theories, for example, asserted that human behavior, including morality, was
formed in a cauldron of subconscious motivations, anxieties, suppressed
urges, and projections of the ego.

Public discourse on morality thus made room for the possibility that
moral conduct was more than a matter of personal will. The burgeoning
field of sociology offered insights to how environmental conditions and circumstances bred social diseases such as crime and prostitution.[9] Scholars,
law-makers, educators, and social reformers intensified their beliefs that
social institutions themselves made monsters of decent people by doing
nothing to alleviate ignorance, poverty, squalor, disease, and unfair working conditions. Many held that education was the key to producing decent
people and engineering a society void of poverty and vice. This rationale for
education was very different from the rationale to engineer an empire.

THE ACADEMY OF EMPIRE

Contemporary federal budgets bear witness to the relatively low regard that
law-makers have for the liberal arts, which is where rhetorical capital has
traditionally been cultivated. The National Endowment for the Humanities,
for example, distributed roughly $425 million in 1979, and only about $150
million in 2018.[10] The National Science Foundation reported that in 2016,
the total of federal agency money for scientific research and development
was over $115 billion.[11] Admittedly, scientific research and development
is more expensive than research and development in the humanities and
liberal arts. This is due to the cost of laboratories and technical equipment.
Yet, the reduction of funding through the National Endowment for the Humanities of 65 percent over 40 years suggests that our elected officials do

---

for good behavior squarely on individuals.

9. Lydston's 1904 book, *Diseases of Society*, developed the thesis that social pathologies cause individual pathologies, and presented a case for moral development as a
product of economic and social conditions.

10. See: American Academy of Arts and Sciences, "National Endowment for the
Humanities."

11. See: National Science Foundation, "Federal Funds for Research and
Development."

not sense the importance of the humanities relative to forming people who are conversant on the great ideas that are foundational to democracy and civility, and who are adept in public discourse.

The narrative that has driven higher education's agenda over the last several decades consistently puts the nation's ability to dominate the global market, remain a military powerhouse, and have a commanding lead in the development of science and technology ahead of all other priorities. When World War II ended, the U.S. and Soviet Union—former allies against the Axis powers— were the most powerful nations on the planet, and they bitterly opposed the expansion of each other's global influence. In 1957, the Soviets put a satellite into space, triggering the space race, which radically shifted the priorities of American higher education. In 1958, Congress passed the National Defense Education Act to produce more scientists. The act represented a new form of government activism in the university, and it pumped millions of dollars into undergraduate and graduate programs in STEM subjects. Federal and state initiatives after Sputnik aimed to overcome what Americans believed was a deficit in the kind of American education essential to national security and economic prowess.[12]

The clarion call for greater numbers of students to earn college degrees in the STEM subjects was reissued in 1983, when politicians and business leaders saw that German and Japanese industries threatened America's might in the global marketplace. The National Commission on Excellence in Education penned that the nation was at risk, as "the educational foundations of our society are being eroded by a rising tide of mediocrity that threatens our very future as a Nation and as a people."[13] The report exclaimed that mediocrity in schools was essentially an act of war as it made the U.S. vulnerable to the economic and military dominance of other nations. It noted that democracy itself was in peril because too many Americans lacked literacies that enabled citizens to understand and solve the world's problems effectively.

A Nation at Risk chastised American education: verbal scores on the SAT were falling; functional illiteracy of 17 year-olds was around 13 percent; high school seniors could not draw inferences from printed material, and 20 percent could not write an argumentative essay. Further, the science achievements of 17 year-olds had declined since 1969; and, between 1975 and 1980, the demand for remedial math increased at colleges by 72 percent.[14] The report called for increases in standards of learning and school accountability.

12. Steeves, et al., "Transforming American Educational Identity," pp. 75–80.

13. National Commission on Excellence in Education, Nation at Risk, p. 1.

14. Ibid, p. 3.

At the time *A Nation at Risk* was issued, the public's regard for government missives about their wellbeing was sharply divided. On one had was the post-Watergate narrative that this report was just one more Cold War petard issued by old men defending the American empire. On the other hand was the enduring Cold War narrative that the world would go to hell in a handbasket if the U.S. was not economically, politically, and militarily strong enough to prevent communism from gaining ground.

Other reports followed, including the *Spellings Report* (2006), which complained that colleges and universities abroad were producing greater numbers of people with advanced degrees than the U.S. It also stated that there were "disturbing signs that many students who do earn degrees have not actually mastered the reading, writing, and thinking skills we expect of college students."[15] In 2012, the President's Council of Advisors on Science and Technology called for an additional one million more graduates in STEM disciplines by the year 2022. The document noted that students who drop out of STEM majors find entry level STEM courses difficult. It called on colleges and universities to create incentives for students to enter and persist in STEM programs for the sake of the nation's economic well-being.[16]

The bumpy road along which liberal arts traveled has been continuously maintained and resurfaced. Americans never gave up the idea that without sound liberal arts instruction, democracy itself was in peril. Ironically, however, democracy itself contained the seeds of decline in the valuing of liberal arts. With confidence that democratizing higher education would create a more enlightened citizenry, produce a more highly skilled work force, and demonstrate the nation's commitment to equity and social justice, colleges and universities flung open the academy's gates to welcome the masses. However, many who enrolled when new opportunities presented themselves treated higher education as would a consumer shopping for something cheap, easy, and convenient. Remarkably, many institutions accommodated them.

AN ELASTIC GOLDEN GATE

The democratization of higher education refers to several phenomena: 1) strategies to increase the number of individuals who enroll post-secondary institutions; 2) improving opportunities for under-represented minorities and low-income families to access and be successful in post-secondary education; 3) expanding students' participation in the academy's policy-making

15. U.S. Department of Education, *A Test of Leadership*, pp. vi–vii.

16. President's Council of Advisors on Science and Technology, *Engage to Excel*, pp. i–ii.

processes; 4) designing inclusive curriculum that explores the experiences of populations whose narratives have been traditionally omitted from the canons liberal arts; and, 5) creating instruction that uses diverse methods and strategies as appropriate for diverse styles of learning. In theory, the democratization of higher education would engineer a more just and equitable society, and produce graduates who would engage in democratic processes for the purpose of building a more just, equitable, and humanitarian society.[17]

The democratization of higher education has led to the upward mobility of millions of Americans. It has improved rhetorical capital by adding to the perspectives represented in public discourse and challenging scholars to address social justice in the curriculum. The Serviceman's Readjustment Act, 1944 (G.I. Bill) and federal loan programs of the 1960s and 1970s resulted in the enrollment of millions of college students.[18] At present, there are approximately 4,300 two-year and four-year colleges and universities.[19] As of 1940, less than 10 percent of Americans between the ages of 18 and 24— roughly 1.5 million—were enrolled in college. That number dramatically increased to 2.4 million ten years later, as more veterans took advantage of federal programs for them, and as more women sought college degrees.[20] In 1965, nearly 6 million were enrolled in college, and that figure reached almost 20 million by 2018.[21] Roughly 75 percent of those enrolled in college attend a public institution.[22]

Increases in the number of students enrolled in public institutions translates into the demand for billions in tax revenue at the state and local level to pay for higher education, which many believe might be a poor investment.[23] Paradoxically, the democratization of higher education has contributed to the depletion of rhetorical capital by lowering standards of mastery in areas of literacy, epistemological development, writing proficiency, and critical analysis. This is a very serious charge, one not made without respect for the complexity of the issues. Many institutions have lowered standards, but that certainly does not mean that all college graduates are bankrupt in rhetorical capital. It does, however, mean that in the zeal to award more degrees to more people, many institutions have adjusted their expectations for

17. Watts, "Democratizing Higher Education," pp. 15–29.

18. Youn, "Introduction," pp. ix–xx.

19. Moody, "A Guide to the Changing Number," para. 1.

20. Snyder, *120 Years of American Education*, pp. 64–66.

21. Statistia, "College Enrollment," charts.

22. Ibid.

23. In 2013, the federal budget for higher education was $65 billion, but states often bear the greater burden. See Pew Charitable Trusts, "Federal and State funding for Higher Education" for more details.

learning, and have made it possible for many students who lack substantial rhetorical capital and who do not read proficiently to obtain a college degree.

The democratization of higher education changed higher education in three important ways. First, it resulted in open enrollment and a reduction in institutional selectivity, which increased the demand for remedial courses to help students who were ill-prepared for tertiary education. Second, by way of institutionalizing student evaluations of teaching (SET), it gave students a greater role in determining whether instructors would achieve tenure or lose their jobs. Third, it increased the pressure put upon professors to award good grades to boost the institution's rate of persistence to degree, and to secure favorable student evaluations.

The increase in college enrollment over the last 50 years is partially the result of open admissions initiatives. Open enrollment is a policy that automatically admits to a two-year college anyone with a high school diploma or its equivalent. Some four-year colleges also practice this policy. A pioneer in this practice, City University of New York (CUNY), initiated open enrollment in 1970, which it claims was highly successful, as it increased the employment options and incomes of many disadvantaged individuals.[24] As colleges and universities admitted greater numbers for the sake of improving students' prospects for gainful employment— and thus do their part in building social equality and justice—they faced the reality that many students who deserved to have a college education were not ready for it. CUNY met this challenge with programs for mass remediation and innovative student support services.[25] Despite opposition to the cost of open enrollment and skepticism about the success it would achieve, CUNY's model was imitated by other colleges across the country. By 2017, roughly 80 percent of colleges and universities admitted at least half of all applicants, and 25 percent admitted 90 to 100 percent.[26]

The democratization of higher education created a burden that not all institutions shouldered evenly. Colleges and universities with the highest admissions rates and the lowest selectivity often bore the highest cost of programs to assist individuals who required remedial coursework. In 1962, the average student admitted into the most selective 5 percent of colleges and universities (such as those in the Ivy League) had an SAT or ACT score in the 90th percentile, and by 2007, the average score for that same student was in the 98th percentile. Conversely, in 1962, the average student who

24. Lavin and Hyllegard's *Against the Odds* traces the development of, opposition to, and outcomes of the endeavor.

25. Lavin and Jacobson, "Open Admissions," p. 2, 45.

26. Desilver, "A Majority," para. 1–4.

enrolled at the least selective 5 percent of colleges and universities scored at the 50th percentile of the SAT and ACT, and by 2007, that same average student scored at the 30th percentile.[27] Thus, students with the greatest remedial needs were concentrated in institutions with low selectivity.

Institutional spending per student varies by institutional selectivity. Whereas in 1976 the colleges and universities with the lowest selectivity spent about $3,900.00 per student, and highly selective colleges and universities spent about $17,400.00 per student, in 2007, spending in less selective institutions was $ 12,000.00 per student and in highly selective institutions was $92,000.00. This means that the least selective colleges and universities—the ones that are most likely to admit students with remedial needs—had far fewer resources than highly selective colleges and universities with which to address those needs.[28]

Critics of open enrollment claimed that the practice reversed a long-standing tradition of admitting students on the basis of merit, and that it would lead to a decline in learning.[29] Others asserted that by lowering admission requirements, institutions may be enrolling individuals whose established academic record suggests they may be unable to actually persist to degree. At present, the graduation rate of students enrolled in two-year colleges after four years of study is just 28 percent.[30] The graduation rate for students attending four-year institutions after six years of study is roughly 60 percent.[31]

EXTORTION EXTRAVAGANZA

For the purpose of achieving a "greater good," many colleges and universities practice the soft extortion of unspoken, mutually agreed upon compromises. Administrators, for example, look the other way when instructors inflate grades and lower standards because they are interested in increasing the numbers of student who persist to degree. Many instructors who inflate the grades and lower their standards proceed with the understanding that such practice may contribute to favorable student evaluations, and so enhance the chances of earning tenure. The strategic plans of state governors and chancellors of college and university systems typically do not dwell on the discrete accomplishments of students relative to reading, writing, and rhetorical proficiency.

27. Hoxby, "Changing Selectivity of American Colleges," pp. 97–102.

28. Ibid, 108–114.

29. Karabel, "Open Admissions," p. 38.

30. Chen, "Catch 22 of Community College," para. 1–2.

31. National Center for Educational Statistics, "Undergraduate Retention and Graduation," para. 1.

There are no state or federal exit exams for college students. When pressed to explain why they do not have this kind of accountability, many say that they are confident that the professors' grades accurately represent students' proficiency, and that the diploma itself is evidence of learning sufficient to the requirements of the institution. State officials are ordinarily interested in lowering the cost of education, and justifying the cost of education by pointing to high graduation rates. Many invest special effort in producing large numbers of graduates from underrepresented minorities, and graduates who majored in STEM subjects, because these are the things that catch voters' and donors' attention.

Grade inflation is serious business. In 1960, "As" represented 15 percent of college course grades, and by 2009, "As" represented 43 percent of college course grades. This is an interesting phenomenon given the fact that the demand for remedial reading during this time frame dramatically increased.[32] This distribution applied to institutions across selectivity standards, and has called to question the meaning of high marks.[33] Grade inflation is sometimes the result of soft extortion, whereby instructors award high marks to students in exchange for favorable course evaluations, or a reduction in students' demand for the instructor's time and assistance. Some educators call this a "disengagement compact" whereby students agree to reward the instructor if the instructor agrees not to make the work load too strenuous.[34]

Grade inflation greases the wheels of democratization of higher education because it enables students with poor and mediocre academic achievement to earn degrees. Though widely practiced, the term "grade inflation" is often not used to describe what is happening in college classrooms around the country. Sometimes instructors and administrators use euphemisms for grade inflation that do not have the negative connotation of grade inflation. Some faculty regard "student-centered practice," and "equity" as code words for lowered expectations.

In the 1960s and 1970s, as students demanded greater input about the quality of instruction and course offerings, SETs acquired leverage in the retention, tenure, and promotion processes.[35] SETs are especially important to the adjunct instructors who are hired on a semester by semester basis.[36] Many instructors are convinced that if they assign too much reading or

32. Wright, "Many College Freshmen," p. 3.

33. Rojstaczer and Healy, "Where A is Ordinary," p. 4.

34. Kuh, "What We're Learning, p. 28.

35. Both Costin, et al., "Student Ratings" and D'Agostino and Kosegarten, "Reevaluating" track this development.

36. Sonner, "'A' is for Adjunct," pp. 5–6.

writing, students will give them bad ratings.[37] Some say that they inflate grades and lower standards to avoid the untrue accusation that they are racist, sexist, or elitist. As one professor with over 25 years of teaching experience stated, "I admit I inflate grades . . . I don't want to be the one who is accused of spoiling someone's shot at the American dream."

Grade inflation and awarding diplomas to students who can barely read and write much beyond what the NAAL calls the "basic" level does not necessarily bother colleges and universities.[38] As one professor quipped, "As long as we produce a celebrity or superstar on a regular basis, it doesn't matter that so many are mediocre or really low-achieving students. . . The shining star steals the spotlight, and the market will eventually sort out the rest." In many cases, families do not care about whether their child has mastery of disciplinary knowledge and abundant rhetorical capital. They are often so proud that their child has received a college diploma, that whether their child has stagnated in his or her literacy and intellectual development is irrelevant. The mystique of a college diploma often neutralizes criticism about the quality of the education. Diplomas tell the community, "my kid is smart," and they symbolize access to high paying jobs. The mystique can be intoxicating and cause educators to ignore serious deficits in teaching and instruction.

SMORGASBORDS AND ZOMBIES

The democratization of higher education left a few bruises on the liberal arts. This is due in part to the belief that liberal arts education is barrier to students who want to quickly accumulate credits in their majors and get going with their careers. Many see the liberal arts as a quaint, but annoying remnant of a pre-industrial society.[39] Though general education (GE) has been conceptualized and operationalized in a variety of ways, many institutions look to their GE programs to articulate its own values and beliefs relative to liberal arts and civic engagement.[40]

In previous incarnations of liberal arts education, GE was represented by a set of courses required of all undergraduates. These typically included courses such as English Composition, or surveys of United States history. The point of such curricula was to ensure that all

37. See: Howard, et al., "Academic Reading," and Sappington, Kinsey and Munsayac, "Two Studies."

38. For a snapshot of the NAAL's four levels of reading competence, see National Center for Educational Statistics, "National Assessment."

39. Ferrall, Jr. *Liberal Arts at the Brink*, pp. 7–12.

40. Warner and Koeppel, "General Education Requirements," 241–244.

students went into their specialized studies with the same understanding of the world, fundamental principles of science, basic math and language skills, and an understanding of U.S. legal traditions and institutions. The curricula standardized baccalaureate studies, and was very Western in its world view.

At present, GE is not represented by a fixed and universal set of course requirements. Instead, it is sample platter of items taken from a menu of GE courses organized into liberal arts disciplines. Students may select from a variety of courses in "menu columns" to satisfy requirements in disciplinary groupings such as: Social Studies/Sciences; Language/Literature; Mathematics/Quantitative Reasoning; Physical and Life Sciences; and, Fine/Creative Arts. In addition, some institutions require students to take courses that have "overlays" that target certain issues, such as social justice, global perspectives, or critical thinking.

This "smorgasbord" approach to GE drew criticism from the American Council of Trustee and Alumni (ACTA), which studied over 1,100 colleges and universities that describe themselves as liberal arts institutions. The ACTA wrote that colleges and universities "offer unstructured and chaotic curricula," for the sake of letting student choose courses with "vague outcomes" based on personal interests, and self-discovery.[41] Only one third of the institutions in the study merited high scores (an "A" or a "B" in their rating system), which evaluated the rigor, cohesiveness, and clarity of curricula and requirements.

The ACTA charged that core requirements can often be met by taking courses that are only obliquely related to core competencies. For example, at one Midwest institution students were able to fulfill their literature requirement by taking a course on "The History of Comics" or "Game Design for Non-Majors." Students at a prominent university in the Great Lakes region earned credit for their Humanities requirement by taking "Global X: Zombies!"[42] Many courses use pop culture as the sugar that makes the medicine of liberal arts curriculum go down.

The zombie trope is popular in many institutions. At a university in the Southwest, students could satisfy science requirements with "Zombie Apocalypse: Biology of Disease," which used the textbook, *Zombie Human Biology*, a real title by real biologists.[43] The course, "Zombie Ethics," offered students at a Midwest college an opportunity to earn credits in the

41. American Council of Trustees and Alumni, *What Will They Learn*, p. 1

42. Ibid, p. 18.

43. See: Hertweck, "Zombie Apocalypse."

humanities and think about morality and what it means to be human.[44] As the legend goes, zombies are reanimated corpses that serve the masters who resurrected them.[45] The morbid creature is a metaphor for people who have lost their humanity to capitalist culture, and are mindlessly enslaved to work, consumption, debt, and greed.[46] The living dead are powerful metaphoric figures, as they connote apocalypse and damnation of the soul. As educators often cater to students' demands for curriculum that is little more than ersatz and pabulum, it may be argued that professors themselves are contributing to the "zombification" liberal arts.[47]

The smorgasbord approach to core curriculum in GE programs has a wee bit of zombie in its DNA. This is true to the extent that colleges and universities design courses and set curriculum requirements that lean more toward pleasing the "customers"—students—than meeting high academic standards relative to the liberal arts. Data from studies of student reading proficiency presented in the previous chapter confirms that students can be very successful in their college courses without demonstrating proficiency in critical reading. When asked to justify the liberal arts and humanities, faculty readily recite their thoughts about the value of being knowledgeable in a wide variety of subjects, building a foundation for learning across disciplines, or endowing students with the critical thinking and rhetorical skills necessary for civic engagement. The zombie lurks in gap between their rhetoric and practice. Many instructors have confided in consultations that the rigor of GE courses is far less than that of advanced courses in a major, and frequently require very little reading, writing, and critical thought. As one professor said, "I don't even grade the assignments and exams. . .students can do them as many times as they need to with open books. . .If they turn something in, they get full credit."

Liberal arts curricula is controversial. Conservatives accuse liberal professors of using GE courses as a platform to indoctrinate students and promote liberal social engineering.[48] Liberals accuse conservatives of wanting to burden students with course requirements that do not represent what students find relevant, and that slow their progress towards their degrees.[49] The most cynical say that GE programs in the liberal arts are only in place

44. See: Johnson, "Zombie Ethics."

45. Lauro, "Introduction, pp." ix–x.

46. Lauro and Embry, "A Zombie Manifesto," pp. 851–68.

47. See Whelan, Walker, and Moore, *Zombies in the Academy* for essays about this phenomena and its effects.

48. Stover, "There is No Place," para. 1–6.

49. Harris, "Why the Liberal Arts May Not Survive," para. 10–13.

to employ the professors of "obscure" and "arcane" subjects like literature, history, and philosophy.

The smorgasbord approach to liberal arts education leaves many holes in undergraduate studies. It is possible in some colleges and universities, for instance, to satisfy liberal arts requirements without taking a course that introduces students to the principles of democracy, the substance of the U.S. Constitution, and daily operations of our government. It is possible to graduate without taking a course in world religion, and without a course in society and media. More to the point, the holes in undergraduate curriculum are about the ignorance one ideally overcomes in a liberal arts education in a democratic society. There are no shortages of GE course descriptions that declare students will examine the Constitution and key court decisions, for example, but whether these courses actually dispel student's ignorance about the core document of our democracy, and about how power operates within, around, and above it is another story.

A 2016 national study of college graduates found that 60 percent could not identify the process for creating laws and adding amendments to the Constitution, and roughly half did not know the length of terms for Senators and Representatives.[50] This is to say nothing about whether graduates can identify congressional committees, the extent of influence that foreign business leaders and governments exercise over Congress and executives, and the ties between lobbying, campaign donations, and legislation. The irony in this scenario is that our society wanted so much to democratize education for the purpose of creating a more equitable and just world, yet has become relatively complacent about the reality that many college graduates do not know much about how our government works .

The controversy over GE and liberal arts is much more profound than what many educators themselves realize. The controversy is not about which subjects to teach, or how many GE credits represent an adequate "immersion" in liberal arts. The controversy fundamentally about the meaning of our humanity.

That may sound like ridiculously inflated language, but is true. In education, every decision about what knowledge and skill set to teach, what learning experiences ought to be facilitated, what kinds of assessments ought to be administered, and what criteria ought to be applied to the evaluation of learning tells us something about the value we place on humanity and how we envision the purpose of our lives. Where the highest purpose of life is material, and where the value of human beings lie in their service to the state and their consumer potential, rhetorical capital matters only to the

50. American Council of Trustees and Alumni, *Crisis in Civics Education*, pp. 4–5.

extent that it facilitates material transactions. Where the highest purpose of life is spiritual or humanitarian, and where the value of human beings lie in their potential to bring the love of God to bear on Earth, rhetorical capital is not only important to material survival, but for building and sustaining caring relationships, just societies, and self-improvement.

DEMOCRATIZING CURRICULUM

In the 1960s and 1970s, students called for curriculum reform that would teach students about the experiences of traditionally marginalized populations and about how to activate social change to eliminate injustices in the democratic process. Three distinct curricula emerged: 1) Ethnic Studies; 2) Multicultural Studies; and, 3) Critical Pedagogy. In their own way, each of these curricula drew from disciplines such as history, sociology, literature, and anthropology to construct courses that spoke to immediate controversies and the lived experiences of a diverse student body. These curricula aim to promote an understanding of the complexity and richness of the human experience, empower individuals who have been marginalized, and to help students comprehend the biases that often taint the construction of knowledge, and reduce bigotry in general.[51]

Ethnic studies concentrates inquiry and discourse on the experiences of a specific ethnic group. Multicultural studies takes a thematic approach to curriculum by focusing on diversity that transcends race and ethnicity, and explores the culture of groups that have developed as a result of social dynamics and unique features of that group. Whereas ethnic studies programs might offer courses such as "Asian-American History," and "Native American Literature," multicultural courses might include, "Religious Minorities in the American Legal Tradition," or "Family Values and Same-Sex Parents."

Critical pedagogy is a construct that represents both a means and end of teaching and learning. The overarching objective of critical pedagogy is to liberate individuals from ideas and assumptions that have resulted in their oppression and exploitation.[52] It challenges both formal educational paradigms and social norms that sustain them. Critical pedagogy aims to transform society by helping people understand how politics, language, religion, literature, rhetoric, historical narratives, popular media, science, and technology can be conduits of injustice and inequality. It asserts that all relationships are vulnerable to exploitation and the struggle of one to subordinate the other.

51. LaBelle and Ward, *Ethnic Studies*, pp. 1–9.
52. Darder, Baltodano, and Torres, "Critical Pedagogy: An Introduction," pp. 2–10.

Critical pedagogy's roots run in various directions. Origins reach back to University of Frankfurt, Germany, where philosophers used theories of Karl Marx and George Hegel as a basis for critiquing capitalism and its indifference to human suffering and social destabilization.[53] Strains of critical pedagogy appear in the works of W.E. B. Dubois, whose essays were foundation to critical race theory, and in the revisionist history of Charles A. Beard, whose 1913 thesis asserted that the authors of the U.S. Constitution insinuated their private economic interests into the document.[54] Noam Chomsky's studies in linguistics during the 1950s paved the way for critical discourse analysis, which investigates how language manipulates perception and thinking, and reinforces prevailing distributions of power and authority.[55]

The works of the French West Indian psychiatrist and revolutionary, Franz Fanon, and the Brazilian philosopher and teacher, Paulo Freire are also foundational to the development of critical pedagogy. Fanon's *Wretched of the Earth* (1961) illuminated the ghastly abuses of colonization that corrupted both the individual's and the nation's regard for life. Freire's *Pedagogy of the Oppressed* (1968) focused on education as a conduit of social control. He held that traditional instruction reinforced class power and privileges, and that teachers had a moral obligation to help students find their voices, and confront the paradigm of competition and exploitation that others insisted represented a fixed and objective cosmic order.

Critical pedagogy is immediately concerned with how knowledge is constructed and how it can be used to disenfranchise and control people. Critical pedagogy is broad in scope, and may be easily integrated into courses that analyze the news, social media, political speeches, historical narratives, television scripts, fiction, scientific articles, government reports, and pedagogy itself.

Rhetorical capital is vital to critical pedagogy. As Ira Shor, Professor of Composition and Rhetoric, noted, critical pedagogy is concerned with: "Habits of thought, reading, writing, and speaking which go beneath surface meaning, first impressions, dominant myths, official pronouncements, traditional clichés, received wisdom, and mere opinions, to understand the deep meaning, root causes, social context, ideology, and personal consequences of any action, event, object, process, organization, experience, text, subject matter, policy, mass media, or discourse."[56] Rhetorical capital makes

---

53. Kincheloe, "Foundations of Critical Pedagogy," pp. 46–48.

54. Fishetti, "W.E.B. DuBois, pp. 33–36. Also see: Beard, *An Economic Interpretation*.

55. Van Dijk, "Principles of Critical Discourse Analysis," pp. 249–283; also see: Chomsky, *Language and Politics* and Herman and Chomsky's *Manufacturing Consent*.

56. Shor, *Empowering Education*, p. 129.

critical pedagogy possible. Without the ability to detect in speeches and writing the biases, assumptions, implications, inaccuracies, irrelevance, and distortions, one is likely to see only the surface of pedagogy, which is largely concerned with transmitting declarative knowledge.

Ethnic studies, multicultural studies, and critical pedagogy have five things in common. First, they all embrace the notion that educators are agents of social engineering, and that educators must challenge the status quo to engineer a better world. Second, they believe that authentic learning occurs when individuals unlearn distorted representations of the world and their place in it. Third, all seek to empower individuals to become effective self-advocates by understanding how power operates in both institutional ways and in the dominant narratives of a society, and by developing strategies to overcome marginalization and invisibility. Fourth, all acknowledge the negative aspects of capitalism and their impact on democracy and the democratic processes. Fifth, all share a special concern the well-being of the poor, vulnerable, and despised.

In theory, ethnic studies, multiculturalism, and critical pedagogy represents hope that, when we are made aware of the reality that human suffering and oppression happen by design, the common citizen will resist all forms of discriminatory behavior for the sake of creating a just and equitable society. In theory, these curricula champion open, honest, and fair debate. In practice, however, these curricula have sometimes fallen short of their ideals, as they become instruments of demagoguery and entangled in political correctness.

Chapter 5

Seeking the Unattainable

KNOTTY PEDAGOGY

It is difficult to say where critical pedagogies—including ethnic studies, multicultural studies, and gender studies— ends and politically correct curriculum begins. In public discourse, critical pedagogies are often synonymous with political correctness. Critical studies and politically correct curriculum can be hostile to all things Western. The anti-Western disposition, however, is complicated, as many people who represent multicultural artists, authors, and scholars are were born in the U.S., and were influenced by Western world views to some degree. A reading list for a literature course, for example, might include non-white authors, such as Langston Hughes, Maxine Hong Kingston, Maya Angelou, James Baldwin, Sandra Cisneros, and Toni Morrison, and, while each of these authors bring unique perspectives to our understanding of the human experience and nonwhite culture, their work may also resonate with respect for some aspects of Western culture, such as the valuing of natural rights, individualism, Judeo-Christian values, and rule of law.[1] True to the American experience, there is diversity within diversity.

Critical pedagogies teach people to resist corporate culture, the abuses of capitalism, and the political marginalization of the masses. Resistance is characterized as non-participation in economic systems and transactions that are designed to maximize profit for the few at the expense of the many. It is also characterized by participation in democratic processes for the sake of reforming or abolishing capitalism's abuses (some would argue capitalism

1. Banks, "Multicultural Education," p. 23.

itself), and for the purpose of increasing inclusivity in law-making and public over-sight of government. Some argue that critical pedagogy is so preoc-
cupied with identity politics that it neglects learning in academic disciplines
and cognitive development.[2]

Sol Stern, Senior Fellow at the Manhattan Institute, has penned some
of the sharpest criticism of critical pedagogy, and takes aim at teachers who
indoctrinate their students to reflexively abhor U.S. foreign policy. He described the conduct of a fifth grade teacher who taught his students about
U.S. intervention in Latin America, then took students to a demonstration
against U.S. Latin American policy. He told students that the right way to
think about U.S. intervention was to side with revolutionaries and reformers not the United States.[3]

Stern's outrage over the lack of the teacher's objectivity appears to be
spot on. In the academic setting, students should be encouraged to examine
all sides of an issue, determine their positions, and argue their case with credible evidence. The strategy of taking students to a public protest also raises
many questions about the teacher's intentions. Most ten-year olds probably
lack the cognitive skills and knowledge to contextualize what they see and
hear, and to grasp the nuances of the issues. Thus, they are vulnerable to
believing what they thought the teacher wanted them to believe, especially
if agreement produced favorable grades. The teacher deserves some measure
of empathy, however, as curriculum and instructional materials in American
schools often do not contain important information about how people outside the U.S. experience U.S. policies. Teachers are often in a tough spot. They
can either go by the book and ignore those experiences, or supplement their
lessons with facts and perspectives textbooks do not provide.

Having taught social studies for 23 years, I argue that curriculum is
made conservative largely by the omission of information that could be
used to marshal defenses for both liberal and conservative view points.
High school students typically do not undertake a rigorous social studies
curriculum. While nearly 95 percent study U.S. History, about 43 percent
take a basic economics course, approximately 60 percent study world history, and roughly 30 percent study either sociology or psychology.[4] Many
students do not understand what the Federal Reserve does, and that it is
a private bank that generates profit. Many cannot explain how the nation
acquires debt, and what that does to the domestic economy. Many do not
know about key tax legislation and Supreme Court decisions that have an

2. Rochester, "Critical Demagogues," para. 1–3.

3. Stern, "Propaganda in Our Ed Schools," para. 3–4.

4. Walstad and Rebeck, "Status of Economics," p. 101.

immediate impact on their economic opportunities and obligations. Many cannot describe how foreign policy is made, what interests drive U.S. foreign policy, and how geography impacts foreign policy. They also lack an understanding of which private entities have extraordinary influence over law-makers and public opinion by way of media ownership, foundational operations, and campaign contributions.

In my experience, students are readily critical of "the system," but lack sufficient information about the specifics of how "the system" operates. Many teachers and professors are poorly trained to fill the gaps in students' knowledge. Many do not care much about social studies because they see no relationship between the knowledge it offers and getting a good job.

Critical pedagogies can be abused. For example, revisionist history lessons that portray American colonists as blood-thirsty, greedy invaders of the Americas can lead students to believe that nothing good ever came of European settlement of the Americas. Sometimes critical pedagogy ends up perpetuating a very dualistic world view that blinds people to nuances and complexity. Sometimes is encourages students to focus on who was the most oppressed of them all, rather than focus on the common threats to our humanity that stretch across all demographic groups.

In a casual chat with a colleague, I raised my concern that critical pedagogy has reactionary elements that are often uncontested. After I was accused of being a "neo-colonialist," I said to my friend, "Do you ever ask the students who condemn Western civilization which aspects of it they are prepared to go without? Would they like to live in a non-democratic society and without civil rights? Go without modern sanitation and medicine? Would they like to forsake central heating, combustible engines, jet planes, cell phones, or the Internet?" My friend smiled wryly and mumbled, "That' not what I meant." I replied, "I think it's important for students to understand that the freedom to criticize comes with the responsibility to be fair—it doesn't make much sense to damn the West and then scramble like mad to have what the West has."

Critical pedagogy is not a magic bullet that will kill what ails us. What we want from the material world, and what we offer as justifications for those wants, however, could kill us. It is easier to condemn "the system" than it is to chastise our own vice. Critiques of society and Western institutions are not always balanced by critiques of individuals' material ambitions and appetites. They do not always scrutinize whether equity and social justice means that everybody has a chance to live an affluent middle class life, and whether the planet could support that outcome for 9 billion people. Moreover, such curriculum sometimes deteriorates into a debate about which group is entitled to things that other groups may not "legitimately" claim.

If critical pedagogy does not culminate in the recognition of the needs, experiences, and values that diverse communities have in common, than its outcomes could reinforce isolation and non-cooperation, rather than unification and collaboration.

In some ways, political correctness is rhetorical choreography. Each step is determined by a director, who interprets the music, and then designs movement to suit the mood of each scene. As in real life, directors, music, scenes, and dialogue regularly change. We may find ourselves doing a waltz at work, the Turkey Trot at the school board meeting, and the Twist with our buddies at the tavern. It's all in a day's rhetoric. Whether the various rhetorical tapes we play are doing us any good or simply keeping us from having to face the tough stuff about who we are is worth deep reflection, even if only for the sake of assessing how authentic we are to ourselves.

DANCING TO A POLITICALLY CORRECT BEAT

The definition of political correctness is a slippery fish and references a broad range of policies, values, and attitudes.[5] At present, it generally pertains to left-leaning orthodoxy in thinking, speaking, and acting. It holds that multiculturalism, ethnic studies, and critical pedagogies are vital to education, and that education must produce people who will re-engineer society to be more equitable and socially just. The academic goal of making the world a better place is praiseworthy. The temptation to indoctrinate from the podium, however, sometimes leads instructors to dictate how people should feel about something, rather than facilitate open dialogue that leads to autonomous decision-making.

Political correctness has also been defined as the politicization of all aspects of life, intolerance for dissent, a rejection of violence as a means of change, and greater interest in culture and social norms than business and economics.[6] Currently, in higher education, political correctness is currency among liberals and progressives. It is "certification" of one's "proper thinking" about everything from affirmative action to prohibiting corporate coffee vendors on campus. In dancing to the politically correct beat, however, many institutions have—wittingly and unwittingly— recalibrated their own academic standards, and have contributed to the depletion of society's rhetorical capital.

Historically, the "political correctness" describes efforts to sanitize language as to eliminate offensive and prejudicial discourse.[7] The term was used

5. Roberts, "Paulo Freire and Political Correctness," pp. 84–88.

6. Coleman "What is Political Correctness," p. 22.

7. Hughes, *Political Correctness*, pp. 3–11.

in the 1930s by German Jewish socialists, who criticized their fellow German Jewish socialists for their support of the Nazi-Soviet Nonaggression Pact.[8] The implication was that support for the nefarious agreement was merely blind obedience to communism rather than a well-reasoned ascent to the principles for which the document stood.[9] Political correctness is in the eye of the beholder, and sways in political winds. During the McCarthy hearings of the 1950s, to be politically correct was to be staunchly conservative. Publically condemning "pinkos" and gossiping about whose liberalism had "gone too far" was socially acceptable. At that time, however, conservatives did not use the term "politically correct" to refer to anti-communism. Anti-communism was so deeply normed in the U.S. that it was presumed to represent the only moral, objective, and rational position to take.[10]

Political correctness is dependent on the context in which is used for meaning. Because political correctness is subject to popular trends in thinking and values, it technically cannot rightly claim to represent a fixed set of principles. The principles that represent political correctness today may be politically incorrect ten years from now. Consider current discourse on women's rights and segregation, for example, and one may see that what was regarded as politically correct a hundred years ago is not politically correct today.

Political correctness can be very confusing. Racial profiling, for example, is politically incorrect, because, as it is currently practiced, it places African Americans under special scrutiny with the assumption that they are more likely to commit crimes than are Caucasians. . The practice of profiling whites is largely unthinkable, because we have been conditioned to fear people of color. In theory, the correctness of profiling any group would be justified if there existed overwhelming statistical evidence that a certain group typically behaved in certain ways. Medical history records represent a politically correct way to profile people, because data linking certain behaviors to certain illnesses has met a scientific threshold for predicting medical outcomes. If we applied that same logic to profiling various groups for public safety, and used crime statistics to back up our claims, we would be more aggressive in profiling whites and males. Consider the numbers:[11]

8. The pact was signed on August 23, 1939 and assured neutrality between Germany and the Soviet Union. The Soviets then occupied Lithuania, Latvia, Estonia, Finland, and eastern Poland, while Germany occupied western Poland. The peace ended when Nazi forces invaded the Soviet Union on June 22, 1941.

9. Feldstein, *Political Correctness*, p. 4.

10. Ivie, "Defusing Cold War Demagoguery," pp. 81–102.

11. Crime Data Explorer, "United States," see figures by topic. Percentages here are rounded off and represent the portion of offenders who provided demographic

- 78 percent of all violent crimes in 2018 were committed by males
- 77 percent of all homicides were committed by males; 49 percent by blacks and 37 percent by whites
- 93 percent of rapes were committed by men; 61 percent of rapists were white and 26 percent were black
- 83 percent of robberies were committed by males; 61 percent were committed by blacks and 29 percent were committed by whites
- 71 percent of mass shootings between 1982 and 2018 that took the lives of at least four people were committed by white males[12]
- 96 percent of white collar crimes, such as fraud, tax-evasion, kickbacks, bribery, price-fixing, money laundering, market manipulation, false advertising, violations of corporate regulations about public and environmental health and safety, and embezzlement are committed by white males[13]

Crime statistics do not portray white men in flattering light. The majority of white collar crimes are committed by white males, and some speculate that this is because white males are disproportionately positioned in corporate jobs that give them opportunities to commit certain crimes that cooks and janitors are not in a position to commit.[14] In any event, public discourse about racial profiling typically does not reference white males. The very thought of it seems absurd. Imagine such profiling in the chatter between dispatch and a patrol car in Manhattan:

Dispatch: I got a complaint about a white male in a Desmond Merrion three-piece due west on Wall at William. He's packin' an over-sized brief case, an over-stuffed duffle bag; appears to be talking into his lapel. He looks like the guys who did the hedge fund heist a couple years back.

Patrol: 33 copy that at 40 Wall. Have suspect in sight. Appears to be headed for Morgan Building. Wait. . .Suspect also wearing huarache sandals. Could be a wash-n-wear.

Dispatch: Huarache sandals. Uh huh. Proceed with caution.

Patrol: Suspect has suspicious object in his pocket. Maybe tickets for Caribbean. I can't be sure.

---

information to authorities. Not all offenders were apprehended.

12. Follman, Aronsen, and Pan, "A Guide to Mass Shootings," para. 1–8.

13. Gottschalk, "Gender and White Collar," pp. 369–371.

14. Wheeler, et al., "White Collar," p. 345.

Dispatch: Sounds like a Cayman caper headed for the rinse cycle. Stay with
suspect. Could be money laundering in progress. Calling for back-up.

This scenario pokes fun at our stereotypes, and it is perhaps a little
silly. There is, however, nothing silly about the annual cost of white collar
crime in the U.S., which ranges from $250 to $660 billion.[15] There is nothing
silly about the total bailout for the failure of banks and investment firms in
2008, which all by themselves is estimated at $498 billion.[16]

The pervasiveness of stereotyping criminality in the U.S. was punctuated
in a lesson that I taught to high school students. Before I began a class discussion on criminal behavior, I asked students to draw a picture of a criminal.
They were given a few minutes and encouraged to draw the first things that
popped into their heads and to be honest. When students shared their pictures with the class, a pattern emerged. The figures were all male, some were
males of color, and all of the criminals were dressed in shabby clothes, had
menacing grimaces on their face, and looked to be under the age of 30. In the
subsequent discussion, the class explored why their images looked as they did.
They were generally astonished at themselves for not thinking about white
collar crime, law-breakers over the age of 60, and female perpetrators.

In his book, *Slouching towards Gomorrah*, former Solicitor General
Robert Bork denounced "radical individualism" as a dangerous element of
liberalism and politically correct thinking.[17] He saw radical individualism as
anti-authoritarian and reviled what he believed was its tendency to promote
vulgarity and hedonism. Bork applied the concept of "radical individualism" only to the behavior of select groups, such as anti-war demonstrators,
civil rights agitators, and feminists, while leaving the corporate variation on
the "radical individualism" theme untouched.[18] His rhetoric helped to distract Americans from the reality that hippie hedonism and corporate greed
have something in common: they both believe that individuals have a right
to indulge their wants, even if it is injurious or offensive to others. Radical individualism is thus a nonpartisan player. White collar crime is often
invisible because folks in white collars want it to be invisible. White collar
criminals are typically well-educated and well-connected, and thus have the
resources needed to influence what media and authorities say about them.[19]

---

15. Friedrichs, *Trusted Criminal*, p. 50.

16. Harbert, "Here's how Much," para. 1–8.

17. Bork's *Slouching towards Gomorrah* explores these phenomena in education,
sexuality, and Affirmative Action.

18. Schwartz, "The Bork Legacy," para. 3–10.

19. Gottschalk, "Gender and White Collar," pp. 363–64

FULL CIRCLE

Political correctness often squashes discourse and debate that are vital to our understanding of the world. Political correctness is especially sensitive to assertions about universal and objective truths, in part because people fear that believing in universal and objective truths will lead to totalitarianism.[20] For many of these individuals, morality is always relative, and so spending time on analyzing and evaluating ideas is perceived as wasteful. Alan Bloom, author of *Closing of the American Mind*, argued that scholarly discourse about virtue, morality, and truth are persistently short-circuited by the belief that such conversation is by definition a means of indoctrinating students. He found that, rather than wrestle with complex and problematic aspects of the human condition, students prefer the idea that there is no such thing as right and wrong. Recent events, however, suggest that students—and society in general—are not absolute in their rejection of absolutism. Instead, people are doing what people have always done; they are being conditional in their commitment to ideologies, and cherry-picking their morality from the trees that meet those conditions.

At present, students are now marching to the beat of politically correct drums that call for universities to ban speakers on campus. The irony is staggering. In the 1960s, politically correct college students loudly championed the right of every voice to be heard, and they risked police beatings, arrest, and expulsion from universities to do so. The Free Speech Movement (FSM) that began at the University of California, Berkeley (UCB) was sparked by student activism to end segregation. As some San Francisco businesses refused to hire blacks, students organized sit-ins and protests. In the fall of 1964, UCB administrators banned all political activity on campus, including the solicitation of donations for civil rights causes, invitations to rallies, and distribution of campaign literature for both presidential candidates, Lyndon Jonson (D-TX) and Barry Goldwater (R-AZ). UCB also allowed FBI agents to collect data on what FBI Director J. Edgar Hoover asserted were "radicals" conspiring to overthrow the government.[21]

Participants in the FSM were largely white middle class individuals who subscribed to non-violent strategies of civil disobedience. Mario Savio, a devout blue collar Catholic, saw the FMS as a moral issue. In the summer of 1964, he volunteered to register black voters in the South, and had been physically assaulted for his efforts.[22] Savio delivered one of the movement's

20. Bloom, *Closing of the American Mind*, p. 25.

21. Rosenfeld, "Mario Savio's FBI Odyssey," para. 1–2.

22. Cohen's, *Freedom's Orator* shines a light on Savio's youth and life's work for social justice.

most iconic speeches in which he contested the humanity of the university. He chastised its bureaucracy for making faculty middle management in a system where students were "raw material," not human beings, and where managers were accountable to the Board of Regents, not the community. "There's a time," he shouted, "when the operation of the machine becomes so odious, makes you so sick at heart that you can't take part. . .you've got to put your bodies upon the gears and upon the wheels. . .and you've got to make it stop!"[23]

The FSM utilized non-violent tactics and civil disobedience to make their point. As President Johnson escalated the war, and as race riots erupted across the country, the rhetoric of protest became vulgar and aggressive, and protesters attacked others and destroyed property. At one extreme of dissent, rhetoric called for a violent revolution against the government. Protesters' use of obscenities, insults, and threats did little to nurture public sympathy for their cause, and soured interest in dialogue about the nation's sins.[24]

To a large extent, the rhetoric of protest was managed by the owners of news media, who exploited the spectacle of social unrest at the expense of offering the public an objective and thorough analysis of dissent.[25] Cameras were quick to record images of rioting youth, but slow to document clerics and their communities praying rosaries for peace. The war offered cause to educate Americans on the effects of Western imperialism in Southeast Asia, but mainstream journalism generally did not linger on those lessons. Journalists whose coverage of the war and protest movements conveyed empathy for victims of war were sometimes accused of disloyalty and blamed for America's defeat.[26] Even though thousands of protestors remained committed to non-violent strategies for change, many who viewed news coverage of riots and demonstrations concluded that the commotions were proof that dissenters were not really interested in dialogue and peace, but anarchy and destruction.

At present, we have come full circle. Politically correct college students vehemently insist that they have the moral authority to prohibit free speech and open debate. Whereby students once participated in the FSM sought to broaden public discourse about war and peace, we now have students who want to restrict such discourse. In the full circle, we may see that the question of whether the university ought to be a safe haven for open debate on all issues is never-ending, as each generation confronts the

23. Savio, "Sit-in Address," para. 8.

24. Gustainis and Hahn, "While the Whole World Watched," p. 203–205.

25. Gitlin's *The Whole World is Watching* documents how news media manipulated public opinion about dissent and war, and functions as a political force that tells people about how the world works and what matters.

26. Herman and Chomsky, *Manufacturing Consent*, p. 169.

conflict between their most prized convictions and the freedom of others to tell them that they are wrong.

By definition, the university lives in tension between two obligations. On one hand, it must pursue and sustain open debate and fair representation of diverse perspectives without partisan prejudice. On the other hand, it must serve the needs of the community that makes its existence possible. If the university offends its dearest and wealthiest sustainers, it risks its well-being. Occasionally, prophetic thinking breaks through the political correctness of moral relativity and the ethos of "keeping the customer satisfied," and college campuses facilitate wonderful conversations that address repressed feelings and unpopular ideologies. This, however, was not the case in some recent events.

In 2016, the Mayor of Jerusalem, Nir Barkat, was harassed and insulted by pro-Palestinian students attending his speech at San Francisco State University. The Mayor cancelled plans to speak at the same venue in 2017 because the University would not advertise the event and responded to the previous tumult by restricting access to the speech.[27] Earlier in 2017, police at the University of California at Davis cancelled a speech to be given by Breitbart's conservative commentator, Milo Yiannopoulos, because student protest had become violent and unruly.[28] Students at Middlebury College in Vermont disrupted a lecture to be presented by Charles Murray, political scientist and author of the controversial book, *Losing Ground: American Social Policy* 1950–1980. Students chanted, "Racist, sexist, anti-gay; Charles Murray go away!"[29] The lecture was cancelled on the spot. In 2019, Beloit College cancelled a speech to be given by Erik Prince, the founder of Blackwater, a private security agency.[30] Students protested Prince, the former Navy Seal and brother of Secretary of Education, Betsy DeVos, as they held his company responsible for murdering innocent civilians, opposing efforts to increase Blackwater's accountability, and gouging taxpayers with excessive compensation for service.[31] Student protests were so frequent and vitriolic that state legislators explored legislative options to protect the right of guests to speak on campus.[32]

27. Melendez, "Mayor of Jerusalem," para. 1–8.

28. Associated Press, "Protests at U.C. Davis," para. 1–7.

29. Jaschik, "Shouting Down," para. 1–5.

30. Bauer-Wolf, "Another Speaker Shut Down," para. 1–13.

31. Scahill's *Blackwater* documents the creation of the corporate army, how it undermines domestic security and side-steps congressional oversight, why it is a threat to international security, and who profits from their existence.

32. Bauer-Wolf, "Free Speech Laws," para. 1–8.

Some people insist that there are individuals whose voices should not be given a public platform. The stock list of those who should be denied free speech include members of neo-Nazi organizations and Ku Klux Klansmen. As an educator, I am deeply troubled by momentum to ban any speech, because it reflects a colossal failure of my profession. To my way of thinking, the failure is twofold. First, it is a failure to teach people how to listen to ideas that are offensive and cruel, and to respond with courtesy, good will, and a sincere interest in resolving conflict through dialogue. Second, it is a failure to help students be deeply introspective and to acknowledge that sometimes their own attitudes and biases fuel public interest in totalitarian ideologies and hate speech.

Teachers and professors are supposed to be gatekeepers of enlightened civility. Ideally, they produce individuals who deeply understand the human condition, the world, and what is necessary to sustain collective well-being. We are the ones who, in theory, teach first-graders to pay attention, share, and say "please" and "thank you." We are also the ones who, in theory, teach college students to pay attention, share ideas with open-minds, be grateful for and respectful of diverse perspectives, suppress the urge to dominate, and apply reason and fairness to discourse. We are the ones who are supposed to teach people how to scrutinize both that which is glorified and that which is despicable, so that judgement is free from bigotry. No idea should get a free pass in the academy just because it is popular or institutionally normed.

At the end of the day, we might feel good about censoring vile and vicious rhetoric, but there are consequences to pay for not talking through it. Censorship legitimizes intolerance, and political correctness promotes the notion only one group is in possession of the truth. In our nation's haste to retaliate against the terrorists in the 9/11 attacks, for example, federal officials disseminated rhetoric that demonized not only what the terrorists did, but *everything* about the terrorists—their religion, their way of life, their perception of America—nothing about them or their culture was seen as redeemable. The dominant narrative declared that Americans do not negotiate with terrorists, and it blamed them for destroying opportunities to settle differences by any means other than military intervention. This is the kid's version of history—the one wherein good guys, who are always right, reluctantly shoot up the town, so that the bad guys, who are always wrong, do not win.

The adult version, the one that looks objectively at conflict between the U.S. and the Arab world, intelligence reports, covert U.S. agendas and activities in the Middle East, and diverse perspectives of the conflict has existed for generations, but gets little press.[33] It is the narrative in which good guys

33. See: Scott's *Road to 9/11* documents how private investments in oil and strategic

are not absolutely good and bad guys are not absolutely bad. It is the narrative of nations whose economic and militaristic interests drive them to do business with each other, even to the point where one nation is using the other to do dastardly things. One nation prolongs global dependence on fossil fuel at the expense of global warming, and the other prolongs the repression of human rights. The businessmen of these nations become very rich, and both are willing to kill to protect what they have. Every time a university permits students or anybody else to shut down open debate, it loses the opportunity to help people see that the world is not black and white.

OUR CHILDREN ARE CRYING

The democratization of higher education brought new voices to the conversation about the purpose and quality of post-secondary curriculum and instruction. It also amplified the voices of the younger generation and their concerns about the world they inherited. Students articulated an urgency for change, and their rhetoric was a formidable assault against the dominant narrative about what the best and brightest in our universities should be doing with their talent. It is impossible to understate the power that the dominant culture's narrative has on our sense of self and purpose. To find their way to humanity and spirituality, each generation is challenged to break the spell of mythmakers who conjure worlds that are so dangerous, that the only way to prevail and prosper is to compulsively compete against each other, fear our differences, and feed war machines that devour over 50 percent of our federal budget's discretionary spending.[34]

Baby boomers gave us the *Port Huron Statement*, an eloquent document that captures the prophetic voice of students in the 1960s, who found it necessary to protest what they believed was a betrayal of American ideals by the institutions that were supposed to protect them. Composed in 1962 as a manifesto for Students for a Democratic Society, it was an indictment against war, the military-industrial economy, racism, materialism, and poverty.

The Port Huron Statement was its generation's thesis about the conflict of interests between citizens and the state, and the conflict between being a republic and an empire. It was received by some as shocking and radical discourse, yet, it articulated dissent that took shape in prior decades. Clerics, scientists, scholars, and concerned citizens had in the 1940s and 1950s

---

interests are at the root of U.S. foreign policy and the way it is packaged and sold to Americans; Wright's *Looming Tower* explains the shock and disruption Arabs experienced as U.S. interest in the Middle East increased, and how it led to 9/11.

34. National Priorities Project, "Federal Spending," para. 4–6.

publically demonstrated their opposition to atomic bombs, segregation, McCarthyism, and the abuses of labor.[35] *The Port Huron Statement* was another chapter in American rhetoric that responded to the enduring question of what it means to be human, and what it means to be democratic.

Rhetoric of the 1960s tugged at America's conscience from several directions. John F. Kennedy's speeches about the moral obligation to desegregate, and to make peace with the Soviets, and Martin Luther King Jr.'s call for non-violent civil disobedience and condemnation of the war in Vietnam challenged people to deepen their commitment to peace and justice. George Wallace's petition for segregation, and Curtis Lemay's advocacy for bombing communists into smithereens reinforced old prejudices and justifications for aggression.[36]

Rather than relying upon elected officials and authorities to orchestrate change from on high, *The Port Huron Statement* called for participatory democracy and grass roots activism to lead the way to change.[37] It was hopeful and rich with empathy for the poor, marginalized, and vulnerable. It told readers, "We are people of this generation, bred in at least modest comfort, housed now in universities, looking comfortably to the world we inherit. When we were kids America was the wealthiest and strongest country in the world. . .Many of us began maturing in complacency."[38] The authors saw that foreign ownership of American land, utilities, and economic institutions was a threat to democracy, as was the conversion of America' economy to a permanent war economy that depended on armed conflict to sustain employment.[39] They saw a world in which people were terrorized by the possibility of nuclear war, totalitarianism, hunger, and racism, and concluded that American had at some point abandoned its interest in building a better world wherein the least of our brothers and sisters could thrive with dignity.[40]

The manifesto echoed what many clerics and religious organizations were preaching at the time about the dignity of the human person.[41] "We oppose the depersonalization that reduces human beings to the status of

35. DeBenedetti's *American Ordeal* is a superb presentation of dissent in the 1950s and 1960s.

36. See: Kennedy, "Civil Rights Address" and "Commencement Speech;" King, "Letter from a Birmingham Jail" and "Beyond Vietnam;" Wallace, "Segregation Now;" and, Coffey, *Iron Eagle*.

37. Hayden, *Port Huron Statement*, pp. 1–6.

38. Ibid p. 45.

39. Ibid, p. 78; 131; 138.

40. Ibid, p. 47.

41. See: John XXIII, *Pacem in Terris*; King, M. L. *All Labor has Dignity*; and Heschel, *Who is Man?*

things," the *Statement* declared, "We oppose, too, the doctrine of human incompetence because it rests essentially on the modern fact that men have been competently manipulated into incompetence" not only by automation, but by the very act of seeing human beings as machines.[42] The rhetoric excoriated corporate greed and declared that it disrupted the social order and was inhumane. It argued that the restoration of morality "cannot be overcome by better personal management, nor by improved gadgets, but only when the love of man [sic] overcomes the idolatrous worship of things by man [sic]."[43]

The manifesto acknowledged the place of the university as an institution positioned to have great influence over society's values and attitudes, and accused it of being part of the machinery that engineered war, exploitation, and injustice. It charged that the university was an apparatus of the military-industrial complex and corporate paradigm. It chided the academy for perpetuating the arms race and nuclear threat by entering into contracts with the defense industry, and for failing to teach individuals about how to become effective agents of social improvement.[44] The manifesto ends with the passage, "If we appear to seek the unattainable, as it has been said, then let it be known that we do so to avoid the unimaginable."[45]

Nearly sixty years after *The Port Huron Statement*, we face the unimaginable. The unimaginable is real and our children see it. Fighting back tears and rage, Greta Thunberg chastised world leaders at the Climate Action Summit at the United Nations on September 23, 2019. The 16 year-old proclaimed:

> People are suffering. People are dying and dying ecosystems are collapsing. We are in the beginning of a mass extinction, and all you can talk about is money and fairy tales of eternal economic growth. . .How dare you! For more than 30 years the science has been crystal clear. How dare you continue to look away and come here saying that you're doing enough when the politics and solutions are nowhere in sight.[46]

The students who protested the abuses of power in the 1960s are senior citizen now, and our children are still crying, in their own way, with their own

42. Hayden, *Port Huron Statement*, p. 51.

43. Ibid, pp. 52–53. See: Bunzel, *New Force on the Left* which presents Hayden's biography and writings.

44. Hayden, *Port Huron Statement*, pp. 165–169.

45. Hayden, "Crafting the Port Huron Statement," p. 18. Also see: Cohen, R. "New Left's Love-Hate."

46. NBC News, "Read Greta Thunberg's," para. 3–4.

words, for grown-ups to stop obsessing about wealth and power, and to lead the way to peace, ecological sustainability, and economic sanity. Neither higher education nor political correctness stopped the unimaginable from invading our lives. Even a 16 year-old can see that. The unimaginable is here because we either denied its presence or rationalized that it is no big deal.

The unimaginable is manifest in so many things: it is that we are killing the planet; it is that war is our way of life; it is that our police officers shoot unarmed and innocent people; it is that our schools and houses of worship are ground zero in mass shootings; it is that a typical corporate executive's salary has increased by 940 percent since 1978, while the typical employee's salary increased by 12 percent;[47] it is that over 12 percent of Americans live in poverty; it is that people bring children into the world that they do not want and cannot care for; it is that one out of every ten elders over the age of 60 in the U.S. have been abused;[48] it is that soldiers kill and torture people for sport;[49] it is that we take pride in our anti-intellectualism, and then deny that our ignorance of the world and each other is killing us.

The unimaginable is that generations of Americans have not been given the rhetorical and intellectual skills to combat propaganda, and are now swarmed by stinging lethal social media and corporate hogwash designed to sabotage our good will and reason. The unimaginable is that we often do not use our marvelous digital technology to enlighten ourselves and cultivate unity and mutual respect. The unimaginable is that we—the Americans who believe that divine providence set us up to lead the world to decency and civility—use our words and communication technology as megaphones for toxic discourse, lies, and the debasement of humanity.

47. Mishel and Wolfe, "CEO Compensation," para. 1.
48. National Council on Aging, "Elder Abuse Facts," para. 2.
49. Cole, et al., "'Repugnant' Phots Emerge," para. 1–10.

Chapter 6

Let's Play Chicken

A SACRED COMMODITY

If higher education is not fully up to the task of building and refining our rhetorical capital, perhaps mass media can lend a hand. It is a reasonable supposition. After all, most Americans have television and are connected to the Internet. In theory, with information immediately available at our fingertips, we can become walking encyclopedias and great critics of what we read, hear, and see. In reality, however, many do not want to become walking encyclopedias and great critics. Instead many want to be entertained, distracted, and soothed by the lullabies of echo chambers. Those who want to be well-informed and analytical consumers of news and information are challenged by the fact that news and information is a corporate product, and as such, "is a commodity, not a mirror image of reality."[1]

In 1983, 50 corporations owned the majority of media in the U.S., and by 2000 that number dropped to just six corporate entities. This type of ownership means that most of America's newspapers, TV stations, cable companies, film studios, book publishers, cinemas, magazines, and radio stations are controlled by individuals who have a vested interest in protecting their parent enterprises and companies within their conglomerates from bad press. The men and women on corporate media boards decide what is newsworthy, who is a credible source, what angle of the story matters, and how deep the reports go.[2] As Ben Bagdikian, former Dean of Journalism at

1. Hamilton, *All the News*, p. 7.
2. Graber and Dunaway, *Mass Media and American Politics*, pp. 7–26.

UC Berkeley reminds us, "With the country's widest disseminators of news, commentary and ideas firmly entrenched among a small number of the world's wealthiest corporations, it may not be surprising that their news and commentary is limited to an unrepresentative narrow spectrum of politics."[3]

New media is essentially concerned with information, and information ultimately is about power. Naturally, the powerful and those who seek power have an interest in controlling news outlets.[4] What people know and believe about their world, and about the people who exert the most influence over it, affects whether citizens and workers will be as compliant to dominant narratives as anesthetized pets, or become people who bear their teeth in rebellion. Our freedom of speech and the abundance of news outlets does not guarantee that we have the truth. We live in a world where whistle-blowers and journalists who tell the truth about government and corporate operations risk their careers and, in some cases, their lives. Truth is a guarded commodity.

In the material world, there is an alliance of power that weds private interests to mercenaries, corporate lobbying, investment firms, government, and the intelligence community. Those who conduct business in the alliance do not always have love of neighbor in mind when they craft public policy or wheel and deal behind closed doors.[5] They do, however, care about the transparency of their operations, and how they might spin public discourse to their advantage. The powerful know that the public must be convinced that those in the alliance are patriots and benevolent stewards of democracy, and must believe that there is free flow of information in the republic. News media is in an excellent position to reinforce narratives about who we are and what we must think and value. They are also in a position to withhold information that might be vital to our well-being.

From a spiritual perspective, news is hallowed ground. It is a space wherein we encounter others—their experiences, thoughts, feelings, and needs—with the potential that encounters will enlighten us, temper our judgement, and arouse our compassion. What we know about others shapes our humanity, and so truth itself takes on a sacramental aspect. Pope John XXIII wrote:

3. Independent Lens, "Who Owns the Media?" Bagdikian's *New Media Monopoly* explores how media corporations have interlocking board members with major industries, including energy and defense, and how this relationship impacts the news. For a global view, see Noam, *Who Owns the World's Media?*

4. Philips, Peter, "Beyond the New American Censorship," pp. 35–52.

5. Bill Moyers' *Secret Government*; Katherine Olmstead's *Challenging the Secret Government*; and, Peter Schweizer's *Secret Empires* shed light on how democracy is subverted, who benefits, and what is at risk.

> Man [sic] has a natural right to be respected. . .He has a right
> to freedom in investigating the truth, and—within the limits of
> moral order and the common good—of freedom of speech and
> publication. . . He has the right also, to be accurately informed
> about public events. . .
>
> Human society. . .demands that men [sic] be guided by jus-
> tice, respect the rights of others and do their duty. It demands
> too, that they be animated by love as will make them feel the
> needs of others as their own, and induce them to share their
> goods with others, and to strive in the world to make all men
> [sic] alike heirs to the noblest of intellectual and spiritual values.[6]

The pontiff recognized that information is vital to moral conduct, and that
where truth is compromised, there is always a threat to decency and dignity.

John F. Kennedy also recognized the crucial role of information and
communication in a republic. He said to a gathering of television broadcast-
ers, "The flow of ideas, the capacity to make informed choices, the ability to
criticize all of the assumptions on which political democracy rests, depend
largely on communications. And you are the guardians of the most powerful and effective means of communication ever designed."[7] Kennedy recognized that societies are built on certain assumptions which may or not be
true, and so we need to verify assertions for our own good.

At the Republican National Convention in 1964, Former President
Dwight Eisenhower appealed to Americans to never let ourselves be "led
astray by meaningless slogans, labels, preconceived notions, and prejudices," and to scorn "sensation-seeking columnists and commentators."[8]
He observed the potential for rhetoric to lead people away from democratic
principles, and the reality that journalists often targeted emotions rather
than the intellect.

We are vulnerable to news media. Companies have an incentives to
distort and hide the truth. The people who own the media and who sit on
their executive boards are often the same people who sit on the boards of
oil industries, energy companies, banks, investment firms, arms industries, pharmaceutical manufacturers, chemical industries, and agricultural
corporations. The status of being a public media enterprise does not immune such entities from editorial pressure to ignore or distort the facts, as
public stations often rely on donations from private corporations to say in

---

6. John XXIII, *Pacem in Terris*, para. 12, 35.

7. Alger, *Media and Politics*, p. 87.

8. Eisenhower, "Transcript of Eisenhower's," para 58–60.

business.[9] Public Broadcasting Service (PBS), for example, enjoys a reputation for objective and substantial reporting, but it is not purely objective and inclusive. In 2015, roughly 75 percent of the board members of PBS's major affiliates, such as KQED in San Francisco and Boston's WGBH, were corporate executives, and most were white males.[10] A 2017 study of 129 episodes of PBS's *Morning Edition* found that the show leaned to the right, as 37 percent of the featured guest commentators came from conservative or center-right think tanks, while 19 percent came from think tanks that were progressive or center-left.[11]

News monopolies tend to create echo chambers. In 1996, Congress passed the Telecommunications Act, which relaxed rules that prohibited monopolies and allowed corporations to acquire multiple stations, even in the same market. Large corporations that already had many investments in the media were able to amass greater numbers of stations than smaller companies with fewer investments, and their companies tended to offer the public more favorable press about the Telecommunications Act than did the others.[12] Newspapers owned by television stations were also more likely to present positive coverage of the Supreme Court's ruling in *Citizens United v. Federal Election Commission*, which declared that, like individual citizens, corporations have civil rights including freedom of speech.[13] This decision cleared the path for corporations to speak freely from their wallets, and to enjoy unlimited spending on political campaigns, which many believe is tantamount to buying influence.[14]

Television plays a huge role in getting people elected and helping them hang on to power. Fox News, one of the most powerful media conglomerates on the planet, is credited with fortifying conservatism in the United States. Since its founding in 1996, Fox has helped to increase the visibility of and public support for Republican candidates.[15] Not to be outdone, Sinclair Broadcast Group, David Smith's media titanic, owns roughly 192 TV stations in the U.S. with a reach of 39 million viewers. Smith, a conservative, assured Trump, "We are here to deliver your message," and that news coverage of Trump's campaign and presidency would be scripted to promote

9. For details on the cross-pollenization of boards, see FAIR, "Interlocking Directorates."

10. Guerrero, "National Plutocrat Radio," para. 2–5.

11. Holycross and Riggio, "Morning Edition's," para. 2–4.

12. Gilens and Herman, "Corporate Ownership," pp. 377–383.

13. Bailard, "Corporate Ownership," see findings.

14. *Citizens United v. Federal Election Commission*, 558 U.S. 310, 2010.

15. Cassino, *Fox News*, pp. 1–25.

him and to disparage his foes.[16] In 2004, Smith prohibited his stations from airing a *Nightline* special "The Fallen," which addressed the cost of the war in Iraq, and in which Ted Koppel read the names of U.S. soldiers killed in the war. Senator John McCain (R-AZ) published an open letter to Smith chiding him for disrespecting those who bore the cost of war, and calling his action "unpatriotic."[17] During George W. Bush's presidency, Smith required his stations to air editorials that lambasted the "angry left," "clueless academics," and "wack [sic] job" peace advocates.[18]

Corporate news is all about the bottom line. General Electric (GE), one of the nation's top defense contractors and manufacturers of nuclear plants and weapons, was once part owner of NBC. GE had a record of sabotaging efforts to inform the public about the hazards of nuclear energy that included cancelling guest appearances of scientists and scholars who held critical views of nuclear energy on NBC shows. In 1987, NBC aired a documentary called, "Nuclear Power: In France it Works."[19] The narrator did not tell audiences that GE was part owner of NBC, and the program was essentially a commercial for nuclear energy. When the *New York Times* wrote about how GE earned $14.2 billion dollars in 2010 and paid no taxes on their loot, NBC affiliates did not cover the story.[20] Even when GE is not the owner of companies that produce and distribute materials addressing nuclear energy, it wields its monetary sword to cut funding for broadcasting entities, including PBS, when those entities want to air programs that criticized the nuclear industry.[21]

Changing the channel does not necessarily enlighten us. Since we do not know what we do know, we may have the impression that we are well-informed when we are not. Everything we see and hear is packaged to be consumed in a given cultural milieu. From the perspective of those who own a great deal of the nation's wealth and resources, what we are allowed to know about the world must be carefully managed as not to arouse discontent with the status quo and consumer dissatisfaction.

16. Kolhatkar, "Growth of Sinclair's Conservative," para. 10.

17. Ibid, para. 24.

18. Klinenberg, "Beyond Fair" para. 5.

19. Martin & Solomon, *Unreliable Sources*, pp. 75–84.

20. Fahri, "On NBC," para. 1–2.

21. Schrader-Frechette, *Taking Action*, pp. 61–63.

CREATURES FROM PLANET LIBERAL

News companies invest lots of time and money encouraging us to distrust and dislike our fellow human beings. Fanning the flames of partisan discord is big business. Audiences gravitate toward news, debates, and editorials that feature violent confrontations and vulgar outbursts. Reality shows that spotlight dysfunctional relationships and celebrities behaving badly are very popular. People seem mesmerized by drama, and the more spectacular the conflict, the more we look. This is especially prominent during election seasons and times of crisis, wherein folks get caught up in loud and belligerent rhetoric, and join the hunt for scapegoats to blame for whatever has gone wrong with our world.

On October 15, 2019, CNN hosted the fourth debate of Democratic presidential candidates and generated accusations of being biased in their moderation. Critics charge that the CNN editorial board orchestrated the debate in a way that would maximize controversy and conflict in order to boost viewership.[22] At times during the event, moderators appeared to be baiting the candidates into verbally attacking each other. As in many other televised debates at that time, the candidates sometimes appeared driven by an urgency to hold the spotlight.[23] The televised debate is not designed to be fair, it is designed to get ratings. It is designed to force the candidates to assert their uniqueness in ways that accentuate divisions in the political party rather than highlight the consensus. This sometimes leaves audiences with the impression that a political party is more fractured than it is. In addition, the candidates do not all get equal time to speak. In the October, 2019 Democratic debate, for example: Elizabeth Warren (D-MA), got about 23 minutes; Joe Biden (D-DE) got 17 and a half minutes; Amy Klobuchar (D-MN) got nearly 14 minutes; while former Housing and Urban Development Secretary Julian Castro (D-TX), Representative Tulsi Gabbard, (D-HI), Entrepreneur Andrew Yang (D-NY), and Businessman Tom Steyer (D- CA) all got less than 9 minutes.[24]

In the extreme, journalists and television talk show hosts (both liberal and conservative) spew personal insults of elected officials, their staff, and their followers for the purpose of publically shaming them and their supporters. The public appetite for verbal fisticuffs and personal degradation of their adversaries keep the airwaves crackling with animosity. If they wanted to, station owners, editorial boards, and journalists could adopt policies to

---

22. Sinclair Broadcast Group, "Former CNN Staffer Claims," para. 1–3.

23. Ali, "At the Democratic Debates," para. 1–7.

24. Torres and Walsh, "Elizabeth Warren gets Most," see chart.

produce a kinder, more enlightened way to use the gift of modern communication technology. They are, however, under considerable pressure to sustain the spectacle of conflict because it sells.

The strategy of distracting audiences from key issues caught the attention of House Speaker, Nancy Pelosi (D-CA). In an interview with Jane Meyer of the *New Yorker Radio Hour*, she responded specifically to the way the press has dealt with President Trump's behavior.[25]

> Mayer: I know you've been quite critical of the press—the mainstream media—nothing like the way the President talks about it, but I've seen that you've thought that we have in some way—I don't know, if we've been used or if we give too much attention to him— or what is it that you think we've done wrong, and what should we be doing differently?
>
> Pelosi: The press have been enablers of the Trump agenda. . .But on a daily basis, he's the master of diversion; he throws something and for 24 hours we hear about this, that, or the other thing, without really paying attention to what else is going on. Now, maybe that's what the market wants, and that's been catered to, I don't know.
>
> Mayer: So, you think we should ignore the Tweets more. . .
>
> Pelosi: No, I think you should talk about what else is going on. . .There are other things that are going on aside from what he does at three o'clock in the morning. . .Its deadly serious for our country. He has dumbed down the discussion of what public policy is about—the Bill of Rights, the First Amendment, freedom of speech, and the rest—it's the tactic of an autocrat to undermine the press, and then to dominate the news, so no matter what's happening, you're talking about "me." Even if it's terrible, you're talking about "me," you're not talking about what they're doing that that would be good for the country.

Distraction is a magician. It makes serious threats to our well-being invisible. It can be achieved by way of explicitly calling attention to something or someone, it can be achieved by omission and censorship. Pelosi speaks of a very serious form of distraction, but there are another forms that may in the long run be robbing us of truth that we need to hear and see.

Consider, for example, the news reports in mainstream media that have "covered" mass shootings. Readers and viewers typically get the shocking headlines, and learn about the number of people killed or wounded. They hear from survivors about how horrible it was to be attacked, and see friends shot. We hear from parents who lost their child. What we do not see, however, is what police and medical personnel see. We do not see a child's head halved by single bullet, or the mangle of shattered bone and tissue

---

25. Remnick, "Nancy Pelosi," (podcast), 21:37–23:10.

that once was a young man's leg. We do not see or hear on a regular basis about how people managed after several surgeries, or what it is like to live in wheelchair for the rest of one's life because somebody aimed an assault rifle that fires three bullets per second toward the crowd and shredded a spinal cord. We do not see or hear much about the depression, anger, and grief of survivors that is sometimes so debilitating it drives people to suicidal thoughts and actions.

Is it not a curious phenomenon that Americans spend so much time creating and consuming violent television shows, films, and games that graphically display dismemberment, bloodied bodies, exposed viscera, and brain splatter, but do not get to see real carnage? If the media were truly liberal, and truly wanted the public to know the full story of what assault rifles do to people, would we not be given the full picture?

For decades, people have complained that the news media has a liberal bias. Some see the liberal perspective in the news media like an alien virus that has infected what was once whole and pure. Before we light up our torches and sharpen our pitchforks for a good old fashioned monster hunt, however, it is important to remember that our way of life is predicated on liberal ideals. The Constitution of the United States was built on liberal philosophical principles. It establishes a legal system that asserts the right of the people— not the pope, the king, the corporation—to govern. It is liberal because it protects individual liberty by imposing checks and balances on the powers of government and courts, allows people to elect their representatives, and holds all people—regardless of wealth, status, and position—accountable to the law. Americans who demonize liberals enjoy the freedom to so because they live in a liberal republic.

At the core of liberal philosophy is the idea that it is better to suffer the mistakes of the people rather than to be denied the freedom to make them. Self-governance can be disastrous when people are denied information, or when people refuse to acknowledge what is happening and who is responsible. Where information is concerned, traditional liberals opt for transparency, because they have faith that truth will ultimately lead to better outcomes than lies.

If the news media were dominated by radical liberals, news programs and newspapers would give the public a daily report on the activities of our elected representatives and their administration. We the people would read, see, and hear the following: the latest details about which lobbyists visited which congressional member that day; which private foundations and think tanks presented which congressional member with a draft of a bill to introduce and why; how much money government officials took in for campaigns that day or that week and where the money came from; how much money was spent in the last 24 hours on foreign and military aid and how it was spent; which conflicts of interest exist relative to our leaders' goals and policies; how foreign ownership of U.S. land and businesses affects the nation; and, how many people died in the U.S. over the last 24 hours due to homelessness and hunger. If the press is so liberal, why is this information not presented to the republic on a daily basis?

Liberal journalists and conservative journalists are both guilty of sabotaging decency in dialogue. It is painful to hear conservative author and pundit Ann Coulter joke that Timothy McVeigh, who bombed the Murrow Building in Oklahoma City in 1994, should have bombed the *New York Times* building, or declare that the only question about President Bill Clinton's "obvious guilt" relative to the Lewinsky affair was "whether to impeach or assassinate."[26] It is just as painful to hear the liberal Chuck Todd of NBC's *Meet the Press* impatiently shout over his conservative guests, and be sarcastic or judgmental in his remarks.[27] Todd admits that journalists have their biases, but believes that they have been blamed for political scandals for so long that it is time for them to fight back.[28] His objective does not justify his strategy. Shouting more loudly than one's adversary does not establish credibility.

The hell that is created in news shows, political commentary, and journalistic analysis is in part due to the speed at which people communicate. Time on air cost money, and so limits on conversations and debates are imposed. This breeds an urgency to create soundbites and to rush through complicated issues in ways that cannot possibly illuminate and address the implications and nuances of anything. Perhaps the reason why so many audiences do not tolerate patient intellectual inquiry or ambiguity is because audiences have been taught to be impatient with thoughtful and nuanced discourse. Even on issues that affect their lives most profoundly, many people are irritated if the logic of an argument takes time to unpack, and prefer a rush to judgement rather than patiently waiting for the fullness of truth.

Every day, hundreds of news items receive less coverage than what they deserve, and many of these stories concern how power is used or abused, which, ideally, should be the concern of both liberals and conservatives. Project Censored identified some of the most under-reported stories from 2017 and 2018. They included stories about the FBI hiring Geek Squad employees (Best Buy) to provide them with information about customers and their computer files. They included stories about drug manufacturers

---

26. Alterman, *What Liberal Media*, p. 4, 107.

27. Chuck Todd's interaction with Senator Ron Johnson (R-WI) on *Meet the Press*, October 6, 2019 is on YouTube at https://www.youtube.com/watch?v=Xzgs2kyNpW0.

28. Todd, "Its Time for the Press," para. 16–25.

targeting poor urban areas with high concentrations of minorities for aggressive marketing of opioids, and stories about pharmaceutical companies
spending millions on lobbying Congress for deregulation while thousands
of people died or went broke trying to pay for their addictions. They included stories about $21 trillion—yes, *trillion*—dollars' worth of spending in the
Defense Department and Department of Housing and Urban Development
for which there is *no accounting*.[29]

The current paradigm of news programing sometimes encourages
people to use labels and stereotypes to summarize the fullness of a person's
character and world view. This tends to trivialize the complexity of our
identities, and distort reality. The term "socialist," for instance, has been demonized in ways that beg the question of what people actually know about
it. T-shirt and bumper stickers colorfully announce that, "Socialism is only
as strong as its laziest citizen," and, "You can have socialism or you have
freedom, you can't have both," and that, "The American dream is not about
a handout." There may be some truth to these slogans, but when viewed in
the light of the U.S. economic system, they seem very odd and ill-informed.

Since the U.S. has a mixed economy, it is already in part "socialist." Our
government already uses public tax dollars pay for roads, schools, hospitals,
parks, libraries, police, fire fighters, national defense, veterans' services,
courts, jails, care for the disabled and elderly, environmental protection,
sanitation and waste management, and transportation. What would it cost
the country to private these items? In addition, public tax dollars also find
their way into private companies as subsidies. An example of this "socialist"
practice comes from the U.S. Department of Agriculture, which subsidizes
American farms to the amount of roughly $20 billion dollars annually. The
public money is distributed over about 2.1 million farms, with the greatest
slice of the pie going to mega-farms with thousands of acres that produce
soy beans, corn, wheat, and cotton, and not to small farmers with a few cows
and a tomato patch. In a purely capitalist economy, mega-farms would have
to compete with all other farms on an level playing field, without subsidies,
and accept their success or failure as a matter of market preferences. [30]

When rhetoric can convince people that socialism is only about able-
bodied free-loaders sticking their hands into our pockets for welfare and food
stamps, and not about corporate bailouts and subsides, or about public services and resources that we all use, then we must consider that something has
gone terribly, terribly wrong with either our education, political discourse, or
our attitude towards the truth, and, in the end, it might be all three.

29. See Project Censored, "Top 25 Censored Stories of 2017–2018."
30. Edwards, "Agricultural Subsides," para. 1.

RIPPED FROM THE HEADLINES

There is no way we can know everything about every event, policy, or issue that impacts our lives. This is a significant matter because information is vital to how we make decisions that have moral and material implications for ourselves and others who share the fallout of how we vote, consume, and work. History teaches us that people are often willingly do rationalize evil deeds because they "did not know" about the consequences of their actions, or because they were complying with the law, or because "everyone was do-ing." The matter of when a perpetrator knew that an act was likely to cause injury or loss of life is therefore a pivotal point in litigation to establish the perpetrator's guilt.

It was not that long ago that the entire world was caught up in the con-troversy over how to punish Germans—citizens and Nazi soldiers alike—for their role in the genocide of six million Jews. Many who were indicted in the Nuremberg trials declared that they were "just following orders," or that they "did not know what was happening."[31] Their defense hung on two suppositions. First, that culpability ought to be mitigated when individuals were forced to do things that they would not normally do or face injuri-ous consequences; and, second, that blame cannot be assigned to those who were unaware of events, even if all the evidence supports the assertion that they should have known. The Nazi apparatus worked hard to prevent German citizens from knowing the details of death camps, torture, and de-praved acts committed in the name of the "Fatherland."[32] They believed that if people knew the details, they would not support the regime. The moral of the story: public opinion plays a significant role in the capacity of the state to perpetrate war crimes and crimes against humanity.

News reports and analysis are especially vital to democratic societ-ies because in those societies people have the right to determine laws and policies that impact the quality of life for everyone. What we know about the conditions of other people's lives influences our attitudes about them. How we tell the stories about businesses, labor, race relations, criminal justice, education, the environment, health care, national security, sexuality, aging, war, and energy have the potential to determine how we see so many things. Our narratives cue us as to which implications are salient, which issues are urgent and which can be ignored, whose interests matter the most, and to

31. Johnson and Reuband's *What We Knew* is an oral history of Germany during World War II that examines the eerie and blurred lines between knowing and not want-ing to know.

32. Ibid, pp. xii–xiii.

who ought to bear responsibility for mistakes and criminal acts, and who are above reproach.

The following is a transcript of a news story aired on National Public Radio on August 16, 2019. It concerns a restaurant proprietor who knowingly employs undocumented immigrants. The discussion of this story is a small illustration of how news reports might shape public discourse and attitudes towards issues by way of what is explicitly reported and what is omitted from the report.

Restaurant Owners Grapple With Hiring Undocumented Immigrants[33]

> The immigration and customs enforcement raids at a chicken processing plants last week reignited an old debate: who will do these jobs if not undocumented workers? In Mississippi, workers dismember poultry for eleven to twelve dollars an hour—brutal dangerous work. Across the country immigrants often do manual low-paying jobs, and employers say they have no choice but to rely on them.

> NPR's John Burnett spent some time with one restaurant owner wrestling with this very issue.

Burnett: It was mid-afternoon at a small popular restaurant in a city somewhere in Missouri. The lunch rush was over, and only a few diners remained. The cook was cleaning up. The proprietor, Lynn, asked that we not use her full name, the restaurant's name, the kind of cuisine, or the city to avoid arousing the attention of federal immigration agents. At least four of her six employees. . .gained entry to the United States without the requisite inspection; they're undocumented. The kitchen manager, Jaime, has been using a fake Social Security number since he came to the US from Mexico 21 years ago. He paid an underground seller 60 dollars for it and didn't ask any questions.

Jaime: Well we had to pay to get a Social—we know there is illegal [sic], but we don't have that, we not gonna have jobs, we not gonna have nothing else. So, we had to do that to work.

Burnett: Lynn and I sat at the serving counter, Jaime was standing in the kitchen wearing a black chef's uniform and a ball cap. Jaime said every immigrant he knows is constantly fearful of ICE, and we had our conversation before the Mississippi plant raids.[34]

Jaime: We just need a careful about everything [sic]. If we do something not correctly we gonna have troubles.

33. Morning Edition, "Restaurant Owners Grapple."
34. ICE stands for Immigration and Customs Enforcement.

Burnett: Lynn said she's plugged into the restaurant community in her Midwestern city, and she states flatly all of them hire undocumented workers.

Lynn: You cannot hire an American here that will show up to work—they will not be coming into their jobs. In America restaurant work is not a serious profession.

Burnett: The administration says they're deporting undocumented citizens like Jaime because he's taking job from Americas.

Lynn: That is the biggest joke—I know—I hear it all the time. And I couldn't hire someone—we put ads on Craig's List, Facebook, in the window, in the newspaper. The people that come in and apply to take our jobs will show up for one shift, they will not be clean, they will not probably be sober, they will ask for their money at the end of the shift, and they will not come back for the second shift.

Burnett: In contrast, Lynn describes her employees—all of whom came from central Mexico—as loyal, dependable, and incredibly hard-working. She says she pays her dishwashers eleven-fifty an hour and sixteen dollars for cooks. That's more than minimum wage, but they get no insurance, vacations, or sick pay. The Pew Research Center says there are seven and a half million unauthorized workers in the United States. They're concentrated in agriculture, construction, and the hospitality industry. But would they chose another line of work if they were here legally? (To Jaime) If you had a green card, would you still be working here for sixteen dollars and hour?

Jaime: Oh Yes. I like to cook, and then I like to work.

Burnett: Even if your boss wasn't standing here, would you work here if you were a lawful permanent resident?

Jaime: Ah, I will [sic] like to do something else, like, uh, I don't know, something different.

Burnett: Jaime didn't say what work he might choose if he had papers. Truth is, there's no path to citizenship for him. I turned back to Lynn, who was nursing a glass of Pinot Grigio after another long day of overseeing the restaurant. (To Lynn) What would happen if ICE were to deport all the undocumented workers in this city tomorrow?

Lynn: We'd close. I mean I couldn't—I'd just sell everything for whatever amount of money we could get for it, and we would close, because there's not enough talent of people [sic] who really do know how to cook.

Burnett: According to the Pew Center, ten percent of restaurant workers are unauthorized. That's one point one million employees. Lynn and thousands of other restaurant owners across the country say they cannot find enough suitable workers in the legal labor pool, especially for their kitchens. But administrative hardliners say, 'the law is the law.'

Krikorian: Whether you're talking about a chicken plant with 200 plus illegal workers, or a little restaurant that has half a dozen illegal workers, the issue is the same.

Burnett: Mark Krikorian is Executive Director for the Center for Immigration Studies, a Washington, D.C. think tank that favors lower immigration. He says there are US citizens who will do these unattractive jobs, and he cheers on Trump's ICE raids.

Krikorian: And if that means ah, a little restaurant somewhere ends up closing, that's unfortunate, I wish that on no one. But restaurants close every day, and if the labor market is tighter, what that means is that restaurants that do come up with a way of recruiting and retaining legal workers will have a competitive advantage.

Burnett: I called Lynn back this week, and asked her thoughts about the big ICE raid. She said her restaurant is too little for ICE to target, but that doesn't means she's not effected. She said now, she's afraid the cost of chicken is about to go up.

FOWL PLAY

Readers' reactions to the story may be influenced by some analysis. There are at least five things to consider. First, the story is presented in the context of a national debate over immigration. It is possible that without the controversy, the story, even though it is probably true, may not have made its way to the airwaves. Undocumented workers like Jaime have been in the U.S. for decades with little media attention. Somebody somewhere decided that it was time to tell this story.

Second, the story is part of at least four larger narratives in the US. Whether each is blatant or nuanced in the story, and whether the issues are adequately addressed in the story are debatable. The first narrative concerns immigration, the second concerns the American labor force, and the third is entrepreneurialism. The fourth, buried deeper than the others, is the tale of how laws are made, enforced, and ignored. Each narrative has implications for the others. Every narrative is made up of characters who interact with each other, and whose actions often affect the well-being of or outcomes for other characters. Sometimes characters remain invisible or do not have any explicit lines as the plot unfolds. In this story, readers hear about how others' actions have impacted them, but those others are not present to speak for themselves. For example, Burnett mentions that "administrative hardliners" want to enforce immigration law, but instead of introducing members of the current federal administration to share their thoughts, he interviewed a member of a conservative think tank. The implication is that the think tank speaks for the administration.

A third thing to consider is that, in this story, the cook felt his survival depended on breaking the law. Readers do not learn anything about why he did not follow immigration laws when he made his way to the U.S., nor do we know about whether the Social Security number he obtained resulted in someone else's troubles with collecting or applying for Social Security benefits. Readers do not learn what the cook thinks about how his choices impact American workers, or the worker's family, which may be living south of the border. These details may be important when wading through the feelings that are aroused when hearing stories like this one, and trying to determine who deserves the lion's share of our empathy.

Fourth, readers learn that the proprietor is trying to sustain her business, and feels proud of the fact that she pays some of her workers more than minimum wage. Readers can only speculate about why she does not pay for health insurance or other benefits, as her thoughts on those matters are not part of the story. Readers also learn that she does not have a high opinion of American workers, but holds immigrant workers in high esteem. Lynn offered stereotypes of American and Mexican workers without being asked to explore their accuracy. Listeners do not hear from Americans who worked for her and then quit, and they are not present to defend themselves against Lynn's stereotypes. Her descriptions of these two groups are dualistic. That is always a red flag in discourse, because it signals the speaker may be biased.

Readers also see that Lynn's assessment—at least as represented in this published piece—is based on what kind of worker is best for her business interests. This interest is legitimate, but might be different from an interest in the well-being of the American working class. That issue is not explored in the story. Readers may wonder, "Does she believe that people can live well on eleven-fifty an hour—$460.00 a week for 40 hours—and no benefits?" Readers may also wonder if the proprietor has thought about what kind of social dynamics are created when people make exceptions for themselves to obey the law. What kind of internal reasoning has excused her from complying with federal regulations? Readers have no information about the restaurant's profit margins, and whether the proprietor could afford giving a greater share of her profits to her employees and still live comfortably. The way the story is framed may give the reader the impression that the most important aspect of the story is economic, and that all the characters in the drama are hapless pons in the game of supply and demand. Might the story also be about morality or politics? Might it be that the invisible hand of the market is actually a series of decisions made by real people with real interests in creating advantages for themselves?

Fifth, in this story, the law is pictured as an agency that *must respond* to a crisis rather than as an agency that *helped create* the crisis. The story exposes a business woman who is breaking the law and an undocumented employee who owns a counterfeit Social Security card. In this story, the listener is confronted with the unspoken question of whether all this law-breaking is OK. In this story, listeners learn nothing about how law-makers may have contributed to the problems. Their contributions might include the passage of bad immigration laws, the willingness to ignore deportation in order to win Hispanic votes, the favor shown to lobbyists who represent agricultural titans who depend on migrant labor, and the inability of the U.S. government to work with its neighbors to the south to end the terror and poverty that drive so many souls north. The educational value of the story is limited, but it does provoke emotion.

In Krikorian's remarks, readers learn that many in the current federal administration believe that if employers were to improve what they offer workers, American workers would gladly take "unattractive jobs." The assertion suggests that private businesses are not taking on their share of responsibility for the immigration crisis. Shortly after ICE raided poultry plants in Mississippi on August 7, 2019, over 200 people applied for work in the plants that lost workers. Applicants told reporters that they were offered wages that were similar to wages in the area, and that the jobs often provided opportunities to advance.[35] Apparently, despite Lynn's assertions, American workers are willing to take "unattractive jobs" for low wages under certain conditions.

WHAT RULES THE ROOST

It is normal for readers to project themselves into stories. When reading the case of Lynn in a city somewhere in Missouri, we know that she worries about the status of undocumented workers because she connects their status to the price she will have to pay for chicken and labor, and we know that Jaime worries about staying in the U.S. and having a job. Who triggers the strongest gut-level empathy: Lynn or Jaime? Readers who eat chicken may project themselves into the story and feel a little irritated about the possibility that ICE raids might increase the cost of their nuggets and wings. Readers who have jobs that pay minimum wage may have much more sympathy

35. Gates, "More than 200 People Applied," para. 1; Vicory, "Job Fair," para. 11–12.

for Jaime than they have for Lynn and wonder whether minimum wages will ever keep pace with the cost of living. Readers who believe that it is wrong for people to get away with breaking the law may be angry because they believe this sort of thing encourages disrespect for rules and fair play.

What readers and listeners were not able to think about as the great chicken chronicle unfolded is the role of Joseph Grendys, the owner of a fowl empire, Koch Foods, which processes poultry. How is it that Grendys, who is worth $2.4 billion (more than the Gross Domestic Product of some of the poorest nations on Earth[36]) cannot afford to hire legal workers for decent wages and benefits, and still sell his chickens for a reasonable profit?[37]

Joseph Grendys represents the thousands of corporate executives whose strategies to make money and whose profit margins rarely make it into news stories. Whether those stories concern the great chicken empire or any other multi-million dollar industry dominated by a handful of families, the details about what it actually cost the families to do business and what they actually profit after expenses are paid are typically omitted from the story. The lack of transparency makes it difficult for audiences to put the woes and miseries of the business class in perspective. Further, it reinforces the mental mind-set that the problems faced by the Lynns and the Jaimes of the world are disconnected from the Joseph Grendys of the world, when in reality they may be closely linked.

The smaller the framework we use for our stories, the more distorted the narrative becomes. The news that we daily consume is nowhere near the whole picture. This means that our moral judgment is often on shaky ground because it is founded on fragments of the story rather than the full picture. Half-truths and distortions are the life blood of hate speech. They are valuable, nonetheless, because they sustain a certain narrative. Consider, for example, the rhetoric of white supremacists in the U.S. who claim that immigrants are taking "their" jobs. The assertion assumes that one is entitled to a certain job by virtue of birth-place or ethnicity. While the *Universal Declaration of Human Rights* (1948) states that, "Everyone has the right to work, to free choice of employment, to just and favourable conditions of work and to protection against unemployment,"[38] there are no federal and state laws that reserve jobs for individuals based on birth place and ethnicity.

Religious organizations have said that people have a right to work, but do not assert that God has reserved certain jobs for certain people. Catholic

36. Statistics Times. "List of Countries by GDP," Table International Monetary Fund.

37. Forbes, "135 Koch Foods." Note: Koch Foods has no relation to Charles and David Koch, the energy moguls who support Libertarian policies, and give hundreds of millions of their $42 billion fortune to favored candidates.

38. United Nations, *Declaration of Human Rights*, Art. 23, Sec.1.

popes and bishops have traditionally taken the position that human beings need work to fulfill their duties to family and to maintain the dignity of providing for oneself. They admonished employers who cheat and exploit workers, and chided individuals and institutions for their role in creating conditions in which honest, hard-working people cannot survive.[39] The Jewish tradition also makes clear that human dignity is edified by labor, and that individuals have the right to work, eat, be compensated when sick or injured, and to be paid on time with decent wages.[40]

A second assumption embedded in the exclamation that immigrants are "taking my job" is that the people who are taking these jobs are selfish individuals who are taking advantage of weaknesses in the U.S. position on immigration. The blame for "lost jobs" is thus concentrated onto a specific demographic population—a very vulnerable population— rather than other individuals who have exercised their power and authority to shape minimum wage policies, immigration laws, immigration law enforcement, and corporate regulations. Blaming the workers deflects attention away from the chicken kings and other corporate chieftains. In the U.S., some of the most powerful lobbyists include those representing agriculture and construction— industries that hire many undocumented workers according to the PBS. These lobbyists are not pleading with law-makers to expel undocumented migrants or mandate higher wages for Americans. They want policies that protect their bottom line.[41]

The cost of catering to corporate potentates is generally not part of the American narrative about jobs and immigration. Many do not know that the paltry price of poultry is linked not only to woeful wages for undocumented and documented workers alike, but also linked to federal welfare programs that dole out food stamps, health care, and subsidized housing when people cannot find work, or cannot earn enough money to support their families, even though they are working.[42]

39. See: Leo XIII, *Rerum Novarum*; Paul VI, *Popularum Progressio*; and, United States Catholic Bishops, *Economic Justice for All*.

40. Perry's, *Labor Rights in the Jewish Tradition* delves into the theology supporting Jewish principles.

41. The bottom line is also enhanced in the production of meat, milk, and eggs by horrific agricultural practices that can only be described as cruelty to the animals and the Earth. See Solotaroff, "In the Belly of the Beast."

42. Boeri, Hanson, and McCormick's *Immigration Policy and the Welfare System* contains essays jam-packed with data that reveal how the government alliance with private industries and the demand for public welfare sustain conflict over immigration and whether the government will enforce immigration laws.

A COMPARTMENT FOR ALL SEASONS

The story about restaurant owners and immigration supports the cultural narrative that the laws of supply and demand rule supreme, and that there is little we can do about that. Many of the stories we tell each other about the human condition begin and end with this notion. In these fables, personal responsibility is a bit player, a minor character with a low profile, who is incidental to the "real" story. The spiritual aspects and implications of our interactions, and the invitation to bring the love of God and humanity to bear on Earth are crowed out of our cultural narratives. Is there place for the spirit, humanism, the grace of God, and love of neighbor, in the narratives of our public lives? Is there a place for spirituality in a story about chickens?

Burnett's story of the entrepreneur and her undocumented worker does not explicitly raise the issue of morality. Listeners may project moral dimensions in to the story, but matters of right and wrong, God's will, or humanitarian obligations were not literally featured in the story. The market for labor is the framework in which all players act out a scene. Whatever struggles people have with life and each other are colored only by the crayons in the market box. Wages, immigration, profit margins, law enforcement, and the cost of running a business are all determined by the demand for labor (cheap yet industrious) and the supply of labor (unreliable if American).

Burnett could have asked questions that prompted Lynn and Jaime to discuss the ethical dimensions of their conduct, or how they saw their actions in relation to their faith, but that might have set the story on thin ice. Journalists are supposed to be objective, and to introduce God and ethics might seem preachy or judgmental. Americans are selective in their use of preachy and judgmental rhetoric. Such rhetoric is generally acceptable when condemning Islamic fundamentalism and abortion, but not typically acceptable when condemning the sale of automatic rifles and tax breaks to the ultra-rich.

Many people think about religion, humanitarianism, and spirituality when they listen to rhetoric and discourse. Some reference sacred teachings in their meaning-making, while others take a humanist approach and ponder the principles of charity and tolerance. Sometimes news stories address religion, especially if there is a major religious controversy or conflict in progress. Covering religion and covering the spiritual dimensions of our thinking about secular issues, however, are not the same.

Subsequent to the 1970s' and 1980s' Great Wakening that saw millions of Americans turn to "born-again" Christianity as a way to find meaning and wholeness in their lives, news agencies began to increase their number of reporters who covered religion. As one journalist put it: "Many editors have decided that they can no longer overlook the mounting evidence that Americans—whether they embrace Catholicism, Judaism, Hinduism, animism, Godless worship, yoga, channeling, spiritualism, or love of nature—are very religious people."[43] The coverage was a response to a social trend, an increase in people's interest to fill a void in their lives with something that brought them a sense of purpose, hope, and security in the world. Increased coverage of religion also helped people understand that religious zealotry often encouraged Americans to nudge democracy in the direction of theocracy.

Covering religious events, personalities, and movements, however, is not the same as covering the religious or spiritual aspects of a story. In covering the religious event, personality, or movement, journalists operate in socially acceptable perimeters of compartments into which we organize the experiences of our lives. We normally have a compartment for God and religious experiences, which is different from the compartment for our political life, our professional life, our private life, and our social life. Life is messy, however, and the content of our compartments spill over into each other quite naturally, as if we were designed to have no compartments. The spillage seems to tell us that our wellness and social well-being was always contingent on whether we were the same person with the same principles and ethos no matter where we were or what we were doing.

Arguably, compartmentalization can breed lies, double-standards, and hypocrisy. It allows us to juggle our values and principles at will, and adopt one set of values and principles in one circumstance, and another set in a different circumstance. This places our integrity on a slippery slope. An individual who inconsistently applies principles— even in order to do good things— risks the loss of one's principles altogether. Compartmentalization also breeds its own rhetoric and narratives, because when we dis-integrate our lives—when we dis-associate our beliefs, morals, and principles from our circumstances—we need a language to justify our conduct. In many instances, justifications become norms, and norms become "truth."

As we compartmentalize our lives, we also compartmentalize people, and we create narratives that allow us to treat others in ways that often contradict our espoused faith and humanitarianism. Sometimes we sort people based on the value they hold for us, and sometimes we sort people based on our perception of their potential for redemption. Many Christians struggle with the idea that they should have unconditional love for others because, rather than risk humiliation, injury, and perhaps even death to defend a

43. Shepherd, "Media Get Religion," p. 21.

scoundrel's potential for redemption, they would rather believe that they can make the world perfect by destroying scoundrels.

In the end, Burnett was under no legal or professional obligation to ask Lynn and Jaime about the morality of their actions or thinking, nor to inquire about how their thoughts and actions represent their relationship with God. The story was not explicitly about a religious experience or event. Having not met the criteria for that compartment of the human experience, it was logical for Burnett to ignore the spiritual and moral aspects of the story.

One may wonder what would happen to our discourse if more journalists and editors raised the question of spirituality, humanitarianism, and morality in reports concerning secular issues. What might listeners have learned if Burnett had asked Lynn and Jamie about their faith and how it informs their humanity? Imagine reporters asking people—not just authorities and experts—but everyone, to discuss the intricacies of how their conscience works, and what evidence they might offer to support claims that they love their neighbors as themselves. It is possible that many would be offended by the questions. It is also possible that we might discover that we have more love and compassion for others than what we have been led to believe.

Chapter 7

The Church of St. Exceptions

I WOULDN'T BET ON IT

If we cannot always count on the news media and higher education to build and refine our rhetorical capital, what about civic leadership and the public discourse of our elected officials? Are those things likely to build rhetorical capital and help improve the quality of our communication? The archives of the United States history, after all, are oozing with political rhetoric that references God and good will, and elected officials at all levels still invoke principles of fairness and justice in their speeches. Might it not be possible then, that our elected officials and civic leaders hold the key to improving rhetorical capital because they are so often in the public eye, and they are, by virtue of being a leader, a moral example for us all? It is possible, but I would not put money on it.

The notion that elected and government leaders will restore and revitalize our rhetorical capital is a bad bet, because secular leaders throughout history have waged war and committed other despicable acts while declaring it was God's will to do so. It is estimated that roughly 7 percent (123) of the 1,763 wars that have been documented in world history have been overtly caused by religious conflict.[1] About 12 million people perished in the Thirty Years War (1617–1648), as Catholics and Protestants contested each other's faith and territorial possessions.[2] Pope Innocent III launched the Fourth

1. Axelrod, *Encyclopedia of Wars*, Vol 3, p. 1484–85.
2. Wilson's *Thirty-Years War* documents the horror of this event, which consumed Europe on a scale never before seen. The war rearranged the political geography of

Crusade (1202–1204), wherein Christian soldiers looted churches, pillaged government treasuries, raped nuns, and murdered civilians before burning Constantinople to the ground.[3]

In the modern era, religion is still bloody business. Christianity was used to defend slavery.[4] It was used to kill, enslave, and force Native Americans to forsake their own religious traditions and beliefs.[5] Protestants loathed the idea of a Catholic president, and anti-Semitism was, and continues to be an American fixture.[6] Everywhere one turns in history—including the 21st century—God is busy hating somebody. Leaders who are serious about improving our rhetorical capital and public discourse would have to change the American narrative substantially. They would have to convince many Americans that the U.S. is not anointed by God to unilaterally determine Earth's fate. They would have to abandon the myth that the nation is a perfect example of democracy.

Leaders that want to restore and rejuvenate our rhetorical capital and public discourse face the serious obstacle of national sanctimony. Our secular leaders operate in a society that has for nearly 250 years cultivated a narrative that places the U.S. on a pedestal at the right hand of God. This narrative is not introduced nor defined in a single formal document, yet it places a striking amount of force upon popular attitudes and values, as it norms the idea of American exceptionalism. The American narrative is found in many sources, and it has been articulated in various ways by various generations. The narrative is relentlessly optimistic and positive. The American narrative tells friends and foes alike that Americans built a sterling civilization with blood, sweat, and tears made holy by our endless good intentions and Christian virtues. It tells the world that every obstacle America overcame bears witness to the superiority of American character, and God's favor. The narrative is a national myth. It is part of America's civil religion, a set of beliefs about our existential purpose, and a set of ideals that transcends all faiths and denominations.

Europe and set the stage for subsequent wars of imperialism.

3. Phillips, Jonathan, *Fourth Crusade*, pp. xiii–xxii.

4. See Morrison, "Religious Defense."

5. Tinker's *Missionary Conquest* examines Christianity's relationship with white supremacy and genocide.

6. See: Michael's, *Concise History* for a survey of anti-Semitism in the U.S. to 1945, and Lipstadt's *Antisemitism* for an exploration of current anti-Semitism in the US and how Americans deny its existence.

AMERICAN CIVIL RELIGION

Religion is a complex and dynamic construct that is the subject of anthropological, sociological, psychological, theological, literary, philosophical, historical, and etymological inquiry and debate.[7] The meaning of religion may never be fully apprehended, as mysticism, psychological phenomenon, metaphors, symbols, superstition, science, the "revealed word of God," transcendence, and assimilation are constantly colliding inside our minds, as we humans reach to the "without" and to the "within" to understand what is meant by "God."[8]

In American culture, the mystical aspects of religion are widely eclipsed by the pragmatic aspects of religion that provide moral guardrails for our conduct. For many Americans, mysticism, the Tao, and the Zen of life are peculiar and esoteric. Americans are practical people and often do not know what to do with mystical and transcendent aspects of life. We are not as interested in "being" as we are with "doing" even when our doing destroys our being. The social dimension of our civic religion teaches us how our ideals ought to be manifest in governance, civic interaction, and foreign relations. Our civil religion is so firmly welded to nationalism that it struggles to bear the light of mysticism and transcendental teachings telling us that we are one with all creation. One cannot be one with all creation when one is busy fighting over creation for national advantages.

As a social construct, religion and its attributes, including nomenclature, rituals, symbols, and doctrines are profoundly influenced by the physical and metaphysical experiences of the community of its origin. Religion in the traditional sense provides individuals with an explanation for why things are as they are, and why one must believe these explanations. It provides societies with a purpose and a sense of identity, which is often endowed by a divine and omnipotent being. Typically, religion is characterized by rules and obligations that govern people's relationship to God, the community as a whole, and "the other" or non-member. In many traditions, religion reconciles mankind with God and offers humanity a way to be with God. Religion also binds people together through ceremonies in which members of the group collectively and publically affirm their commitment to a certain creed and ethos.

Theologian Paul Tillich held that every human being is religious because every human being is driven to the "ultimate concern," which is the matter of one's orientation to life. He believed that the "ultimate concern" is

---

7. Guthrie, "Religion," pp. 412–415;

8. Crawford, *What is Religion*, pp. 1–8.

not material and immediate, but fixed on the questions of what it means to *be* and *exist*, which lead inevitably to God.[9] For Tillich, to make a nation, a political ideology, or science the "ultimate concern" is idolatrous. Civilization expresses a collective "ultimate concern" that maybe alternately sacred and secular, but always concerned with ideals. Sociologist, Emile Durkheim wrote, "A society can neither create nor recreate itself without creating some kind of ideal by the same stroke."[10] Civil religion embodies ideals and defines the "ultimate concerns" of a society. It creates myths and legends of a glorious national history that will sanctify what the "high priests"—secular leaders and officials—of civil religion say should be sanctified.

Civil religion serves many of the same functions of traditional religion with a decidedly secular essence. In civil religion, God becomes a generic figure, a higher power frequently stripped of tribal affiliations and Christological attributes. Civil religion also provides individuals and society with a sense of identity and purpose. It embodies an ethos, principles, and values.

Civil religion in America is the product of many ingredients and has evolved over time. The Enlightenment principles which promoted reason, religious tolerance, and civility for the mutual benefit of all are central to American civil religion, as is the idea that there is a God and divine providence. Another key ingredient is the belief that, regardless of our ancestry and national origins, Americans have been called to work collectively to create a model of democracy and decency for the world. Another element of America's civil religion is the belief that liberty is essential for the human being to thrive both materially and spiritually. Though the U.S. Constitution originally gave special legal status to white male property owners, it grafted into itself great flexibility that allowed for future generations to stretch its meaning and application. The ability to amend the law allows for future generations to embrace broader conceptualizations of justice, common good, and human dignity than what previous generations had to offer. In its ideal form, the American republic was conceived and organized for the people. What was meant by "the people" evolved over time as bullets and legislation took turns enfranchising the marginalized.

America's civil religion defines the nation's place in the world as one uniquely suited to global leadership. It announces American exceptionalism to the world and waves banners of achievement in law, industry, humanitarianism, and culture—all of which justify the nation's affluence. American civil religion is expressed in the Great Seal of the United States. On one side there is an eagle clutching arrows in one talon and an olive branch in the

9. Crockett, "On the Disorientation," p. 4.
10. Durkheim, *Elementary Forms*, p. 425.

other. In the eagle's beak, a banner reads "E Pluribus Unum," Latin for "out of many one." On the flip side, there is an unfinished pyramid over which sits an all-seeing eye that radiates light. This side reads, "Annuit Coeptis," meaning "Providence has approved of our endeavor," and "Novus Ordo Seculorum," meaning "New order of ages." For nearly 250 years, these symbols have declared to the world that the people of the United States believe that God has anointed their nation to build a new world order that unites people from all over the earth under one enlightened shepherd.[11]

The traditional narrative of how America became the mightiest and most honorable nation on Earth tells the tale of a country with humble beginnings, and of a people who simply wanted to worship the Lord and work with honest hands to earn their daily bread. Historians in the American orthodox school portrayed the U.S. as a benign and benevolent nation, one that reluctantly went to war, and always for self-defense. In the narrative of American civil religion, America did not seek greatness, rather, divine providence saw fit to impose greatness and global leadership upon it.[12]

America's civil religion is reinforced by various types of rhetoric and discourse about the greatness of America's people, principles, causes, and way of life. Its rhetoric assumes the authority of sacred scripture and is implicit in the archives of Congressional Records, U.S. Supreme Court decisions, political speeches, campaign ads, campaign speeches, memorial sermons, and campaign slogans. Civil religious scripture is embedded in popular movies, news media, television shows, biographies, history books, and school curricula. The rhetoric consists of many stories that all lead to a single conviction: with God's blessing, America is the hope of the world, and shall use its might as it sees fit to extinguish evil, and to establish a world order where peace and liberty may prevail.[13] America's civil religion personifies the nation not as God's ancillary, but as a living conduit of God ordained at its conception.

Sociologist Robert Bellah called attention to President John F. Kennedy's Inaugural Address as an example of civil religion's rhetoric. Kennedy declared:

> For man holds in his mortal hands the power to abolish all forms of human poverty and to abolish all forms of human life. And yet the same revolutionary beliefs for which our forefathers fought are still at issue around the globe—the belief that the

11. Haberski, *God and War*, p. 5.

12. May's *Imperial Democracy* and Steel's *Pax Americana* illustrate this interpretation of the United States.

13. Bellah, "Civil Religion in America," pp. 5–8.

rights of man come not from the generosity of the state but from the hand of God.

Let the word go forth from this time and place, to friend and foe alike, that the torch has been passed to a new generation of Americans—born in this century, tempered by war, disciplined by a hard and bitter peace, proud of our ancient heritage—and unwilling to witness or permit the slow undoing of those human rights to which this nation has always been committed, and to which we are committed today at home and around the world.[14]

Kennedy entered the presidency as a strident cold warrior, and his speech suggested that America was God's right hand in seeing that liberty and human dignity were honored around the globe. He spoke of bearing burdens and making sacrifices for the sake of human rights. He told listeners that their reward for undertaking the American endeavor was not the possession of a magnificent empire, but "good conscience" and solace in having done much to help others.

Kennedy's speech placed the U.S. at the forefront of global transformation and echoed the confidence of his predecessors that America brought light to the world that was brighter than the lights of all others. His rhetoric suggested that peace, prosperity, and liberty would follow wherever the U.S. left its footprint. The civil religion of America made it generous with foreign aid, and inspired its global outreach of compassion through the Peace Corps and Alliance for Progress, which helped foreign countries develop their infrastructure, schools, hospitals, and economies. American civil religion, however, has not transformed the world at its most radical base. In some instances, America's pious rhetoric has been a Trojan horse that smuggled ruin and oppression into foreign nations, and carried the disease of empire wherever it went.

To restore and rebuild rhetorical capital and public discourse, elected and appointed officials alike would have to admit that the traditional and popular narrative of America as a reluctant and unselfish hero is not 100 percent accurate. Leaders would have to admit that America's critics were, in many instances correct about the death, destruction, and tyranny that followed American intervention and investment. They would have to come clean about why so many Americans around the country do not have access to the best education, health care, housing, and nutrition possible. They would have to do so because to restore and rebuild rhetorical capital and public discourse requires a re-establishment of trust in public figures to tell the truth. They would have to win the trust of the marginalized that

14. Kennedy, John F., "Inaugural Address," para. 2–3.

whenever they spoke about the nation's conditions and needs, they spoke with accuracy and included voices from the margins. Part of the reason why our rhetorical capital is fragile and futile is because too many promises to lift up the poor and despised that were declared in the heat of a political campaign have not come to fruition.

Whether elected leaders like it or not, their words have an impact on the extent to which we are willing to make sacrifices for the common good, put in an honest day's work, pay our taxes, and obey the rules. We are not all so benevolent that we rise above the specious, egotistical, and vulgar speech of those in high office. Rather, many of us are impressionable and have no problem rationalizing our own dishonesty, self-centeredness, and vulgarity because this is how our own leaders communicate. When leaders feed the public belligerent discourse and rhetoric that is not fair and accurate, it alters the norms for leadership and the substance of our civil religion. A steady diet of lies, prejudice, and undeveloped reasoning tells the public that leaders do not respect the people they govern well enough to tell them the truth and give them thorough and cogent discourse.

THEY BOWED THEIR HEADS AND DOUBTED

Michael Medved's two books, *The American Miracle* (2016) and *God's Hand on America* (2019) assert that American history "proves" the republic is central to God's plan to redeem the world. In his interpretation of American history, every event, however bloody and barbaric, was carefully crafted by divine hands so that the United States could made the world ready for Jesus' return to Earth. The problem with the thesis is not that God might use the imperfect to work divine will, nor the notion that redemption is an unfolding process. The problem is that it is elitist and offers no substantial evidence that God was not also working with other societies and nations to work God's will. The thesis regards the U.S. as an exceptional nation, one that is above the accountability of men and their laws, and one that may rightly refuse to collaborate with other nations for the sake of "doing the will of God."

Many elected officials and community leaders in the U.S. have bowed their heads to ask God's blessing. They have prayed for fallen soldiers, for victims of hurricanes and fires, and for the casualties of mass shootings. Historians tell us that presidents have leveraged religion to obtain popular support for policies and candidates, but reveal little about how faith informed their policies and judgement.[15] Government leaders have

15. Bass, Rozell, Whitney, "Introduction," pp. 1–12.

often blended institutional religion with civil religion, and nearly always to achieve material objectives.

Presidents have consistently used religious rhetoric to unify the country, and to secure mass support for a given course of action. When presidents invoke God in public, they offer assurance that divine providence has been consulted on matters, and that cosmic forces are aligned with their objectives. George Washington is said to have knelt in prayer at Valley Forge to pray for victory against the British.[16] Knowing the power of faith to unite people, and knowing Americans needed assurance that the new republic was anchored in reverence for God, roughly one third of the sentences in his Inaugural Address contained religious references.[17]

Thomas Jefferson admired the teachings of Jesus, but wholly rejected the idea that Jesus was divine. He created his own bible, which included the teachings of Jesus, but not the stories of miracles or the resurrection.[18] Knowing how bitterly he would be received by the general public should his beliefs about Jesus be known, he was very private about his faith. He regularly used religious rhetoric to assure people that the separation of church and state did not obliterate his piety and the sanctity of the American endeavor.[19]

Abraham Lincoln admitted that he was "an open scoffer of Christianity," but was perhaps the most pastoral and prophetic of all American presidents.[20] He believed that religion moderated passion and impulses that were detrimental to society, and he used religious rhetoric to unify the people with each other, even though he believed that religion should only be about uniting people with God. Lincoln reviled religious zealotry as it tended to close dialogue rather than widen and sustain it. He found it absurd that people on both sides of the Civil War prayed to the same God for victory, and audacious that people prayed to protect slavery.[21]

DIVINE STARS, DIVINE STRIPES

The U.S. transition from being a nation that shined its messianic light brightly enough for others to see at a distance to being a nation that brought

16. Scott, "The Faith of George Washington," pp. 13–44.

17. Shogun, *Moral Rhetoric of American Presidents*, pp. 47–48.

18. See: Jefferson, *Jefferson Bible*, which includes Jefferson's notes on Judaism and Deism.

19. Buckley, "Thomas Jefferson and the Myth," 45–58.

20. Morel, "Lincoln's Political and Religions Politics," pp. 83–106.

21. Ibid, pp. 94–94.

that light right up into the faces of other nations whether they sought it or not, was due in part to the presidencies of Theodore Roosevelt and Woodrow Wilson. The two were children during the Civil War, and by the time they were young men, the U.S. was an industrial force with considerable interests abroad. Like many of their generation, they believed that God had spared the nation total destruction in Civil War, and reserved for it a special place as the world's captain of democracy and decency. They held that the wealth gained from industrialization and appropriation of foreign territories in Hawaii, the Philippines, and Latin America at the turn of the 20th century underscored God's favor.

President Theodore Roosevelt is remembered for muscular acts of nationalism, building the Panama Canal, establishing a modern navy, charging into battle against the Spanish with his "Rough Riders" in Cuba, and keeping Japanese ambitions in China and in the Pacific in check. He was also a progressive who championed federal regulation to improve the safety of food and medicine, and who created the National Forest Service and National Parks. His upbringing was religious and filled with social activism that honored virility and science as key elements in social progress.[22] In 1916, he published a book, *Fear God and Take Your Own Part*. He preached that to fear God meant to "respect and honor God," and that "all of this can only be done by loving our neighbor, treating him justly and mercifully, and in all ways endeavoring to protect him from injustice and cruelty. . ."[23] Of foreigners he pontificated, "We must treat other nations as we would wish to be treated in return. . ."[24]

In many ways, Roosevelt was a man of his times. Like many of his generation, he was influenced by the Darwinism, and the idea that natural selection had rendered some members of the species to superior to others. Colonialism in his era was seen as a necessary bridge between barbarity and civility, as tribal, non-industrial people had to be "groomed" for their liberties.[25] On Memorial Day, 1902, as the U.S. fought Filipino nationalists seeking independence from American hegemony, he proudly announced that the war was fought for the "triumph of civilization over forces which stand for the black chaos of savagery and barbarism."[26] Estimates of the

22. Hawley, "Theodore Roosevelt," pp. 1–19.

23. Roosevelt, *Fear God*, p. 15.

24. Ibid, p. 16.

25. Van Ells, "Assuming the White Man's Burden," 607–611. Rudyard Kipling's poem "White Man's Burden" lauded the sacrifice of nations that took seriously the moral duty to "save" societies living in "darkness."

26. Kramer, "Race-making and Colonial Violence," p. 169.

number of Filipinos who died in that war are as high as 700,000.[27] His loath-
ing for Native Americans was well-known, and he described the wars to
remove Natives from the plains as wars against savagery.[28] Some historians
say that Roosevelt did not think that any race was "inherently or biologi-
cally inferior" to others, but instead, found that some races were socially and
economically "inferior" to whites, having not yet "reached a high degree of
education, economic success, and cultural achievement as had the majority
of white societies."[29]

Woodrow Wilson was the grandson, son, and nephew of Presbyterian
ministers. Rejecting a career in the ministry, he opted for academia and
politics. He brought his faith to bear in his public life, having never abandoned the idea that the material world was filled with opportunities to serve
God and improve the soul.[30] In his first term (1913–1917), Wilson's rhetoric
raged against political machines that were greased by patronage and made
to do the bidding of big business.[31] It resonated with muckrakers, preachers of the Social Gospel, urban reformers, and famers' alliances who cried
that banks and railroads were squeezing the life out of American families.[32]
Wilson shared Roosevelt's desire to see the U.S. take its place on the world's
stage, and World War I took Wilson's nationalism to new heights. It made
him an apostle for world peace, and a crusader for the ill-fated League of
Nations. Wilson harbored hope for the perfectibility of the world, which
many historians argue is fatal in a president.

Like Roosevelt, Wilson was racist. As with many Presbyterians, he
believed the Bible sanctified slavery. He felt that emancipation was unfortunate because slaves were ill-prepared for their freedom, but that education,
vocational training, and jobs would eventually lead blacks to equality and
prosperity.[33] While President of Princeton University, however, African
Americans were quietly compelled to withdraw their applications. When
Wilson moved into the Oval Office, segregation, which had not existed since
the Civil War in federal workspaces, was revived. His stance on segregation

27. Gates, "War-Related Deaths," p. 367.
28. Gerstle, "Theodore Roosevelt," p, 1283.
29. Skidmore, "Theodore Roosevelt on Race and Gender," p. 42.
30. Thorsen, *Political Thought of Woodrow Wilson*, pp. 4–5.
31. Cooper, *Warrior and the Priest*, pp. 174–184.
32. Muckrakers were journalists who exposed corruption, abuse of power, and the
suffering of the poor. See Weinberg and Weinberg, *Muckrakers*. See: Morgan, "The Development of Sociology and the Social Gospel."
33. Blumenthal, "Woodrow Wilson and the Race Question," pp. 1–2.

was so odious, that black Americans mobilized votes against him, and in 1916, Democrats, Wilson's party, lost control of the House and Senate.[34]

In his most messianic role, Wilson attended the Versailles peace talks after World War I, and was given a hero's welcome. He brought the U.S. into the war in 1917 with rhetoric declaring that the war would "make the world safe for democracy." He saw Versailles as an opportunity to establish world order and peace through disarmament and cooperation. The instrument of such cooperation was his brain-child, the League of Nations, an international council that would resolve conflicts without war. To Wilson, the League was a sacred "covenant" to prove that men had not died in vain, but died as part of a "crusade" to liberate the world.[35] Wilson pitched membership of the League to the U.S. as a God-given path forward to "free every nation from unworthy bondage."[36]

Those who were in "unworthy bondage" and hopeful that Wilson was serious about decolonization included Ho Chi Minh and Mahatma Gandhi. Minh sought participation in the peace talks for the purpose of liberating Vietnam from France, and was refused.[37] Gandhi, was disappointed as the Treaty failed to liberate India from Great Britain.[38] The rhetorical crusade to make the world safe for democracy had been just that: rhetorical. Black soldiers in the U.S. army who fought for democracy thought segregation would end, but like British and French colonial subjects, they learned that the rhetoric of liberty meant only what white men said it meant.

American political rhetoric at the turn of the 20th century illustrates the durability of the American narrative in which the U.S. is consistently a bystander, minding his own business until a poor, defenseless people are attacked by rapacious nations, and then, out of pure benevolence, takes gun in hand to vanquish the menacing foe. Consistently, God approved of the American savior. Our presidents told us so. In the last half of the 20th century, America acquired so much military and economic power, that it could assert its narrative with far more force than ever before. The U.S. clung to the durable Puritan narrative that it could redeem the world and make it anew in its own image.[39]

34. Ibid, pp. 14–15.

35. Wilson, "League of Nations," para. 17–18. Fearing the loss of national autonomy, the U.S. Senate voted against joining the League.

36. Wilson, "Address to the Senate," para. 27–28.

37. Macmillan, *Paris 1919*, p. 59.

38. Cohen, "Gandhi's Concept of Non-violence," p. 35.

39. Gamble, "Savior Nation," pp. 8–9.

THE DULLES BOYS

In the aftermath of World War II, the U.S. was a military and economic superpower unlike any that had ever existed. It had atomic bombs, and by virtue of escaping the destruction of its factories in World War II, commanded the world's economy. America civil religion during the Cold War positioned God as the advance guard of democracy and capitalism.[40] As popes denounced Marxism and dictatorship in their encyclicals, and religious magazines demonized communists, children prayed in schools for the liberation of people living under Soviet tyranny.[41] Reverend Billy Graham and other evangelicals declared that communism was the anti-Christ, and warned Americans that their patriotism and military might were vital to their faith and their soul's salvation.[42]

Anti-communist rhetoric marshalled support for police actions, coups, assassination, torture and other covert activities in foreign countries. It helped to tighten the grip of American investments around the world. American control of foreign resources was typically reinforced by friendly dictators who oppressed and impoverished their own people while living in luxury made possible by U.S. support.[43] Anti-communist rhetoric propelled the House Un-American Activities Committee hearings, which presumed that even an intellectual interest in alternatives to capitalism or union membership was proof of one's treachery against the nation.[44]

Among the most ardent cold warriors were two brothers, John Foster Dulles, former Secretary of State (1953–1959), and Allen Dulles, former Director of the CIA (1953–1961). They were the face of national security, and firmly believed that the U.S. was destined to create a new world order.[45] Their rhetoric assured Americans that God was behind the stars and stripes all the way.[46] John was also a member of the Federal Council of Churches, an international organization dedicated to spreading the Gospel and building good will between nations.

40. Preston, "Peripheral Visions," pp. 111–113.

41. Chappel's *Modern Catholic* chronicles the Catholic response to modern capitalism, Marxism, fascism, and cultural shifts regarding values and civil rights.

42. Aiello, "Constructing Godless Communism," para. 5–13.

43. Bacevich's *American Empire* explores the imperious U.S. foreign policy of modern presidents and their 19th century antecedents.

44. Schrecker's *Age of McCarthyism* surveys HUAC's history and includes many documents.

45. Kinzer's *Brothers* and Immerman's *John Foster Dulles* shed light on the Dulles boys' agenda.

46. Hoopes, "God and John Foster Dulles," pp. 159–162.

Both John and Allen were attorneys at the investment firm Sullivan and Cromwell. The Wall Street firm litigated cases concerning foreign investment, mergers, anti-trust law, and derivative regulations. It also created international cartels and holding companies, and lobbied to secure favorable investment climates. Wall Street was, in some respects, an ideal prep school for future CIA operations.[47] Prior to the two World Wars, the Dulles brothers were confident that, under the stewardship of the U.S., all of humanity would be elevated by way of colonial development and the avoidance of extreme nationalism.[48] Early in the Cold War, John petitioned the Federal Council of Churches to work for greater moral restraint in war, and favored placing atomic bombs under international supervision. He held that when Christian nations felt free to use atomic weapons, others will see atomic war as the new norm.[49] A decade later, John not only flipped his position on atomic weapons, but he and his brother became fierce cold warriors that pursued a new world order by any means necessary.

The transformation of John Foster Dulles took place between 1946 and 1952. The shift was like that of a father who tries to correct his son's errors first with tenderness and good counsel, then, having lost his patience, pins the kid against the wall and roars, "If you ever do that again, I'll break every bone in your body!" Up to 1946, John was relatively respectful of the Soviets. They endured extraordinary suffering during the war, lived under Nazi occupation for nearly three years, and lost over 20 million lives. He was puzzled by Soviet mistrust of the West, and seemed to forget that the U.S. supported the Czar in the Bolshevik Revolution.[50]

By 1946, the Soviets had an unwelcomed presence in territory east of Berlin. To buffer themselves against future German invasion, the Soviets forced Eastern European countries they occupied to adopt communism and take orders from the Kremlin. They had refused to relinquish oil-rich occupied territory in Iran, and supported communists in Greek's civil war. At a 1946 session of the United Nations, Soviets asserted that the Anglo-American presence in the Middle East and Asia caused wars against colonialism. As historian Mark Toulouse noted: "After 1946, Dulles no longer talked about the interdependence of the world as a whole. Rather, as he came to see it, the world was now divided into two irreconcilable faiths."[51]

47. Kinzer, *Brothers*, pp. 37–62. See: Lisagor and Lipius, *A Law unto Itself*, and exposé of Sullivan and Cromwell.

48. Toulouse, pp. 99, 105, 125–26.

49. Ibid.

50. See: Fogelsong, *America's Secret War*.

51. Ibid, p. 213.

The Dulles boys were knights in a war between good and evil. Atop the moral high ground, they fought communism with unforgiving righteousness. They embraced the doctrine that that atomic assaults for Godly purposes were justified.[52] The Cold War reconstituted the crusading spirit of medieval times, during which armies marched long distances to kill infidels they believed God could never love.

THE GOSPEL OF THE CIA

John Foster Dulles announced in 1957 that the U.S. commitment to the defense of democracy was based on religious beliefs that place "exceptional importance to freedom," and "the sanctity of the human personality," and the right of people to "have governments of their own choosing," then qualified his remark by asserting that liberty "can be dangerous license unless it is exercised under the discipline of moral law."[53] The U.S. would naturally determine when liberty had become dangerous in its use. His rhetoric reinforced a dualistic world view in which the U.S. gleamed with incorruptible virtue and the Soviet Union was diabolical beyond redemption. Whether the facts about the characters of these two nations fit the rhetoric was irrelevant; the Dulles boys and their comrades would *ensure* that they fit.

The Dulles' rhetoric seemed rational in the frigid Cold War climate, and millions of Americans, including members of Congress, investment firms, and Pentagon supported it. The CIA co-opted news corporations, including CBS, *Time*, *The Washington Post*, and the *New York Times*, not only to disseminate their views, but to participate in covert operations that provided safe houses to spies, and whereby journalists became couriers of documents and money.[54]

Under the direction of the Dulles boys, the CIA worked with allies around the globe to orchestrate propaganda campaigns, rig elections, and train foreign military in the arts of kidnapping, torture, and murder of civilians. The CIA infiltrated peace and union organizations, faked riots, laundered money, and directed coups.[55] For the sake of protecting Western control of Iranian oil, the CIA led a coup in 1953 against the legally elected

52. Gaddis, "Unexpected John Foster Dulles," pp. 47–78.

53. Dulles, "Challenge and Response," p. 42.

54. Bernhard, *US Television and News*, pp. 184–185; Pearse, "Historical Roots of CIA-Hollywood," pp. 280–310.

55. There are many substantial books on how the CIA manipulated foreign policy and used deceit and religion to secure their objectives, including: Weiner, *Legacy of Ashes*; Kinzer, *Overthrow*; and, Talbot, *Devil's Chessboard*.

Prime Minister Muhammed Mossadegh that included *paying provocateurs to attack mosques* and shout their love of Mossadegh and communism.[56] At the time, news reports accepted the theatrics as historical truth. The CIA recruited Catholic priests to spy on people and deliver CIA-authored sermons in Central America.[57] For the sake of protecting the profits of United Fruit Company, whose board members included Allen Dulles, the CIA launched a coup against the legally elected Guatemalan President Jacobo Arbenz Guzman.[58] The CIA also backed the coup against the legally elected prime minister of the Central African Republic and helped establish a dictatorship under Mobuto Sese Seko.[59]

During the Cold War, the rhetoric of defending democracy around the globe was translated into actions that often diminished the self-determination of nations. Nationalists who were fighting to end colonial occupation found that if their new governments were not friendly to Western interests, they were accused of being communists, and targeted by U.S funded rebels and mercenaries.[60] Sometimes the strategy backfired. For example, cold warriors gave the Mujahideen (Afghani rebels) sophisticated weapons with which to fight the Soviets in Afghanistan in the 1970s. A faction of Mujahideen created the Taliban in the early 1990s, and used American weapons, training, and resources in terrorist assaults against the United States.[61]

President Eisenhower was devout in his commitment to protecting democracy and free enterprise. These things were to his way of thinking perfectly aligned with rights owed to human beings created in the image of God, and were the reasons for his dedication to a life of public service.[62] In his first term, Eisenhower was content to have the CIA manage the dirty business of fighting communism. He did not want a nuclear or ground war, so coups, propaganda campaigns, and assassinations became standard Cold War tactics. In his second term, however, things started to sour. The "missile gap," whereby Soviet nuclear weapons outnumbered U.S. nuclear weapons,

56. Gunn and Slighoua, "The Spiritual Factor," p. 43.

57. See Hertzog, "From Sermon to Strategy," pp. 44–64; Diamond, *Spiritual Warfare*, pp. 207–211.

58. Schlesinger and Kinzer', *Bitter Fruit*, and Chapman's, *Bananas* trace CIA involvement in the coup.

59. Gerard, *Death in the Congo*, pp. 135–155.

60. Weiner's *Legacy of Ashes* and Jacobson's *Surprise, Kill and Vanish* are meaty histories of the CIA.

61. Wissing's *Funding the Enemy* documents how American taxpayers fund both side of the war against terror, the opium trade in Afghanistan, and who profits from such madness.

62. Immerman, "Confessions," p. 328.

was a myth that cost the U.S. millions to "catch up" with phantom missiles. CIA coups in Syria (1957) and Indonesia (1958) had been debacles, and global criticism of U.S. support for totalitarian regimes was increasing. By 1959, Eisenhower regretted that he had not fired Allen Dulles.[63]

Joseph Stalin's death in 1953 presented Eisenhower with a unique opportunity to offer Stalin's successors pathways to peace and cooperation. Eisenhower believed that the arms race was greatest threat to peace, and was interested in negotiating a reduction of nuclear weapons with the Soviets. He resisted hawkish attempts to get him to send forces to Eastern European countries under Soviet control, and believed Eastern European nationalism would eventually make Soviet occupation untenable.[64] John Foster Dulles disliked talk of arms reduction and believed that a divided Europe was "unnatural" and "unstable." Eisenhower thus planted the seeds of détente—a relaxation of tensions between the U.S. and Soviet Union—only to find that hardened cold warriors were ready to pluck them from their soil before they took root. Just ten years into the Cold War, prophetic voices in high places challenged the dominant narrative that the U.S. was called by God to destroy communism and the Soviets. Rhetorically, God was thus on both sides of the Cold War.

EISENHOWER AND DÉTENTE

Eisenhower had been a faithful cold warrior who supported technological innovation in space and weaponry to secure the "free world."[65] He deeply respected the roles of armed services and intelligence community in national defense, and understood that for the sake of peace and order, good guys sometimes needed to play dirty tricks. He also argued for the reduction of atomic weapons and said that atomic energy should be put "into the hands of those who will know how to strip its military casing and adapt it to the arts of peace."[66] In his *Farewell Speech*, he acknowledged the existence of a "military-industrial-complex" in the U.S., and warned:

> In the councils of government, we must guard against the acquisition of unwarranted influence, whether sought or unsought, by the military-industrial complex. The potential for the disastrous rise of misplaced power exists and will persist. We must never let the weight of this combination endanger our liberties

63. Thomas, "Governing with a Hidden Hand," para. 4.
64. Froman, *Development*, pp. 10–17.
65. Taubman, *Secret Empire*, pp. xii–xiii.
66. Eisenhower, "Atoms for Peace," para. 37.

or democratic processes. We should take nothing for granted. Only an alert and knowledgeable citizenry can compel the proper meshing of the huge industrial and military machinery of defense with our peaceful methods and goals, so that security and liberty may prosper together.[67]

Eisenhower also believed that disarmament was an "imperative," and that we needed to learn how to live with our differences with reason and "decent purpose." In his *Chance for Peace* speech to the American Society of Newspapers Editors, he declared:

Every gun that is made, every warship launched, every rocket fired signifies, in the final sense, a theft from those who hunger and are not fed, those who are cold and are not clothed. This world in arms is not spending money alone. It is spending the sweat of its laborers, the genius of its scientists, the hopes of its children.

The cost of one modern heavy bomber is this: a modern brick school in more than 30 cities.

It is two electric power plants, each serving a town of 60,000 population.

It is two fine, fully equipped hospitals. It is some 50 miles of concrete highway.

We pay for a single fighter plane with a half million bushels of wheat.

We pay for a single destroyer with new homes that could have housed more than 8,000 people.

This, I repeat, is the best way of life to be found on the road the world has been taking. This is not a way of life at all, in any true sense. Under the cloud of threatening war, it is humanity hanging from a cross of iron.[68]

The cost of war was not a sudden epiphany for him. While in officer school during the 1920s and 1930s, Eisenhower studied the cost of mobilizing for war. He had seen the horrible carnage and death camps on the Western Front of World War II.[69] His rhetoric for peace was by most accounts genuine, but regarded as "simplistic" and "naïve" by peers and historians who believed that it was unwise to decrease U.S. nuclear might in a world that was so dangerous.[70]

67. Eisenhower, "Farewell Speech," para. 14.
68. Eisenhower, "Chance for Peace," para. 31–39.
69. Thomas, *Ike's Bluff*, pp. 59–61.
70. Immerman, "Confessions," pp. 325–26.

In May, 1960, just two weeks before Eisenhower's Paris peace summit with Premier Khrushchev, CIA spy Gary Powers was shot out of the sky over Sverdlovsk, Russia. The U-2 planes from which pilots snapped photographs of the landscape flew at about 70,000 feet, allegedly out reach of radar and missiles. Speculation that the CIA had orchestrated Power's crash and capture in order to derail the summit bubbled up in high places. Senator William Fulbright (D-AR) remarked, "I have often wondered why in the midst of these efforts by President Eisenhower and Khrushchev to come to an understanding, the U2 incident was allowed to take place. No one will ever know whether it was accidental or intentional."[71]

What was not accidental in 1960 was that the U.S. had 18,638 nuclear weapons and the Soviets had 1,605.[72] It was not accidental that during the 1950s, investments in military industries were twice as profitable as investments in non-military industries.[73] The rhetoric of peace and détente in the 1950s may have had a pious ring to it, but piety's ring was a tiny tinkle compared to the roar of the cash register. Eisenhower's prophetic discourse produced few changes. Would the next president be able to shift the American narrative?

KENNEDY AND DÉTENTE

In times of crisis it is very difficult to know whether rhetoric is true or false. Crisis heightens our anxiety and throws us off center. It also makes us eager to find individuals who seem to know all the answers, and who are willing to act when others are paralyzed. For thirteen days in October, 1962, as Soviets sent nuclear missiles to Cuba, two men held the fate of Earth in their hands. Both believed in God, loved nature, and had lost children to early deaths. Both were veterans of World War II who had fought on the same side against fascism. Both had been stubborn cold warriors who adamantly defended the "righteousness" of their world views. Both executives, President John F. Kennedy and Premier Nikita Khrushchev, were surrounded by military and civilian advisors who wanted a summative confrontation between these Cold War adversaries. Both cringed at the prospect of mutual destruction.

The story of the Cuban Missile Crisis has a happy ending—at least for those who did not want to use it as a pretext for World War III. The U.S. removed missiles it had installed in Turkey, and promised that it would not invade Cuba. The Soviets, who had come to the aid of Fidel Castro after

71. Kelly, "Mayday, 1960," para. 7.

72. Norris and Kristensen, "Global Nuclear Weapons Inventories," p. 81.

73. Brandes, *Warhogs*, p. 275.

the U.S. failed to overthrow him during the Bay of Pigs invasion of April 1961, withdrew missiles from Cuba. Kennedy and Khrushchev used "back-channels" to resolve their differences. Kennedy's brother, Robert, met with Soviet Ambassador Anatoly Dobrynin to ensure that the president's voice could be heard clearly and accurately above the din of saber-rattling in the advisory committee, the Pentagon, and State Department.[74]

Months before the Cuban Missile Crisis, Kennedy and Khrushchev laid the ground work for negotiations that ultimately enabled them to de-escalate the threat of war. On September 29, 1961, Khrushchev initiated clandestine correspondence with Kennedy. His first letter of 26 pages described his feelings about peace and cooperation.[75] He alluded to the pressure of his party to bully the West, and invited Kennedy to share his thoughts. Over the next year, the two were secret pen pals. Each expressed regret for conflict over the Berlin Wall in 1961 that had nearly drawn them to war, and both agreed that while they would never see eye to eye ideologically, they agreed that peaceful co-existence was the best way forward.

Both Kennedy and Khrushchev lived in political worlds where they had to prove their worthiness for holding office by using aggressive rhetoric, and by constantly reciting the superiority of their nations. The letters Kennedy and Khrushchev exchanged helped them resist the temptation to fight. They are rich in empathy, and sprinkled with serious discourse about God, duties to humanity, and reverence for life. Both men were profoundly influenced by the Gospels, and readily used biblical references to make their points.[76]

Missing from many narratives of the Cuban Missile Crisis is what many believe was an attempt to sabotage negotiations for a peaceful resolution. During the missile crisis, both the Soviet Union and U.S. proceeded with scheduled Intercontinental Ballistic Missiles (ICBM) tests, including an 8.2 megaton atomic weapon detonated by the Soviets over Novaya Zemyla on October 22, 1962.[77] On October 26th at 4:00 A.M., an Atlas missile was launched in California *without* authorization from Washington.[78] Some

---

74. Hayes, "RFK's Role," para. 16.

75. Douglass, *JFK and the Unspeakable*, pp. 23–25.

76. Douglass' *JFK and the Unspeakable* presents a fascinating account of the private correspondence between Kennedy and Khrushchev and of Kennedy's communications with religious leaders on the matter of peace.

77. The biggest bomb exploded by the U.S. was Castle Bravo, 1954, at 15 megatons with a cloud surge of 130,000 feet. The largest U.S.S.R. blast was the Tsar Bomb, 1961, at 50 megatons with a cloud surge of 211,200 feet. By comparison, the bomb dropped on Hiroshima in 1945 was 15 kilotons with a cloud surge of 25,000 feet.

78. Norris, "The Cuban Missile Crisis," p. 42.

believe that U.S. Strategic Air Command launched the unauthorized missile as a way to threaten Moscow.[79]

Kennedy pursued his own détente. He fired Allen Dulles in 1961, and in 1963 removed missiles from Turkey, signed the Test Ban Treaty, and issued National Security Memorandum (NSM) 263, which announced plans to remove all U.S. military personnel from Southeast Asia in 1964. Just days before his death, he gave a speech in which he stated that the U.S. Alliance for Progress (an aid program) "did not dictate to any nation how to organize its economic life," and that each nation is "free to shape its own economic institutions in accordance with its own national needs and will."[80] To hawkish cold warriors, this was an abomination, as it implied tolerance for Marxism. To U.S. investors in foreign utilities, mining, and agriculture, Kennedy's words rang with threats to profits and dividends. The day after Kennedy's funeral, President Lyndon Johnson penned NSM 273, which reversed NSM 263, and was a crucial step towards war in Vietnam.

Kennedy exhibited extraordinary courage in offering the world an alternative to the bellicose American narrative of Cold War. In 1963, he would have been applauded in some circles had he publically denounced Khrushchev as "Red Nicky," or called Fidel Castro the "Havana Hotshot," or threatened to "obliterate" Vietnam's economy if they did not comply with his demands.[81] He chose not to travel down those rhetorical roads, and thus demonstrated that one need not crucify the character of adversaries, nor issue ultimatums in order to resolve differences. At the time, public officials often privately cussed adversaries and called them vulgar names, but such talk was kept out of the media in those days, and not the centerpiece of presidential tweets and speeches. Today, things are very different. Elected officials not only publically attack the character of foreign adversaries, they attack members of their own party, and anyone in the press who criticizes their behavior and judgment.

MYTHS UNTO OURSELVES

In 1961, while Kenney and Khrushchev were exchanging secret missives, Thomas Merton, the cloistered Trappist monk who wrote prolifically about peace and the sin of war-based societies, wrote Robert Kennedy's wife, Ethel. "Certainly our basic need is for truth," he penned, "and not for images and

79. Janney, *Mary's Mosaic*, p. 246.

80. Douglass, *JFK and the Unspeakable*, p. 250.

81. Trump threatened to "obliterate" Turkey's economy if it did not follow his directives regarding ISIS; see Vasquez, "Trump Threatens," para. 1–3.

slogans that 'engineer our consent.'" He added: "We are living in a dream world. We do not know ourselves or our adversaries. We are myths unto ourselves and they are myths unto us."[82] Merton saw that people readily project onto others and onto themselves wishful thoughts and presumptions about who they are.

Merton also believed that myths about our identities poisoned the soul by convincing us that they we are not one in the spirit of God, and that it was always "the other" that was dangerous and immoral. Through prayer, music, poetry, and conversation, Merton resisted dehumanization, and in his personal letters and essays decried mind-numbing social conventions and institutional efforts to dodge the truth of our condition. He rebelled against attempts to silence his critiques of militarism, and was unapologetic about his disdain for Wall Street and America's false claim to superiority.[83]

President Kennedy violated the unwritten rules of the Cold War by refusing to mythologize the Soviets as creatures from Kremlin hell. By 1963, he had retreated from the American narrative of divinely ordained exclusivity, and instead wrote a story about adversaries who become brothers. Premier Khrushchev also violated the unwritten rules of Cold War. He refused to mythologize Americans as money-mongering oppressors of the proletariat, and removed his own mask of the Marxist messiah. Both men violated the political rhetoric that defined their paths to power. Both trembled together in secret over their mutual power to turn the Earth in to charred cinders floating in space. Both were humbled by the nuclear terror at their command, and they metaphorically joined hands and refused when high-ranking advisors pressured them to annihilate the other.

Both men paid the price for taking the rhetoric of peace and co-existence seriously. Kennedy was assassinated in November, 1963. Many, including some in the CIA, U.S. armed forces, and other government offices believe that Kennedy was "eliminated" by domestic enemies in order to reverse policies of peaceful co-existence and arms reductions.[84] Khrushchev was removed from office in October, 1964. He had fallen out of favor with powerful party officials by being too conciliatory and friendly with the enemy, and was forced into obscurity.[85]

Following the Vietnam War, the U.S. lost some of its economic competitive edge around the globe. Since the 1970s, American hegemony has

82. Merton, *Cold War Letters*, p. 26–29.

83. Higgins, *Heretical Blood*, pp. 4–8.

84. See: Prouty's *JFK, the CIA, Vietnam*; Janney's *Mary's Mosaic*; Hughes-Wilson, *JFK: An American Coup D'état*.

85. Taubman, *Khrushchev*, p. 1–13.

given way to a political reality in which the U.S. had to learn how to share responsibility and authority with other nations in an "altered, independent global environment."[86] Foreign nations challenged U.S. dominance in industrial production, and by 1985, the U.S. became the largest debtor nation.[87] As of December, 1991, there was no more Soviet Union, and no more reason for a perpetual war economy. As these things unfolded, globalization hastily proceeded with the help of digital technology.

The very concept of "nation" has been disappearing for decades, as multinational corporations and international investments corral countries under one big economic umbrella, and as we are united in consumer appetites. Yet, government leaders continue to flood our ears with the old narratives of "America first" and American exceptionalism. Americans have viewed the world for so long through nationalistic lens that it has difficulty recognizing that exceptionalism does us little good when we face global threats to our existence, such as climate change, epidemics, biological warfare, and nuclear assaults. We have not been humbled by our claim to be God's servant, and that makes us dangerous. We have not used our resources and liberty to steer ourselves and the world away from lethal creeds and lifestyles, and that makes us foolish.

86. Dumbrell, "American Foreign Policy," p. 9.

87. In 1985 U.S. debt was $1.8 trillion, and in 2018, it was $21.5 trillion. See: Reed, "What is the National Debt?"

Chapter 8

The Idolatry of Nationalism

THE RHETORICAL NATION

The idea that the U.S. is an exceptional nation and one that is divinely destined to lead all civilizations to order, prosperity, and morality was well established long before the cold warriors put their imprimatur on the concept, and continues to thrive long after end of the Cold War. The tenacity of these ideas throughout history gives us some understanding of how normal it seems to believe them. Though the republic itself changed dramatically from 1783 to the present by creating an empire and becoming a dominant force in global affairs, the rhetoric concerning God's blessing on the entirety of the nation's ambitions and development never wavered.[1]

At present, the U.S. is challenged to reinvent itself, and to create a new narrative that is more compatible with international cooperation and conservation. Thus far, it is proceeding with the same old narrative that divine providence wants the nation to dominate all others so that it might save all others. The narrative is troublesome. It does not acknowledge the fact that the very concept of "nation" has changed and continues to change as a result of globalized economies and multicultural domestic demographics. As billionaires and millionaires own resources, land, utilities, stocks, and securities that are located outside the nation of their origin, nations "disappear," and in their place emerges international affiliations and multinational concentrations of wealth and power. The narrative is also troublesome

---

1. Hauptman, "Mythologizing Westward," pp. 269–82. Also see: McCartney *Power and Progress* for a discussion of how the U.S. rationalized its imperialism abroad.

because it projects godlike and messianic qualities that traditionally belong to God onto the state.

The concentration of wealth into the hands of a few changes how nations relate to each other, because super-rich corporations can behave in ways traditionally reserved for nations. They can, for example, hire mercenaries and private security services to protect their interests, making it possible for them to protect diamond mines and oil fields in the same way nations protect them.[2] Former mercenary, Sean McFate, wrote that the use of "guns for hire" has become increasingly popular with U.S. administrations as they pursue their military ambitions abroad while honoring congressional caps on the numbers of U.S. troops on the ground. He notes that under Obama's administration, the ratio of U.S. soldiers to private contractors in Iraq went from 1 to 1 in 2009 to 1 to 3 by 2016, and in 2014, 8 percent of the federal budget ($285 billion) went for mercenaries.[3] McFate warned that the practice causes "mission creep," or the expansion of official operations. He also stated:

> No international laws exist to regulate the mercenary industry. What we're left with: If anyone with enough money can wage war for any reason they want to, then new superpowers will emerge: the ultra-rich and multinational corporations. Oil companies and oligarchs should not have armies.[4]

When power is concentrated in the hands of international corporate affiliates, national borders become superfluous, and so do national elections. Since the outcome of political races in one nation has implications for investors all over the world, the international private sector has a stake in the democratic processes of nations that are not their own, and thus an incentive to tamper with elections. In addition, the globalization of the economy and corporations provides incentives to all political parties in the republic to seek the advice and favor of foreign countries who are connected to it by way of trade, military sales, and investments.[5] Public discourse and news reports have not explored this phenomenon nor its implications at length. This means that politicians can arouse voters by rallying for nationalism knowing that the very definition of "nation" is evolving by leaps and bounds, and may not mean what voters think it means.

---

2. Singer, *Corporate Warriors*, pp. 104–107.

3. McFate, "America's Addiction to Mercenaries," para. 5, 11.

4. Ibid, para. 20.

5. Foley, "Is it ever OK," para. 3–5.

The projection of messianic properties onto the U.S. and the American endeavor were once fitted to a concept of "nationhood" that is fast slipping into extinction. Globalization compels those committed to a messianic agenda to think about how to leverage religion to win support for agendas in a world where God is still profoundly tribal in some cultural world views, and is associated with terrorism and oppression. The American narrative is still peppered with God talk, and many citizens demand that political leaders prove their worthiness for office by exhibiting religiosity.

Playing the God card in in national politics has helped some candidates get elected, and prayerful response to tragedies has been helpful to the nation in need of solace and healing. Piety and prayers, however, has not guaranteed that elected leaders would be exemplary in moral conduct. God talk does not necessarily translate into the kind of leadership that makes a nation humane and humble, nor into the kind of leadership required for global stewardship. The public discourse of government officials frequently gives the impression that godliness and goodness are America's "ultimate concerns," and that the nation is merely an instrument of God's will. American conduct, however, gives the impression that an expanding economy and control over the evolving world order are America's "ultimate concerns," and that God is merely an instrument of the nation's will.

ICONS OF CRUELTY

Civil religion represents our ideals and what we cherish as our "ultimate concern." Its rhetoric has inspired people to undertake philanthropic causes and to be good to one another. It has also preached that our "ultimate concerns" are material and nationalistic. For many generations and with relentless propaganda, Americans have reconciled God's will to American ambitions. In many people's mind, the two are one. Confidence that America's "ultimate concerns" are perfectly aligned with God's will has directed our eyes and our minds away from damage resulting from the pursuit of our objectives. Many Americans are not troubled by the means of obtaining our goals, hypocrisy, or double standards. Many are desensitized not only to the suffering of others, but to the private pain that comes each time they censor their own reactions to inhumanity for the sake of fitting in with the crowd.

Sometimes there is a screeching dissonance between the rhetoric and the reality, and the disparity hits us with great force when there are no words, and only pictures. This happened to millions of people in the 1960s and 1970s who hit psychological walls when the photographs of the war in Vietnam slammed into the American narrative that the U.S. was a noble country fighting the enemies of freedom in a distant land. The pictures of napalmed infants, farmers crying as their homes and crops burned, and families reduced to heaps of mangled bowels and shredded flesh did not match the rhetoric of a glorious war to liberate oppressed peasants. Without a word, pictures changed people's minds about the war, and about the people who orchestrated it in the name of God and democracy. More wars and more pictures followed.

On April 28, 2004, *CBS News* broadcast images from Abu Ghraib, an Iraqi prison that the U.S. had commandeered for the purpose of detaining and interrogating Iraqis suspected of terrorism. Pictures from Abu Ghraib shocked congressional members who were investigating allegations of criminal acts. The images revealed a perverse and sadistic element in the U.S. armed forces. They became icons of in the archive of man's inhumanity.

Against the rhetoric about the noble war against terrorism and the hallowed mantras, "we are just," "God is with us," and "we must defeat the evil ones," the pictures appeared.[6] They were surreal. A man balanced on box, cloaked in a black garment with a black hood over his head, his arms extended like he was nailed to an invisible cross while electrodes gripped the tips of his middle fingers. He was a prisoner at Abu Ghraib, and his torture became the amusement of his captors. His body and circumstance made public is now part of the rhetoric that accuses Americans of war crimes, and, perversely, part of the rhetoric that celebrates American militarism. His image is that of a modern crucifixion; it is the summative expression of nationalism gone berserk with its own might; it is the image of humanity deformed by titillation gained from the utter humiliation of another human being.

Other pictures from Abu Ghraib magnified our depravity: prisoners cowering before attack dogs; naked men piled into human pyramids to the thrill of smiling soldiers; prisoners smeared with excrement; detainees in excruciating stress positions, and forced to masturbate in front of their guards. They seem like obscene Stations of the Cross—each station an incremental dehumanization on the road to Golgotha; and, all stations leading to the man in the black hood with arms extended. The scapegoat—a suspect, identified as Abdou Hussein Saad Faleh, who may or may not have committed any crimes—who had to atone for the sin of being Iraqi.[7]

Sociologist Jared Del Rosso posited that political discourse shapes not only a nation's willingness to torture, but how it debates controversies

6. See: Bush's "Address to Joint Session" and "Operation Iraqi Freedom."

7. The identity of the hooded man on the box has been debated. Faleh himself says that he was detained in Abu Ghraib and was forced to wear the same garments as the man on the box, but he is not in the famous photo. See: Adams, "For Harold Morris," para. 7–10.

surrounding the practice. Governments work hard to keep torture far from public view, but when it is exposed, officials must provide a rationale. Some argue that torture is necessary for national security. Others assert that though the practice might be disturbing, other nations do things far more terrible. Some dodge responsibility by quibbling over the definition of torture, as did Secretary of Defense, Donald Rumsfeld, who denied that the U.S. tortured prisoners, stating, "My impression is that what has been charged thus far is abuse, which I believe is different from torture."[8] His remarks came one week following CBS' display of photos from Abu Ghraib. President Bush' rhetoric assured Americans that God is vengeful and that American enemies are God's enemies.[9] When people believe that their aggression is sanctified because it protects God, they do not always see God, as did Jesus, in the eyes of their adversaries.

About six years after the photographs of Abu Ghraib drew national outrage, an American platoon in Afghanistan created their own digital legacy by murdering innocent civilians and taking pictures of themselves beside their bloody bodies. Led by Sargent Calvin Gibbs, soldiers killed Afghanis, disguised the murders by placing weapons near the bodies of the dead (to give the appearance that U.S. soldiers had been attacked), and then posed beside their victims with big smiles. Some soldiers took body parts of the "kill" as war trophies.[10] When Specialist Adam Winfield reported his platoon's behavior, he was charged with murder.

Winfield and others described the conditions that led to murder and mayhem. Gibbs bullied the soldiers, badgering them with accusations that they were not real men until they had a kill. The kill excursions broke the boredom that set in as troops endured assignments to patrol areas where there was little to no active fighting. It gave the men something to brag about. The kill narrative was all about how to be a "real man." It is in essence about the idolatry of masculinity. It presumes that "real men" prove their manhood by murdering innocent people and slicing them up for souvenirs. Very little in mainstream news and commentary addresses the idolatry of masculinity and what it is doing to the world, the men who embrace it, and the people around the men who embrace it.

8. Del Rosso, *Talking about Torture*, p. 29.

9. Bush's "Address to Joint Session" and "Operation Iraqi Freedom" posit the thesis that the U.S. must wage war against the enemies for God and freedom.

10. *Kill Team*, Directed by Dan Krauss, Motto Pictures. DVD 2013.

WE WILL CALL EVIL BY ITS NAME. . .MAYBE

President George W. Bush had a special relationship with God. When asked in the Republican Primaries of 2000 who was his most important philosopher, Bush replied, "Jesus Christ." Four years later, faith was the epicenter of the presidential election, and George W. was its advance guard.[11] Bush once explained that, "When you turn your heart and your life over to Christ, when you accept Christ as the Savior, it changes your heart. It changes your life. And that's what happened to me."[12]

George W. Bush entered the presidency as a "saved" man, one who proudly believed that he was chosen by God to lead and to speak for the Almighty.[13] He firmly believed that life is sacred from the point of conception, and that stem cell research tampered with the sanctity of life, but favored the death penalty because he felt it was a deterrence to criminal conduct.[14] His rhetoric about a changed heart sounded honest and sincere. Then, he launched a preemptive strike against a sovereign nation based on false accusations that it had weapons of mass destruction. He violated the principles of Just War, approved the use of torture, and pursued wars in which thousands of Afghanis, Iraqis, and U.S. personnel were killed.[15] By November, 2018, the number of Iraqi civilians killed in the war to orchestrate regime change was conservatively estimated at 182,000.[16] The legacy of bloodshed and deception caused some folks to wonder: "If this is this what it means to be born-again in Christ, what was Bush like before his conversion?"

Bush also had a special relationship with democracy. When pressed to justify and illuminate the rationale for his foreign policies and war, the president simply stated that he did not need to explain himself to anybody.[17] Bush's rhetoric of redemption has left a bitter taste in many mouths because it placed Jesus and God squarely in the driver's seat of American imperialism. His post 9/11 vigilantism was so unilateral and absolute that it left little room for international collaboration and a humane way to world peace. Bush averred that God had chosen him to lead, and apparently, to Bush's

11. Campbell, "The 2004 Election," pp. 1–12.

12. Aikman, *A Man of Faith*, p. 3

13. Wallis, "Dangerous Religion," p. 28.

14. Singer, *President of Good and Evil*, p. 47.

15. The theory of Just War asserts that war is only justified when certain criteria are met, including the exhaustion of all other options for conflict resolution, war in proportion to the threat, and war that is not offensive. See Mattox, *St. Augustine and the Jut War Theory.*

16. Watson Institute, "Cost of War. Iraqi Civilians," para. 1–3.

17. Woodward, *Bush at War*, p. 145.

way of thinking, that gave him a special capacity to determine what was moral and what was not.[18]

Bush's theological outlook was tribal and dualistic in many ways. Its rhetoric sounded like that of the ancient Israelites who petitioned God to smite their Canaanite enemies, and to exact vengeance upon the wicked. There was to be no turning of the "other cheek." Following 9/11, Bush told the world, "You are either with us, or you are with the terrorists."[19] He added to the prelude to the U.S. invasion of Iraq, "The only way to deal with these people [terrorists] is to bring them to justice. You can't talk to them. You can't negotiate with them."[20] His statements were summative, and all but obliterated the need for Americans to learn about why many Arabs and Muslims hate us. Bush's rhetoric flew in the face of the Gospel's command to love one's enemies and to pray for those who persecute us (Matt. 5:43–44).

To a large extent, Bush's rhetoric against negotiations with terrorists is troublesome because the way we use the word "terrorist" is troublesome. In public discourse, we use the word "terrorist" selectively, and mostly to emphasize the "otherness" of people, which tends to diminish the belief that they deserve empathy. "Terrorism" describes violent acts committed against innocents without provocation. People can get away with using such rhetoric only when they are not willing to examine what provocation looks like from the "terrorists'" point of view.

Bush's administration typically used the word "terrorist" to describe "evil" people who are motivated by jealously and hatred for the freedoms American enjoy. The rhetoric hides from view the reality that for generations, Muslims have been distressed and angry about America's impact on their countries and culture. The rhetoric ignores the fact that Arab nations have communicated their objections to Western intrusions into the Middle East, and have been unable to resolve conflict through petitions and negotiation.[21]

Osama bin Laden outlined Islamic discontent in his 2002 "Letter to America."[22] He stated that Americans are not innocent people, as their taxes and election of imperious officials lead to corruption, pain, suffering, and oppression in the Muslim world. He called attention to Israeli occupation of Palestine and how torture and murder enforce it. He criticized U.S. support

18. Singer's *President of Good and Evil* explores this in depth.

19. Bush, G. W. "Address to Joint Sessions of Congress," para. 54.

20. Toros, "We Don't Negotiate with Terrorists" p. 407.

21. Makdisi's *Faith Misplaced* chronicles Arab-American relations from 1820–2001, and explores the role of oil, Israel, Saudi royalty, Arab nationalism, and Islamic fundamentalism in the love-hate relationship.

22. See Bin Laden, "Letter to America."

for government puppets who profited from business with the U.S., while their own people suffered deprivations. He chastised the U.S. sanctions in Iraq which led to the deaths of innocent people. He excoriated Western decadence, gambling, alcohol, pornography, drug use, and prostitution, and, he called out the hypocrisy of America's espoused love of democracy and its violation of national sovereignty when it became a threat to its financial interests.

Bin Laden's grievances do not justify the attacks of 9/11—no, not in the least—and they certainly do not acknowledge that many Muslims happily drink alcohol, gamble, and watch pornography in private. Nevertheless, his comments deserve attention. Why do Americans reflexively believe that our nation's conduct is above reproach? Why do we react so violently— so dismissively—when others tell the U.S. to stop hurting their nations and their people?

Whatever shame Americans felt as they read bin Laden's letter was not well-represented in public discourse during the vengeful days of the war on terror. Americans were not supposed to empathize with bin Laden. He was a terrorist, and in the hawkish world of Bush and his advisors, including Dick Cheney, Donald Rumsfeld, Richard Pearle, Paul Wolfowitz, Richard Armitage, and Condoleezza Rice, one does not listen to a terrorist's side of the story.[23] In their world, the terrorist side of the story is never legitimate. In the nation's battle with evil, it was heresy to frame events and their antecedents in ways that diverged from the orthodoxy of American righteousness. Journalists who tried to widen the 9/11 discourse for the purposes of exploring what was known or suspected about Saudi involvement were not provided a wealth of column inches in newspapers, nor given abundant time in televised reports.[24] Professors who were critical of U.S. foreign policy were threatened, reviled, and sometimes fired.[25]

Between the lines of Bush's declaration that, "America will call evil by its name," was the assertion that America will also *define* evil, and set the perimeters of what it is and is not.[26] The American narrative has allowed for Americans to admit mistakes, but it adamantly rejects the claim that Americans have ever been evil. Nationalist rhetoric after 9/11 drove a wedge between people who claim that their hearts have been changed by Christ.

23. Mann's *Rise of the Vulcans*, carefully documents the path to war in Iraq that *long preceded* 9/11.

24. Entman, "Cascading Activism," 423–427; Finnegan's *No Questions* documents the post-9/11 contest between journalism that is unconditionally patriotic and journalism that strives for objectivity and diversity of perspectives.

25. Wilson, "Academic Freedom," pp. 119–122.

26. Bush, "Graduation Speech," para 25.

On one side, Christians opened their hearts to the possibility Muslims and Arabs have legitimate objections to American conduct in the Middle East, and that the Islamic faith deserved respect. On the other side, Christians bared their teeth, denounced Islam as inherently corrupt and a violent religion that worships a false god, and denied the legitimacy of complaints about U.S. conduct in the Middle East.[27]

The rhetoric concerning the war against terrorism had the effect of unifying most the country, at least until it became clear that Iraq did not possess weapons of mass destruction, and that the war was going to continue longer than had been expected. Yet, many clung to the belief that, weapons or no weapons, the U.S. had a right to invade Iraq and change its government. The rhetoric allowed for Americans who stood with the president to vicariously experience the "awe" of walking shoulder to shoulder with the executive, and permitted them to at least pretend that they were equals in a sanctified and just war. The notion that common citizens walked shoulder to shoulder with Bush is pure illusion. Average Americans are not and will never be inside the elite circle in which the Bushes of the world spin. The fantasy that the common masses and their concerns are tenderly kept in the hearts of the power elite may comfort folks, but all too often, as war, bank scandals, tax laws, and corporate accountability reveal, common folk are expendable bit players in the national narrative.

Former Secretary of Labor, Robert Reich, who has served in the administrations of Presidents Ford, Carter, Clinton, and Obama, describes how Wall Street and their pals in Washington have "rigged" the economy. His insights underscore the reality that some people own the nation while others can only rent it. He notes that federal laws make it possible for the richest Americans to obtain whopping wealth, while corralling everyone else into an economic purgatory, wherein wages are stagnate, growing numbers of jobs are part-time without benefits, and people rely on credit just to pay the bills.[28] Reich acknowledges that propaganda plays a vital role in convincing average Americans that their government always, without exception, places their well-being ahead of all other interests.

Blessed are those who can tell the difference between theater and reality, for they shall know from whence their enemies come. In order to call evil by its name, we have to know about how things like law-making, law enforcement, government regulation, economic systems, foreign policies,

27. Cimino, "No God in Common," pp. 165–166.

28. Reich's *The System: Who Rigged It, How We Fix It* explores how economic policies, tax laws, bank regulations, and court decisions have helped polarize wealth in the U.S., and how government officials and experts have deceived Americans about the causes of their economic woes with mythic rationales for exploitative policy.

and conflicts of interest work. We have to know more about who controls the national agendas, who benefits from them the most, and who suffers from them the most. We have to pay attention to who is chosen to serve as presidential advisors and cabinet members, because their careers, lives, values, and statements tell us something about the president's true agenda. The powerful are not transparent in the U.S., and so we often know their "ultimate concerns" by their actions. To call evil by its name, we may have to scrutinize our own patriotism and accept that if we dare to call evil by its name, we might be implicated.

The rich and powerful do not have a corner on evil. Each of us embodies the potential to be evil, and so it is important to learn about our own inner theater, personal narratives, and private myths. Not all of us want to play nice all the time, and not all of us want to temper our lust for power, popularity, and wealth. Not all of us want to take responsibility for the messes we create or the damage we do as we consume or claw up the ladder of success. Calling evil by its name is not the same as admitting that we have some kind of personality quirk or neurosis. It is about facing the part of us that *chooses* to hurt others, knowing very well that there are ample opportunities to avoid the injury.

MAKE AMERICA GREAT COMPULSIVELY

In the second presidential debate in 2000, George W. Bush told the audience, "The first question is, what's in the best interests of the United States. . .When it comes to foreign policy, that'll be my guiding question."[29] As did Bush, many have made their way to the White House with promises to put American interests above all others.[30] As America's civil religion holds, the U.S. is the best nation ever—the richest, the most powerful, the freest, and the most ethical—and so deserves to put its interests first. The rhetoric conjures images of the U.S. aloft in the heavens, radiating golden beams of righteousness to muddling mediocrity below.

The rhetoric of America as the envy of the world is detrimental and deceptive to everyone in the long run for four reasons. First, it obscures the ways in which our democracy is not so democratic. We live in a republic wherein some people feel entitled to have a greater say than others. In 1971, future Supreme Court Justice, Lewis Powell, wrote a memorandum to the U.S. Chamber of Commerce, warning that businesses had to find a way to

29. Singer, *President of Good and Evil*, p. 115.

30. Calamur's "A Short History" summarizes the origins and use of the American-first mantra.

protect its interests against a rising tide of liberal criticism of capitalism.[31] At the time, public interest in environmental protection, consumer safety, minority rights, fair employment, and corporate oversight were growing. The Powell Memorandum suggested that the Chamber of Commerce should support new speaker's bureaus, textbook reviewers, and a writer's pool that would generate discourse that countered the liberal rebellion against capitalism.

One of the outcomes of Powell's efforts was the rapid proliferation of conservative think tanks and lobbyists during the 1970s and 1980s, and by 2008, there were 1,776 think tanks in the U.S. Think tanks employ experts to study issues and make pertinent information available to the public and policy-makers. Their political ideologies vary and include progressivism, libertarianism, and neo-conservativism.[32] The number of lobbyist groups has also mushroomed, from 10,308 in 1970 to 23,298 in 1995.[33] Lobbyists are largely representatives of private organizations and industries who are paid to present ideas for legislation to congressional members, and to advocate certain policies that benefit their organizations and industries.

Although lobbyists do not always get what they want, they have the resources to hire researchers, fund-raisers, and lawyers who know how to draft legislation. As political action committees, they can donate money to fund political campaigns. Over half of congressional lawmakers who leave office and find work in the private sector work as corporate lobbyists.[34] The revolving door between private interests and the U.S. Congress ensures that private interests are central in debates over policy and law-making.

The strength of our democracy is compromised by the Electoral College, which can neutralize the majority's will. In 2016, Hillary Clinton got nearly 2.9 million more popular votes than Donald Trump, but lost because of the Electoral College's weighting of delegates.[35] In addition, voter suppression has been achieved by adjusting the perimeters of voting districts, creating shortages of polling facilities, and complicating voter registration efforts.[36]

Second, the rhetoric of "America is the best" inflates global expectations that democracy guarantees prosperity to all. The truth is that millions of Americans who have lived beneath the stars and stripes have lived in poverty and struggled against discrimination that blocks access to opportunities

---

31. "Lewis Powell Memo," para. 1--7; 44–52. Also see: Cray, "Greenpeace Analyzes."

32. Ahmad, "U.S. Think Tanks," pp. 531–539.

33. Rosenthal, *Third House*, p. 3.

34. Zibel, "Revolving Congress," para. 1–3. Full report available on website.

35. Krieg, "Its Official," para. 2.

36. Root, "Voter Suppression," para. 2–6.

for self-improvement. The 2018 U.S. Census revealed that 11.8 percent of people (38.1 million) lived in poverty, and that African Americans and Native Americans are more than twice as likely to be poor as are whites.[37] The report also indicated that the federal poverty line for that year was $12,784.00 for an individual. Given the cost of living, this is an absurd threshold. In many parts of the country, rents are so high that even those earning twice the poverty threshold would be at serious risk for homelessness. In December, 2018, for example, the average rent for a one-bedroom apartment in San Francisco was $3,304.00 per month, or $39,648.00 a year—this was 3.1 times the federal poverty threshold.[38]

Third, the assertion that everyone can and should have an American standard of living is dangerous and shameful. Americans have not set a good example for the rest the world. We consume more than we need and always want more, which does not bode well for global sustainability. The World-watch Institute reports that though the U.S. represents about 5 percent of the world's population, it consumes at least 25 percent of the world's energy (oil, coal, natural gas); and, that the average American uses the equivalent of 9.7 hectares for his or her existence, while scientists indicate that planet can currently afford only 1.9 hectares per person.[39] Americans throw away 200,000 tons of edible food daily and generate 17.7 percent of the world's trash. It would take 4.4 Earths to provide the current global population with an American standard of living.[40] The American dream that has ignited a global desire for luxury and excess makes some people very rich and happy in the short run, but in the end it may kill all of us.

In conversation with a research colleague who teaches courses in business management and studies sustainability by traveling the world to meet with local officials and scientists, I asked whether the people in developing nations are taking their cue for future production and consumption from environmental conservationists and being mindful of sustainability. The professor said flatly, "No. They have assimilated American appetites for a very high standard of living, and they want to consume as we do, and live like we do." I asked about incentives to change. "We all have incentives to change," he reported, "but we don't believe them. . .We don't want to change."

A fourth reason why the rhetoric of America as the envy of the world is detrimental is that it breeds arrogance. By holding our nation up as the paragon of humanity, we readily close our ears to what others have to say

37. Poverty U.S.A. "Population of Poverty U.S.A.," para. 1–8.

38. Rent Jungle, "Rent Trend," para. 1.

39. Worldwatch Institute, "State of Consumption Today," Sec. 8.

40. Hungary Planet, "Ecosystem," see: Information panels.

about their conditions and potential solutions to common problems. In the end, there is little difference between the cold warriors who were willing to destroy the planet because they believed in the motto, "better dead than red," and the contemporary "America-firsters," who are willing to destroy the planet because they embrace the motto, "live large today, to hell with tomorrow."

There is a fine line between the prayer petition, "God bless America" and the idolatry of nationalism. To ask the Almighty to grant favor to our national endeavors differs from the prayer, "Thy will be done." National endeavors might be very different from God's will. Our prayers for God's blessing are often accompanied by quiet bargaining. We might pray for victory in war, for example, with the promise that with victory we will use our power only for good things. Regardless of how popular nationalistic rhetoric is, it is almost always idolatrous. It is idolatrous because it encourages people to place their faith in the state for their well-being rather than to place their faith in God. Nationalism coaxes the belief that the invitation to love our neighbors as ourselves (Matt. 22:39) only pertains only to people inside our own borders or to those who share our world views.

There is an imbalance between the rhetorical capital held by those in power, and the rhetorical capital held by those who do not have power. Most of us are at a disadvantage when the mighty merry-go-rounds of political and commercial propaganda get going. We do not have the resources to broadcast our views on radio and TV, nor to publish and distribute our own newspapers, nor speak with the force of a think tank or corporate lobby. We generally lack the time and training that it takes to be well-informed and a proficient critic of rhetoric. This does not make us bad or immoral people, but it does make us vulnerable to manipulation.

STUCK IN THE GROOVE

There is no reason to expect that public discourse in the U.S. will ever stop asserting that the U.S. is the best nation that ever existed, and deserves to be number one. The U.S. is an empire, and empires that want to stay empires must convince its citizens that it is good to be an empire. It must have a narrative that tells people that an empire is so valuable that it is worth a few sacrifices along the way, including limits on civil liberties, stagnant wages, deteriorating public services, and the cost of war.

The U.S. had an opportunity to change its narrative after the Soviet Union collapsed in 1991. At that point, republics emerged from the dust of communism in Eastern Europe, and Russian commitments to developing nations were in flux. Americans had the chance to take grand steps towards the modernization of developing nations, and to lead the world's efforts towards peace, health, and sustainability. In the absence of Cold War adversaries who competed for world hegemony, many developing nations descended into brutal civil wars. This, in addition to famines, epidemics, religious radicalism, and uncertainty about the location of the former Soviet Union's nuclear arsenal were formidable challenges to global stability and survival.

Upon surmising the multiple threats to international stability, former Secretary of State during the Clinton administration, Christopher Warren, observed that, "As a global power with global interests, it is the United States that stands to lose the most if we retreat." All presidents elected after the fall of the Soviet Union agreed that the U.S. had an obligation to lead the world toward democracy and market economies. There also existed a consensus that the U.S. had to protect its interests by all means, because if the U.S. was compromised in any way, there would be a dangerous void in global leadership. The option to change the American narrative was eclipsed by the desire to fortify it.

The U.S. used humanitarian and military aid to foreign countries and intervention to protect its interests, while also supporting the development of democracy and free markets around the world. President George H. W. Bush assured Americans that democracy would follow wherever free markets prevailed.[41] He also believed that humanitarian intervention would help create conditions where private enterprise might flourish. During the Somalian Civil War, Bush sent 28,000 American troops to Somalia in 1992 to distribute tons of humanitarian aid to fight famine. Calling it "God's work," Bush stated, "We have no intent to remain in Somalia with fighting forces, but we are determined to do it right — to secure an environment that will allow food to get to the starving people of Somalia."[42] Somalian war lords intercepted much of the aid and often used it to purchase weapons.

Bush's successor, Bill Clinton, established a program to end the Somalian Civil War, build schools, hospitals and sanitation facilities, and continue humanitarian aid. He posited that if Somalia could modernize, it would establish a democratic government and end the regimes of war lords. Clinton's hopes were dashed when in October 1993, Somalians shot down two U.S. military helicopters, killed 18 and wounded 77 U.S. soldiers, and dragged the corpse of a U.S. Marine through the streets of Mogadishu.

---

41. Latham, *Right Kind of Revolution*, p. 192.

42. Glass, "Bush Sends Marines," para. 1–4.

Congress angrily called for the removal of U.S. troops to Somalia, where they felt that the U.S. had no compelling interests at stake.[43]

During Clinton's campaign, civil wars raged in Haiti, Bosnia, Chechnya, Croatia, Sierra Leone, Rwanda, Afghanistan, Burundi, Zaire (Congo), and Yemen. The world petitioned the U.S. for intervention and aid. The U.S. petitioned its allies for assistance to pay for the endless task of resolving ethnic conflicts, building democratic societies, and helping dilapidated economies recover from, war, disease, and famine. The American narrative held firm that the best way for developing nations to achieve democracy was for them to join the free market bandwagon, whereby Western investments and loans from the International Monetary Fund would produce economic conditions favorable to the development of democracy. The narrative persists despite evidence that free market capitalism has in many instances thwarted the creation of democracy in developing nations by exacerbating civil wars, increasing national debt, and transferring national wealth to Western banks and corporations rather than using it to improve life in the developing nation.[44]

The 9/11 attacks presented the U.S. with another opportunity to shift its narrative. They called Americans to a deeper understanding of global animosity towards the United States. It was the chance to reach out to other nations and form a more perfect union. Instead, we went with the old chorus line of "America first." As the U.S. mobilized its troops for war in Afghanistan and Iraq, President George W. Bush told Americans that their role in achieving national goals was go out and shop more.[45] Across the country, hundreds of businesses from car dealerships to coffee vendors launched campaigns to increase sales by associating their product with patriotism.[46] It felt like a bizarre carnival of lost souls as barkers seemed to be calling out to us: "Step right up ladies and gentlemen and punch that ol' terrorist in nose with your brand new luxury SUV!"

Arguably, telling people to go shopping after the 9/11 attacks was a sign of decadence. The directive told the world that not even an act of terrorism would derail the American resolve to press on with its "ultimate concern," which is commercial transaction. It said to all nations that we see problems and solutions only in material and monetary terms. It declared that the U.S. interpreted the 9/11 assaults as an attempt to cripple the nation

43. Latham, pp. 197–98.

44. See: Chua, *World on Fire*, a gripping account of how free trade and globalization have shifted wealth from one hand to the other in ways that breed violence, corruption, and indifference to law in nations across the globe.

45. Bush, "Press Conference," para 11.

46. Tsai, "Patriotic Advertising," p. 077–078.

financially, and that we would prove to the world that nobody messes with our economy. Armed with our credit cards and coupons, we would show the world who is boss! The directive was also sad. It conjured images of distressed people filling a psychological and spiritual void by wandering malls in a haze and filling their bags with things—things that they did not need, things that distracted them—things that could never replace the touch of a loving hand, a prayer, a meditation on peace, or a clear and substantial explanation for why so many people in the world were so angry with us.

The war on terrorism replaced the Cold War. President Barack Obama inherited the war from George W. Bush, and then he passed it along to his successor. Though Obama toned down the caustic rhetoric Bush had used to describe American adversaries, he vigorously fought the war. In his first inaugural address he stated that, "We will not apologize for our way of life, nor will we waver in its defense," and that those who "seek to advance their aims by inducing terror and slaughtering innocents" will ultimately be defeated.[47] Obama authorized ten times as many drone missions as did George W. Bush, with 563 strikes in Somalia, Pakistan, and Yemen during his two terms.[48] He also attempted to understand the causes of terrorism, and he relied heavily on targeted kill and surveillance to combat it, which drew criticism that he was too idealistic and overly optimistic about his strategies to end terrorism.[49]

Historian Barbara Tuchman observed that governments often pursue policies that are detrimental, and even catastrophic to their national interests. Why is it, she pondered, that people make the same mistakes over and over, when they know at the time that they are pursuing policies that are counter-productive, and that alternative courses of action are viable and available? The stories of religious campaigns, revolution, and war throughout history, she argues, are filled with leaders who proceeded down paths of lunacy confident that they were immune from the catastrophes that others who took the same paths experienced.

Tuchman found that people often get themselves into trouble for the same reasons they cannot or will not extricate themselves from trouble once they are in it. The first cause is a poor assessment of conditions and facts, whereby individuals insist on preconceived notions rather than objective evidence, and signs that they have misread the situation. A second cause is the refusal to learn from prior experience, and to take seriously the possibility that, even when actors and scenes change, plots and human fallibility do

47. Obama," Inaugural Address," para. 18.
48. Purkiss and Serle, "Obama's Covert Drone," para. 1–2.
49. Stern, "Obama and Terrorism," para. 1–2.

not. Other factors include the vanity of leaders, miscalculations of competence, and under-estimations of oppositional forces. These variables contributed to some of history's most pivotal events, including the Protestant
Reformation, the American Revolution, Hitler's invasion of Russia, and the
Vietnam War.[50]

Like a needle stuck in a record's groove, we go on, reciting the same old
narratives, pursuing the same old agendas, ignoring the same old warnings,
and being surprised by the same old results. Nature and history are telling
us that we need a new narrative. The poor and oppressed are telling us that
we need a new narrative. Clerics and spiritual teachers are telling us we need
a new narrative. In many cases, our own suffering, anger, and alienation are
telling us that we need a new narrative. We keep telling the world that we
are decent, humanitarian, and Christian people, and we cannot seem to stop
yelling at each other and stop stirring up hate, fear, and lies in our public
discourse. We need to change the channel, but do not seem to know how.

50. Tuchman, *March of Folly*, pp. 4–33.

Chapter 9

God Talk

PERSISTENT PIETY

There is no religion in the world that has not been tainted by human errors and ego. With imperfect ears, we have heard the voice of God. With imperfect minds, we have interpreted the word of God. With imperfect motives, we have spread the word of God. Whether or not pastoral and religious discourse will help us to construct a more humanitarian national narrative, a more spiritual personal narrative, and rescue our rhetorical capital from indecency and incivility depends in part on the extent to which materialism and nationalism have influenced religious leaders' spirituality and theological perspectives.

Like politics and advertising, religion is in the business of persuasion. As persuasion goes, religion is disadvantaged by the fact that it is promoting something that cannot be seen, quantified, and empirically proven. It is interested in convincing people that God exists, calls to us to a sacred purpose, and offers us eternal life through reconciliation, faith, and obedience. The more tangible aspects of religion are easier to sell. These include moral guidelines that urge us to forgive each other, be kind to strangers, and be charitable to the poor, the sick, widows, and orphans. Religion is far from being confined to theological discourse in America. It is woven so tightly into our political discourse that the rhetorical threads are often indistinguishable.

Engaging in discourse about religion is difficult in the U.S. for at least three reasons. First, the idea that human beings must rely upon God's favor just to survive is neutralized by our confidence that science and technology will sustain us. Where God is not perceived to be an immediate and essential factor in our day to day existence, God becomes remote and alien. Some posit that religion is superstitious fool's gold, and that those who take faith and God seriously are weak-minded, immature, or too ignorant in matters of science.

Second, many dislike religion because the faithful have tried to force their doctrines on others, and used religion to control and exploit people. Even when discourse about religion is exploratory, academic, and non-evangelizing, some folks think that others are conspiring to convert them. Many of us have experienced ambiguous feelings about sharing our thoughts on God, religion, and spirituality because we fear being labeled a starry-eyed nut bag or worse. Many do not trust that even a well-trained instructor could introduce the concept of religion and facilitate studies of the world religions in an objective and fair way. The absence of academic studies of religion and the spiritual side of the human experience leave individuals open to believing false reports and stereotypes about religion and the people who practice it. The absence leaves many with no clear understanding of why religion has always been central to civilization, what it has added to human development, and why it has consistently caused conflict and war.

A third reason for our uneasiness with religious rhetoric is the reality that so much God talk is filled with hate and ignorance, and is obsessed with earthly riches. It is difficult for many people to absorb religious rhetoric and to be open-minded about other people's spiritual wisdom when preachers are in love with their own celebrity and indulge themselves with mansions and material luxuries. It is also difficult to listen to the instruction of preachers whose knowledge of history, humanity, great literature, culture, and theology is so dreadfully vacuous that it cannot give listeners anything more than sweeping, superficial pabulum and clichés. Many have left their communities of faith because clerics have failed to provide insight to what it means to be faithful in the modern world. Many are offended by the idea that in order to have faith in God, they must shut off their brains and believe whatever the nice preacher says.

Despite the difficulties that come with having faith in things that we cannot see, modern American presidents have echoed the Puritan refrain that the U.S. is summoned by God to be great. Jimmy Carter (D-GA) told Americans, "Ours was the first society openly to define itself in terms of both spirituality and human liberty. It. . . has given us an exceptional appeal, but it also imposes on us a special obligation to take on those moral duties which, when assumed, seem invariably to be in our own best interests."[1] In his inaugural address, Ronald Reagan (R-CA) stated, "To us, as to the ancient People of The Promise, there is given an opportunity: a chance to make our laws and government not only a model to mankind, but a testament to the wisdom and mercy of God.[2] Bill Clinton (D-AR) declared:

> And so, my fellow Americans, as we stand at the edge of the 21st century, let us begin anew with energy and hope, with faith and discipline. And let us work until our work is done. The Scripture says, "And let us not be weary in well doing: for in due season we shall reap, if we faint not." From this joyful mountaintop of celebration we hear a call to service in the valley. We have heard the trumpets. We have changed the guard. And now, each in our own way and with God's help, we must answer the call.[3]

Those who seek public office are aware of the potency of the narrative that the U.S. is God's righteous advance guard, and know that to challenge the myth is to risk votes. Barack Obama (D-IL) was exceptional, as he offered a prophetic alternative to the narrative.

At the National Prayer Breakfast in 2015, Obama invited Americans to embrace certain principles that would guide our thinking about religion and God. His first principle was humility, "not being so full of yourself and so confident that you are right and that God speaks only to us, and doesn't speak to others, that God only cares about us and doesn't care about others, that somehow we alone are in possession of the truth." He added:

> Our job is not to ask that God respond to our notion of truth— our job is to be true to Him, His word, and His commandments. And we should assume humbly that we're confused and don't always know what we're doing and we're staggering and stumbling towards Him, and have some humility in that process. And that means we have to speak up against those who would misuse His name to justify oppression, or violence, or hatred with that fierce certainty. No God condones terror. No grievance justifies the taking of innocent lives, or the oppression of those who are weaker or fewer in number.
>
> And so, as people of faith, we are summoned to push back against those who try to distort our religion—any religion— for their own nihilistic ends. And here at home and around the world, we will constantly reaffirm that fundamental

1. Carter, "Inaugural Address," para. 4, 6–8.
2. Reagan, "National Affairs," para. 13.
3. Clinton," Inaugural Address," para. 16.

freedom—freedom of religion—the right to practice our faith how we choose, to change our faith if we choose, to practice no faith at all if we choose, and to do so free of persecution and fear and discrimination.[4]

The freedom of religion of which Obama spoke is a double-edged sword. There will always be those who embrace the freedom to believe that being nihilistic is better than being heretical.

ASK BIG

A recent study found that two thirds of churchgoers in the U.S. believe that God wants them to prosper financially, and that one in four believe that they have to do something for God in order to receive material blessings. The research also noted that evangelicals, African Americans, and Hispanics are more likely to hold these beliefs than are other Protestants and whites.[5] The Prosperity Gospel preaches that if people have the right faith and right attitudes, God will shower them with material fortune. The promise is especially attractive to the poor and working class, and those who are overwhelmed with debt.

The rhetoric of riches suits American civil religion well, as its focus is on the well-being of the individual rather than the local and global community. It offers simple solutions to complex problems and often promises that, for a small monetary contribution, illnesses will be healed, businesses will thrive, and the wants of private prayers will be fulfilled. It sometimes punctuates the urgency of action by telling people that the end of time is near. The Prosperity Gospel is seductive. It does not ask us to look too deeply at the way we support institutions and lifestyles that hurt or exploit others. It does not question the American dream, nor ask whether it is real, moral, or achieved at the expense of someone else's deprivation and oppression. It does not ask whether the Earth and all of creation can physically, environmentally support an American dream for the 9 billion people who live on this planet. The Prosperity Gospel is about immediate gratification, which is very different from other traditions that ponder whether today's decisions will be good and healthy for several generations to come.[6]

---

4. Obama, "Remarks," para. 17–19.

5. Smietana, "Most Churchgoers Say," para. 3–4; 11–18.

6. Native American wisdom teaches that proper care for people and the Earth require the community to consider the impact of decisions seven generations in to the future. See: Lowe, *Seventh Generation Earth Ethics*.

Joel Osteen, who preaches the Prosperity Gospel, marries the power of positive thinking with the will of God. He asserts that God designed us to prevail in the material world:

> From the very beginning God created you to be victorious, healthy strong, and creative. Your original software says, 'You can do all things through Christ.' He programmed, 'Whatever you touch will prosper and succeed.' He programmed, 'You are the head and not the tail. You will lend and not borrow. You are a victor not a victim.' You were programmed to live an abundant, victorious, faith-filled life. That's how your creator designed you.[7]

Osteen's rhetoric skips past the narrative of original sin into the happy place of original entitlement. He cheerfully trumpets that we should "ask big:"

> When God laid the plan for your life, He didn't just put into it what you need to get by to survive, to endure until the end. He put more than enough in it. He's a God of abundance. We see this all through scripture. . .
>
> Yes, we should thank God that our needs are supplied. We should be grateful that we have enough, but don't settle there. That's not your destiny. He is a more-than-enough God. He wants you to have an abundance, so you can be a blessing to those around you.[8]

Osteen's rhetoric tempts audiences to believe that people who are real victims and real paupers are that way because are not Christians, or because their faith is weak. His rhetoric is very different from the Social Gospel, which calls upon the faithful to create services and resources to relieve the poor, shelter the homeless, and work for social reforms that prevent poverty, illness and ignorance. It paints a picture of faith that is wildly different from the other pictures of faith, including the images of Gandhi fasting for weeks so that rioting and violence would end, and images of clerics and nuns marching peacefully against racial segregation, and images of missionaries murdered by military juntas in Latin America because they advocated economic justice for the peasant masses.

Osteen tells congregants that, "whatever you touch will prosper." What does that mean? How does this square with Jesus' statement that his own followers would be sent into the world "as sheep in the midst of wolves," and hated and persecuted because of him (Matt. 10:16–22). Was Jesus thinking that people might be jealous of Christians because they got rich?

7. Osteen, *Think Better, Live Better*, p. 2.
8. Ibid, p. 218.

The Gospel is clear that while on Earth, the faithful may be victimized and not always "victorious" in the material sense. Jesus also directed the faithful, "Do not lay up for yourselves treasures on earth, where moths and rust consume and where thieves break in and steal, but lay up for yourselves treasures in heaven where neither moth nor rust consumes and where thieves do not break in and steal" (Matt. 6: 19–20). The disparity between Scripture and the Prosperity Gospel reminds us that human beings are capable of rationalizing anything, and that we are free to interpret sacred teachings in ways that neatly support our "ultimate concern."

That God wants good things for people is easy to accept, but telling the faithful that they should not "settle" for what they have because Jesus has a fortune for us, if we could just squeeze greater faith from ourselves, flies in the face of Jesus' directive to sell our treasures and follow him (Matt. 19:21). Osteen's rhetoric suggests that there is a cosmic quid pro quo, whereby God distributes material wealth in exchange for veneration and faith. His message sails past the perplexing question: Why would God send his son to the world to tell people to stop being so obsessed with earthly treasures, then use earthly treasures to reward dutiful believers? The assertion implies that giving your life over to Christ is a stepping stone to a secure and affluent lifestyle. How does that square with Jesus' invitation to the faithful to deny themselves, take up their cross and follow him (Matt. 16:24)?

Studies indicate that the Prosperity Gospel appeals more to those with lower levels of income and education.[9] They also reveal that many who gave evangelists large sums of money as "seeds" of miracles where turned away when they sought the ministries' help in times of sickness and financial crises.[10] Osteen's fortune is estimated between $40 and $60 million.[11]

There are lots of ways to "ask big." In a world that is running low on fossil fuel, destroying precious forests to increase cattle and agricultural production, and warming to dangerous levels, "asking big" might include prayers that we might have the strength and frugality to reverse dangerous consumptions of energy and other resources. Asking big might be supplications that God grant us the strength to resist the temptation to buy mansions we do not need, or to constantly upgrade our gadgets and possessions. It might be prayers for the strength to destroy the economic machinery that keeps the distribution of wealth so radically skewed towards the few at the expense of the many.[12] That would be big.

9. Schieman and Jun, "Practical Divine Influence," pp. 739–744; 746–748.
10. Baker, "Preachers Getting Rich," whole story.
11. Vrz, "Joel Osteen," para. 10.
12. Kurt, "Are You In," para. 1.

The evangelist calling for the faithful to "ask big" in the material sense is not asking much. Anyone can treat God like Santa Claus. That is easy. Asking for really big things that turn our hearts around, is not so easy. Asking big is asking to have the courage, humility, and the love that is necessary to live in a working class neighborhood or ghetto for the purpose of helping that community live with dignity and improve itself. Asking big is praying for the patience and wisdom to be a part of a local public school board and working to improve learning. It is asking for tenderness and compassion to be a volunteer who teaches the incarcerated or feeds the hungry, and cares for the elderly. Asking big is asking to be liberated from envy and relentless obsession with our appearance and popularity. Asking big is asking for the strength to say no to children who feel entitled to have everything on their terms, and who have already made leisure their "ultimate concern" and consumerism their personal religion.

One of the biggest prayers of all lives is the prayer to love others as we love our selves. Osteen's message acknowledges that with abundance, we can be a blessing to others, but what does that imply about those who do not have abundance and those who will probably never have it? Is there a certain threshold of income that if not met, will excuse us from tithing or giving to charity? Are the poor destined to be regarded as pathetic recipients of charity and blessings to no one because they do not have abundance? Are the poor impoverished because they do not love God enough?

The Prosperity Gospel creates a narrative filled with references to "winning," "triumph," and "victory." It is a narrative wherein the primary culprit in our unhappiness, failures, and poverty is not sin or vice, it is a negative mindset. Victory is about getting what we want. Having a mind for victory means verbally and mentally claiming our right to victory, as if to utter the words, "I am not a loser; I am destined for riches" will cause cosmic forces to shower us with money. Very little in Osteen's teachings invite us to care for the dispossessed and the despised. There are prayers for miracles to heal diseases, but not for legislation that will check the cost of pharmaceuticals and health insurance. There are prayers for better paying jobs so families do not lose their homes, but not for changes in rapacious loan policies and minimum wages. The followers of the Prosperity Gospel typically do not quarrel with the kind of capitalism we practice. The rhetoric that says we are communally responsible for each other is a faint whisper routinely muted by hallelujahs for the big ask.

GUERILLA TACTICS FOR THE LORD

In 2004, Senator Charles Grassley (R-IA) led a Senate Finance Committee investigation of excessive profiteering of evangelicals. The combination of some ministers' ostentatious lifestyles and the sprawling enterprise of their churches, foundations, publications, and guest presentations aroused congressional curiosity. At the heart of the legal issues is the reality that religious institutions are tax-exempt, and senators wanted to know whether the personal mansions, yachts, jet planes, luxury cars, and off-shore accounts were paid for with church money. During the investigation, the Senate learned that some ministers had openly campaigned for political candidates, which violates the conditions for being a tax-exempt ministry. The investigation did not result in any penalties or criminal convictions. It did, however, generate congressional motivation to review and revise tax codes related to religious and charitable organizations, and interest in capping the compensations ministers awarded themselves.[13]

Several of the ministers brought before Grassley's committee refused to cooperate and submit financial records. Getting current and former employees of churches and ministries to talk was also difficult. An ex-employee of Kenneth Copland Ministries stated, "The Copelands employ guerrilla tactics to keep their employees silent. We are flat out told and threatened that if we talk, God will blight our finances, strike our families down, and pretty much afflict us with everything evil and unholy."[14] Kenneth Copland Ministries in Fort Worth, Texas were among those Grassley investigated. The ministry employs family members who are paid millions for their services. The Copelands own an 18,000 square-foot mansion, several luxury cars, a jet, and four boats. Kenneth's son John acquired some of the church's property after it was known that oil was under the surface.

Grassley's committee failed to secure radical reforms in the legal oversight of churches and ministries. The five-term senator was denied a seat at the 2008 Republican Convention, largely because many of his Republican supporters in the "Hawkeye State" were upset by the investigation. Many Republicans in Iowa relied heavily on support from the evangelical right during the campaign season, and did not appreciate Grassley's attempt to bite the hand that blessed them.[15]

---

13. Perry, "Senator's Investigation," para. 1–5.
14. "Grassley Withers Under," para. 11.
15. Ibid, para. 27. Also see "Grassley Withers."

The political power that evangelicals wield has implications for foreign policy and national security.[16] The Christian right sees the United Nations as a threat to family values and putting America first. Many evangelicals believe that social justice rhetoric is essentially Marxism in disguise, and see multiculturalism as a threat to white America and its decency.[17] Many evangelicals hold that the U.S. must set the stage for Jesus' return to Earth. At present, numerous Christians believe that Donald Trump will bring about the apocalypse, the end of the age that produces Jesus' earthly regime.[18] Whether the executive believes this or not is unclear, and in some ways what he believes does not matter. What matters is that those who want the end to come soon may support presidential ultimatums and U.S. belligerence with hopes that they will lead to World War III. Of course, candidates cannot openly run on a platform to ring in the apocalypse. Armageddon does not play well in campaign slogans and parades.

LOUSY CHRISTIAN, GREAT LEADER

Among Trump's advisors are Reverend Robert Jeffress, pastor of the First Baptist Dallas, Texas Church. Jeffress believes that people who support Trump are morally and spiritually superior to those who do not support Trump. He has gotten himself into trouble by supporting Trump's wall along the southern border, announcing that Jews are going to hell, and for declaring that Islam encourages pedophilia.[19] Jeffress believes America is decaying because, "We have allowed the atheists, the infidels, the humanists to seize control of this country and to pervert our Constitution into something the founders never intended."[20]

Jeffress contends that liberals have misinterpreted the First Amendment, and takes umbrage at rules that prohibit displays of nativity scenes and other religious artifacts. "The Establishment Clause," he argues, "says Congress shall make no law respecting the establishment of religion," which means for him, that the state cannot impose a particular faith upon citizens, but does not mean citizens cannot express their faith in public.[21] America,

16. Martin, "The Christian Right," 71–79.

17. Anderson, "Evangelicals and Catholics," p. 21.

18. Maza, "Trump Will Start the End of the World," para. 1–2. Also see: Green, "Why Some Christians Love," and French, "Evangelicals are Supporting Trump," para. 1–5.

19. Zhou, "Christians Who Support Trump," para. 7–8.

20. Green, "One Way to Push," para. 4.

21. First Baptist Dallas, "Dr. Robert Jeffress," para. 4–5.

he insists, is a Christian nation, thus, laws banning the expression of faith at public schools and in public places is an attack on the nation's Christian identity. In June, 2018, Jeffress purchased space on billboards to promote a special upcoming event. They announced, "America is a Christian Nation," which prompted angry editorials in the Dallas press. The company renting the billboard space removed the advertising, as people accused the ads of being "hateful," and "divisive."[22]

The billboard controversy teaches us something about how Americans spend their rhetorical capital. Americans are thin-skinned when it comes to billboards with religious messages that promote revivals, or that tell readers that life begins at conception, and very thick-skinned when it comes to billboards that push unhealthy items such as fast food, super-charged caffeine drinks, alcohol, and cigarettes.

America is and is not a Christian nation. Americans are diverse in their faith. Roughly 70 percent say they are Christian, while about 6 percent are non-Christian faiths including Muslim, Hindu, and Jewish, and nearly 23 percent report they have no religious affiliation or are atheist.[23] The rhetoric that America is Christian breaks down not just because the nation is religiously diverse, but because the values and morality of Christians themselves are often so oppositional to the Gospels that the meaning of Christianity is anybody's guess.

Depending on one's perspective, the Gospels are not much help to evangelicals who would like the republic to lean a little in the direction of a theocracy. The Gospels do not explicitly speak about the modern world, with its modern science and technology, or its modern culture. They do not, for instance, specifically discuss abortion, the Internet, pornography, pre-emptive strikes, mercenaries, aid to dictators, stem cell research, rent control, tax loopholes, nuclear weapons, cocaine, corporations, rent control, bank fraud, immigration, monetary settlements for pain in suffering in litigation, communism, capitalism, and a host of things that beg the question of what is evil and what is good. Jeffress appears certain, however, that he and his fellow Christians conservatives have cracked the code of the Gospel's message on all issues foreign and domestic.

In January 2019, as the federal government was shut down pursuant to the president's refusal to sign a budget until he got what he wanted to build a wall along the U.S. southern border, Jeffress told television audiences that the president was "doing exactly the right thing in keeping this government

22. Browder, "Robert Jeffress' Mega-Church Forced," para. 1–3.

23. Pew Research Center's, "Religious Landscape Study" provides a fascinating look at the distribution of religion state by state, and public opinion about moral issues and spiritual experiences.

shut down until he gets that wall." After all Jeffress reasoned, Nehemiah was inspired by God to build a wall around Jerusalem, and "The Bible says even heaven is gonna have a wall around it."[24]

When asked about Trump's bragging about grabbing women by the "pussy," Jeffress admitted the remarks were crude and indefensible, "but not enough to make me vote for Hillary Clinton." When asked about Trump's adultery with Stormy Daniels and the hush money she received to keep quiet about it, Jeffress declared that evangelicals "knew they weren't voting for an altar boy." The pastor has proudly stated, "Trump's a lousy Christian, but he's a good leader."[25] Given his convictions, it is unlikely that Pastor Jeffress will lead the attempt to rescue public discourse from vulgarity and incivility. He has rationalized mean and dastardly discourse because he believes that the president's goals resonate with what God wants, and apparently holds that meanness and dastardliness does not count when one is doing the "will of God."

It seems that Jeffress cares more about the religious message posted on billboards than about the moral message of a president's conduct. Given that Jeffress believes that the founding fathers of the United States wanted the new republic to be a Christian nation and a beacon of morality to all nations, the president's "lousy" Christianity should be a big deal, but it is not. The only thing that seems to be consistent in Jeffress' discourse is that Trump is his kind of warrior, because he is "without a doubt the most pro-life, pro-religious liberty, and pro-Israel. . .president we've ever had."[26] Jeffress has said of Democrats, "Apparently, the god they worship is the Old Testament god Moloch, who allowed for child sacrifice."[27] This is an odd statement given the fact that the Israelite patriarch, Abraham, heard God tell him to kill his son Isaac, and Abraham thus prepared for a human sacrifice (Gen. 22:1–19). It is also a curious statement given the Christian belief that the salvation of mankind *required* the sacrifice of Jesus, "the son of God," on the cross. All theological paradox and metaphors aside, Jeffress uses the criteria of child sacrifice selectively. He apparently does not regard the casualties of war in Afghanistan and Iraq, nor the poverty of American ghettos, rural America, and Native American reservations, nor the lack of health care for sick and dying who cannot afford health care, nor the woefully mediocre public schools as sacrifices to Moloch. Why?

24. Mooney, "Trump's Apostle," para. 3, 5.

25. Ibid, para. 11, 13, 29.

26. Cole, "Pastor Robert," para. 5.

27. Ibid, para. 13.

GRAIN ON THE SABBATH

Another one of Trump's spiritual advisors is Paula White, a non-denomi-national Christian and former pastor of New Destiny Christian Center in Apopka, Florida, author, and television celebrity. White graduated from high school, but has no formal seminary education. She claims she was called at the age of 18 to preach and help heal people whose lives have been broken by poverty, drug abuse, poor judgement, and misfortune. Her ministry is especially popular with people who have experienced crises that have left them despondent and filled with self-loathing. The thrust of her message is hope. It is about facing mistakes and personal disaster, and believing that God has a plan to restore our lives, our self-esteem, and our health. Her church is one of the largest in the nation and features celebrity appearances for fund-raising.[28]

White's outreach to those in crisis is impressive. She has preached in prisons to the incarcerated and counseled the rich and famous who have made train wrecks of their lives. She says that God does not want people to suffer. It all sounds so good until it does not. In defense of separating immi-grant children from parents at the border, White told the Christian Broad-casting Network that, if "Jesus had broken the law then he would have been sinful and he would not have been our Messiah."[29] This might be White's way of saying that he who breaks the law shall be punished, and that when the president separated children from their parents, he did not break the law. White's comment reveals limitations in her legal and theological acuity.

First, the president's actions relative to separating immigrant children from their parents have not been wholly legal. The American Civil Liberties Union (ACLU) sued the Trump administration in federal court in Febru-ary, 2019 for violating codes regulating the incarceration of undocumented immigrants. At that time, the median stay of the 2,654 children in detention was just over five months.[30] Many children were under the age of ten, many were sick, and many suffered because they were traumatized, underfed, un-bathed, cold, and warehoused in filth.[31]

Second, and very importantly, Jesus himself actually broke the law. Yup. He got busted by the Phariseesa couple of times, once for picking grain on the Sabbath (Matt. 12: 1–8) and another time for healing a blind man on the Sabbath (John 9:13-16). Jesus acted out of compassion; his disciples

28. Lee and Sinitiere, *Holy Mavericks*, pp. 115–119.

29. Glenza, "Paula White," para.27.

30. American Civil Liberties Union, "Family Separation," para. 13–14.

31. Rose and Allyn, "Scenes of Tearful," para. 1–4.

were hungry and the man could not see. He broke the law, yet for many remained the messiah. For some, he was the messiah *because* he broke the law. In his defiance, Jesus liberated the faithful from the ideas that the letter of the law is greater than the spirit of the law, which is love. White seemed oblivious to the nuances of the Gospel, and wholly indifferent to the suffering of the detained children.

Evangelicals, members of the Christian right, and Catholics represent the majority of the President's religious advisors, and they are mainly white males who want the U.S. to ban abortion and gay marriage, and to get tough on immigrants.[32] Many advisors are not ordained ministers. The men and women who are on these religious councils include many who are not gathered to explore theology or to created bridges between adversarial faith-based institutions. Instead, they want to help Trump understand what is important to these groups, so that he might win their support.[33]

God talk is often militant, and we need not turn to radical Islamic soldiers to see that. The U.S. has private security corporations that are dedicated to advancing the "Christian" vision at gunpoint. Blackwater, a security services corporation created by Erik Prince is one example. Dedicated to "a Christian supremacist agenda," Blackwater provided mercenaries to fight Islamic terrorism and donated money to conservative Christian organizations, such as James Dobson's *Focus on the Family*, that combat liberalism in U.S. politics.[34] While contracted by U.S. State Department and the Department of Homeland Security, Blackwater battled secularism and non-Christian religions at home and abroad. Blackwater operated on the periphery of rules to which U.S. armed forces are held accountable, and some of its soldiers were found guilty of murdering innocent civilians in Iraq.[35]

Congressional members and taxpayers alike were alarmed by Blackwater's audacity. It has: operated with far less accountability than that of U.S. soldier; billed U.S. taxpayers two to three times that billed for regular U.S. soldiers; established headquarters off-shore to avoid U.S. taxes; and, recruited mercenaries from foreign countries with reputations for gang violence and dictatorships, including Honduras, Chile, El Salvador, Panama, and Colombia.[36] Blackwater's success was made possible because George

32. Schiffer, "Donald Trump Names 34 Members," para. 1–4; also see Banks, "All the President's Clergymen," and Banks, "The Key Evangelical Players."

33. Diamond and Appleton, "Paula White," para. 5.

34. Scahill, *Blackwater*, pp. 81–82. Prince sold Blackwater to an investment group in 2010. It is now called Academi.

35. Grumbach and Fieldstadt, "Former Blackwater," para. 1–4.

36. Scahill, pp. 55–60.

W. Bush's administration supported the privatization of U.S. armed forces to fight terrorism, and because many supported Prince's religious objectives.[37]

Today, there are many religious leaders who serve prophetic causes rather than power and prosperity. Chris Hedges, Joyce Hollyday, and William Barber II are just a few of the Protestant clerics who might offer the executive insights about social justice.[38] There are Catholics chiming in, including Helen Prejean, Roy Bourgeois, and James Martin.[39] There are Jews who walk the path of community restoration and peace, including Stosh Colter and Atalia Omer.[40] A president's choice of advisors reveal whether the president wants an echo chamber or an assembly of broad thinking individuals who bring diverse voices to the process of policy development. The choice also reveals which theology has a legitimate place in America's civil religion and national narrative, and which does not.

WAITING FOR MESSIAHS

President George W. Bush created the Office of Faith-Based and Community Initiatives in 2001, and President Barack Obama renamed the office, the President's Council on Faith-Based and Neighborhood Partnership. These organizations worked with federal and private resources to provide social services at the local level. Obama's council included men, women, clerics, scholars, community organizers, business leaders, Catholics, Jews, Muslims, Sikhs, Mormons, and non-believers. The current councils of religious advisors are narrower in their representation of faith, and have fewer members with scholarly theological expertise.[41]

37. Kuhlenbeck, "Theocratic Mercenary," Para. 3–9.

38. Christ Hedges is Presbyterian minister who has written widely on the subject of poverty and war. Author, Joyce Hollyday is co-pastor of Circle of Mercy, a congregation that preaches peace and justice, and serves the needs of immigrants. William Barber, III is a minister and president of the North Carolina National Association for the Advancement of Colored People, whose crusades to end poverty call for a moral revival.

39. Helen Prejean is a sister in the Congregation of St. Joseph, and founder of SURVIVE, which helps victims of violence heal; she is an activist against the death penalty. Roy Bourgeois is a former Maryknoll priest, and founder of the School of the America Watch, which opposes training of Latin American military to oppress and kill civilians; he supports women's ordination as Catholic priests. James Martin, a Jesuit priest, is an advocate of gay rights.

40. Stosh Colter is the executive officer of Bend the Arc, a progressive Jewish organization working for peace, justice, and community advocacy. Professor of Religion, Atalia Omer is author of multiple books on nationalism, peace, and reconciliation between Palestinians and Israel.

41. Jenkins, "Trump is Dismantling," para. 7–10.

There is a difference between creating religious councils in order to create opportunities for people to receive needed service, and creating them in order to amplify partisan propaganda. There is also a difference between creating them to represent various perspectives on moral matters and creating them in order to give the illusion that diverse perspectives are represented. What is created depends upon who occupies the Oval Office.

Americans have always had a special place for religion in its national narrative and we pay the price for this. Religious vision creates tension between those who want religion to dictate law and policy, and those who do not. Half of Americans say that it is vital for presidents to share their religious beliefs, and 40 percent say that presidents do not share them as much as they should.[42] Some Americans want leaders to share their religious beliefs so that voters can determine whether candidates' views are aligned with their own doctrines. Others want leaders to share their religious beliefs for the purpose of creating a social transformation, from a paradigm of greed, intolerance, and hateful mindsets, to a new paradigm of charity, good will, justice, and sustainability. Some want leaders who share their religious faith for purely sentimental reasons.

Americans invested a great deal of messianic hope in Barack Obama. He was the candidate who had the "audacity to hope" that we could be better than we thought we could be. He kept telling audiences who questioned the nation's potential for change, "yes we can." Many perceived Obama as "the One," a liberator and redeemer, who would, by virtue of being liberal, black, and young, slay the ancient dragons of bigotry and poverty. In his inaugural address, Obama's rhetoric revealed his faith in transcendence, as he called for a new paradigm of national unity: "For we know that our patchwork heritage is a strength, not a weakness. We are a nation of Christians and Muslims, Jews and Hindus, and non-believers. . . . To the Muslim world, we seek a new way forward, based on mutual interest and mutual respect."[43]

Horace Campbell, Professor of African American Studies and Political Science, argues that Obama was not as revolutionary as he may have seemed, but was caught up in a political moment where his charism and the people's need for a savior merged. He wrote:

> Many progressives understood that something was fundamentally wrong with US society, but pinned their hopes on the election of Obama. These elements had no coherent movement. The old Left had virtually disintegrated, with disagreement over whether to support electoral politics or not. In the midst

42. Masci, "Almost All U.S. Presidents," para. 5.
43. Obama, "Inaugural Address," para. 19.

of the indecisiveness of the progressives, the mainstream media took the missionism and messianic traditions of society to
the point of comparing Barack Obama to a black Jesus. Society
was trapped by its religiosity. . . Obama was entrapped within
these traditions of messianism, the presidency, inherited wars,
neo-liberalism, and the incompetence of a class that promoted
religious intolerance and hatred in order to destabilize people.[44]

In other words, Obama appealed to voters in part because they were able to
project their own understanding of his agenda into his candidacy. Campbell
suggests that had Americans approached the election without messianic
expectations, they would have had more realistic expectations about what
Obama was able to accomplish and what was beyond his capacity.

Ultimately, Obama relied on the advisors of his predecessors, who
thrust the U.S. into war and who manufactured the Recession of 2008. He
also relied on the same neo-liberal policies of bailing out banks to prevent
the economy from totally collapsing. He supported an extension of Bush's
tax cuts for the rich, and is criticized for not doing enough to build the
strength of the Democratic Party. The backlash against his presidency probably had less to do with his vision of justice and love of neighbor, and more
to do with his inability to extricate himself from the messes he inherited.
Poverty spiked up to 22 percent during his presidency, and Democrats, his
own party, lost over 1,000 seats in state legislatures and governor's offices.[45]

Obama did not cast himself as a savior, and instead regularly acknowledged the communal nature of leadership and social transformation. He
said to officials, ministers, and community leaders at the 2016 Easter Prayer
Breakfast:

> To do justice, to love kindness –- that's what all of you collec-
> tively are involved in in your own ways each and every day.
> Feeding the hungry. Healing the sick. Teaching our children.
> Housing the homeless. Welcoming immigrants and refugees.
> And in that way, you are teaching all of us what it means when
> it comes to true discipleship. It's not just words. It's not just
> getting dressed and looking good on Sunday. But it's service,
> particularly for the least of these.
>
> And whether fighting the scourge of poverty or joining
> with us to work on criminal justice reform and giving people
> a second chance in life, you have been on the front lines of

44. Campbell, *Barack Obama*, p. 216.
45. Kamarck, "Fragile Legacy," para. 3–4.

delivering God's message of love and compassion and mercy for His children.

And I have to say that over the last seven years, I could not have been prouder to work with you. We have built partnerships that have transcended partisan affiliation, that have transcended individual congregations and even faiths, to form a community that's bound by our shared ideals and rooted in our common humanity. And that community I believe will endure beyond the end of my presidency, because it's a living thing that all of you are involved with all around this country and all around the world.

And our faith changes us. I know it's changed me. It renews in us a sense of possibility. It allows us to believe that although we are all sinners, and that at times we will falter, there's always the possibility of redemption. Every once in a while, we might get something right, we might do some good; that there's the presence of grace, and that we, in some small way, can be worthy of this magnificent love that God has bestowed on us.

You remind me all of that each and every day. And you have just been incredible friends and partners, and I could not be prouder to know all of you.[46]

How often do we remind others that we are proud to be part of their team or their community? How often do we tell each other that, though we falter as sinners and imperfect human beings, we are always within reach of God's grace, redemption, and new beginnings? Do we not all give more, worry less, and put resentments aside when our goodness and dignity is honored rather than mocked and ignored?

Campbell noted with Obama in office, some decreased their activism and slowed the social networking that is vital for creating social change. He observed that bigots and conservatives did not miss a beat, as their websites proliferated and their hate speech was aired in mass media.[47] The right-wing resented prophetic leaders who urged mercy for criminals, charity for the poor, and hospitality to the stranger. Its idea of a savior was someone who would restore the crumbling status quo, wherein Protestant white males could enjoy unassailable privileges.

Arguably, it is not fair to wait for messiahs, because one human being cannot single-handedly change an entire culture and its narrative. The kind of things many Americans wanted Obama to do, including increase taxes on the wealthy and end poverty, are things that can only be done when the vast

46. Obama, "Remarks," para. 28–33.

47. Campbell, p. 217.

majority of Americans are ready to change the traditional national narrative about the nature of prosperity, and the right of individuals to get as rich as they can without government interference. Moreover, what does it profit the people who elect a "messiah," but will not follow his or her lead in by volunteering time for community service, speaking truth to power, and improving what they are able to improve in the workplace? We are all potential leaders, advocates, and agents of change, and this assertion is compatible with both democratic and religious principles.

Greta Thunberg, the sixteen year-old who began a world-wide movement demanding that government and industrial leaders act swiftly to reverse climate change, began her campaign by skipping school and sitting outside the Swedish Parliament with a sign that read, "Strike for Climate." On September 20, 2019, four million people around the world marched to punctuate the urgency of enacting strategies to reverse global warming. Three days later, Thunberg addressed the United Nations Climate Change Summit, and verbally spanked her elders for allowing their greed to dictate environmental policies at the expense of biodiversity and ecological sustainability.[48] She fearlessly "asked big" for corporate executives and national governments to reverse the damage to the environment caused by an irrational lust for wealth.

The world is a scary place. Empires and the domains of strongmen provide cozy places to hide. The faithful, however, are not called to be cozy, but to roll up their sleeves and learn the way of God by loving others. The first generation of Christians had no nation, no police force, no army, no mercenaries, no senators, no lobbyists, and no judges. They were members of a "rogue" religious cult that was persecuted by Roman emperors, yet they ministered to the poor, the sick, and the suffering. Christianity did some of its best work without the government aid and the protection of the state.

48. Ortega, "Greta Thunberg," para. 2–4.

Chapter 10

Empowerment

ADVOCACY AND AGENCY

A great deal of rhetoric in our society promotes personal empowerment. Though there are many ways to define and exercise empowerment, our public discourse normally refers to empowerment as the capacity to access resources and influence the laws and policies that govern us. Efforts to empower individuals and communities have been motivated by inequities in our economic and legal systems. Though we are empowered by the Constitution to choose our representation in Congress, and by civil liberties extended to us in the Amendments, some people lack the knowledge and skills required to use one's empowerment effectively.

In general, empowerment is concerned with the authority to act, judge, and decide on one's own behalf. It is associated with autonomy and the legitimacy in exerting one's own will. It is about taking control of one's own life.[1] Scholars say that empowerment is "both a value orientation for working in the community and theoretical model for understanding the processes and consequences of efforts to exert control over decisions that affect one's life, organizational functioning, and the quality of community life."[2] In other words, empowerment is an ideal and a quality of behavior which has implications for community and corporate endeavors. Empowerment is also a

1. McLaughlin, *Empowerment*, p. 124.
2. Zimmerman, "Empowerment Theory," p. 43.

psychological phenomenon whereby individuals acquire the confidence and motivation to pursue one's interests and objectives.[3]

The use of the term "empowerment" to describe the legal authority of individuals to exert influence over their lives goes back to the 1600s. In modern times, it has been associated with the inclusion of employee input in management decisions, and movements to increase and protect the rights of minorities and women. It is also used to describe privatization efforts and investment in "underdeveloped" global regions.[4] Empowerment has led to positive outcomes. Empowering nurses to have greater input in the procedures of health care, for example, has led to improvements in patient outcomes and nurses' job satisfaction. Empowering teachers has led to instructional innovations and the improvement of learning outcomes. Empowering victims of sexual assault to report their abuse has led institutions to be more meticulous in screening and training individuals who work with children, and in monitoring and reporting wrongful conduct.

Empowerment in the legal and social sense has not always been distributed evenly. Even in democracies, the legal power to exert one's will and one's voice have been denied on the basis of gender, color, and religion. History reveals that agency has been something people acquired by way of protesting discrimination and fighting for civil rights. In addition, the ability to judge wisely and to act responsibly is also not evenly cultivated. Yes, we have the power to choose our senators and representatives. No, we have not all been taught how to decode the candidate's propaganda, nor how to locate and digest scholarly or scientific materials that might inform our decision to support or oppose certain laws and policies.

Research tells us that human beings readily defer to the will of others based on their perception of others' credibility, and that people who exert dominance in communication are often presumed to have expertise and credibility even when they do not.[5] Even when we are "empowered," we are vulnerable to deceit. The mortgage meltdown that triggered the Recession of 2008 was in part caused by manipulative bankers who convinced home buyers that they could afford homes they could not afford. Access to loans and home ownership in our society represents empowerment. It gives families a sense of stability and it builds equity. When banks foreclose on homes, as they did for roughly 3.1 million families in 2008 alone, individuals are not empowered with options.[6] They are instead faced with uncertainty,

3. Zimmerman, et al., "Further Explorations," pp. 707–727.
4. McLaughlin, pp. 2–3.
5. Dunbar, et al., "Empowered by Persuasive Deception," pp. 868–70.
6. Christie, "Foreclosures," para. 1–2.

homelessness, ruined credit, business failures, and sudden dependence on others to help them out of a crisis.[7]

EMPOWERING THE EMPOWERED

One of the ways that Americans exercise their power and agency is in the market. Our choices as consumers have the potential to influence whether companies perish or thrive. When farmworkers in California went on strike under the leadership of Cesar Chavez in 1965, domestic and foreign customers of California grown grapes, lettuce, and other produce supported them by boycotting these items. Many farmworkers at that time worked for wages of less than $1.50 an hour without benefits, pensions, and decent facilities to rest and clean themselves. The boycott helped the farmworkers win wage increases and benefits.[8] The boycott also demonstrated the power of collaboration between labor unions and consumers to change corporate policy. As our economy is currently structured, the tension between the well-being of workers, consumers, and corporations is enduring and formidable.

The cycle of strikes, boycotts, union negotiating, regulation, and reform are fixtures in the American economy. Traditionally, whatever we have done in order to empower ourselves and others economically has been determined in part by the capitalist framework in which we operate. This is to say that we define our economic problems and craft our remedies for the problems in ways that ultimately lock us into the American version of capitalism. Those who offer alternative frameworks and solutions are frequently derided as "socialists," even if their framework and solutions have nothing to do with Marxism or other socialist paradigms.

Embedded in the national narrative is our own special story about capitalism and its potential to empower and enrich us all. Its appeal is that it allows individuals to own private property, be as entrepreneurial as one wishes to be, and to earn money by the simple act of making an investment in somebody's else's business. In theory, private profit translates into employment and taxes that can be used for the public's well-being. In theory, therefore, capitalism greases the wheels of love for one's neighbor, as the entrepreneur's fortune organically flows abundantly into everyone else's pockets. Tax shelters, loopholes, and exemptions on one hand, and government subsidies for gargantuan businesses on the other, frequently turn the abundant flow into a trickle, and the trickle into a drip. We rally around the

---

7. See: Dayen, *Chain of Title*, which reveals how banks committed fraud with empowering language and deceit.

8. See: Bardacke's *Trampling Out the Vintage* for the full story and context.

narrative in any event, because there is always the chance that, if we play the game well, we will one day be on the side of the deluge, not the drip.

Many of our leaders believe that empowering the powerful is a good idea. The Supreme Court Decision, *Citizens United* v. *Federal Election Commission* (2010), for example, stated that corporations are entitled to the same rights as individuals. It determined that contributions to political campaigns represent "free speech," and as such, ought not to be restricted. The decision enables corporations to amplify their political propaganda in ways individuals cannot.[9]

The modern trend of federal activism to empower the powerful was propelled during the 1980s with rhetoric that promised to get government off America's back. Since the Reagan administration, both Republicans and Democrats have relaxed prohibitions against monopolies, and the Justice Department has reinterpreted antitrust laws as to permit massive consolidation of industries.[10] During the 1980s, federal policies also reduced industrial and banking regulations and the power of unions, while increasing the lobbying power of corporations.[11] President Reagan justified these policies as "the best way of ensuring personal liberty."[12]

President Bill Clinton pursued Reagan's goal to reduce government intervention as a way of empowering the people, stating: "I'd like for us to have not only welfare reform but to re-examine the whole focus of all our programs that help people, to shift them from entitlement programs to empowerment programs."[13] He also empowered the powerful by signing the Gramm-Leach-Bliley Act in 1999, which paved the way to the Recession of 2008. The act reversed the 1933 Glass-Steagall Act, which forbid commercial banks from using its assets and deposits to make high risk investments in the global market. Glass-Steagall placed a wall between commercial banks that served the needs of the average American family, and the giant investment firms of Wall Street that served the needs of millionaires. Commercial banks suddenly had a lot of loot to invest in highly speculative businesses and "products" such as derivatives. The ensuing fraud and predatory lending disempowered millions as they lost jobs, homes, savings, and pensions in the Recession of 2008. The catastrophe hit the middle class so hard, that its ability to consume in order to keep the economy going was seriously

9. See: Mayer, *Dark Money* and learn how millionaires have invested in political campaigns and why.

10. Mitchell, "Rise and Fall," para. 9–14.

11. Palley, "America's Flawed Paradigm," p. 7.

12. Reagan, "State of the Union," para. 10.

13. Clinton, "Address before a Joint Session," p. 118.

damaged.[14] Taxpayers ultimately paid about $498 billion to rescue banks and other financial firms that had faltered in the fiasco.[15]

Americans often conceptualize empowerment as the capacity to control external things, such as rules, access to opportunities and resources, wages, and costs. There is another dimension to empowerment, however, one that concentrates on internal things. The Gospels suggest that spiritual empowerment is the capacity to live in the world, and yet, not be of the world. For the faithful, empowering one's self concerns the individual's ability to discipline one's thoughts, speech, and actions. It concerns the resolve of individuals to own their own narrative and stay faithful to spiritual convictions implicit in that narrative. Mahatma Gandhi taught that a thorough love of God liberated individuals from reactionary behavior. Reactionary conduct was a sign that one was not in control of oneself, and that others had gained power over one's emotions, will, and spiritual narrative.[16]

Many Americans do not leap to Gandhi or think about their own spiritual potential when they hear the word "empowerment." In the West, we tend to see the word in the material sense. In the narrative of the Prosperity Gospel, empowerment is the faith and courage to "ask big," and claiming the abundance that we were "designed by God" to have. In focusing on the external factors of our lives, we tend to seek only external remedies for our afflictions and unfortunate conditions, and so lose sight of internal remedies, such as our capacity to be still and listen, our patience, mercy, wisdom, good will, and gratitude. Many of us have experienced the despair that comes when we feel like we have no control in the material world, and see ourselves as victims of circumstance. The danger in the despair is that we become more myopic, more isolated, and more removed from human relationships that may represent encounters with the love of God.

SOUL NOIR

In the American narrative, individualism is nearly a religion unto itself. The individual must always prevail, must be empowered by all means, and must be wholly self-reliant. In its extreme, individualism can be highly toxic to humanism and spirituality, as it situates the individual's wants and will above all other considerations. In this extreme, individualism isolates people from others and throws one's moral compass into disorientation, because one no longer has any point of reference for the human experience except oneself.

14. Reich, *Beyond Outrage*, pp. xii–xvi.

15. Harbert, "Here's How Much," para. 1–8.

16. Iyer, *Essential Writings of Mahatma Gandhi*, pp. 245–263.

The dark side of individualism has been explored by sociologists, theologians, psychologists, and social critics. It has also been the subject literature and film, and there are many representations of individual empowerment gone bad. The super-empowered Dr. Frankenstein, for example, overcame nature and death. He was god-like and his moral outlook was essentially hijacked by his obsession with the idea that he alone—with only incidental assistance—created life where there was none. He was incapable of hearing the warnings of others who feared for his soul and the safety of the community around him.

To a lesser extreme, there are the characters of film noir, a movie genre that gained popularity during the 1940s and 1950s. Film noir portrays the darker side of humanity and the sickly side of the American dream. The noir world is cruel, unforgiving, unapologetic, and corrupt. Noir's protagonists are individuals whose individualism takes them in very different directions than the chivalrous cowboys who saved the West, and cherry-cheeked teens dancing their way through small-town melodrama. They are individuals who get ahead by double-dealing, robbery, murder, and deception. Noir plots challenge the American narrative that everybody can get ahead if they work hard and play by the rules. In Noir, rules means nothing. Cops and judges take pay-offs, unions are dirty, and everything is negotiable until the bullets fly. Noir is a world where decent people do indecent things because they are victims of things that they cannot control.[17] In the Noir world, people do not shake the dust from their shoes and move to a new place where their humanity and spiritual gifts can thrive. Instead, they are consumed by darkness and become one with decay. It is a world where the best thing that people hope for is to survive and to feel good doing it.

The birds and bims of film noir want no serious romantic ties or obligations.[18] Like Humphrey Bogart's character Rick Blaine, owner of Rick's Café in *Casablanca* said, "I stick my neck out for nobody."[19] Rick is all about Rick. The Noir protagonists are motivated by something other than making the world a better place, because they gave up on that ideal a long time ago. What makes them tick? As the detective Sam Spade in *The Maltese Falcon*, Bogart tells the woman who hired him, "We didn't exactly believe your story, Miss O'Shaughnessy. We believed your 200 dollars. I mean, you

17. Osteen, *Nightmare Alley*, pp. 1–3.

18. Bird is noir slang for man, bim is noir slang for woman.

19. *Casablanca*, directed by Michael Curtiz (1942; Burbank, CA: Warner Brothers, 1998). DVD.

paid us more than if you had been telling us the truth, and enough more to make it all right."[20] Self-interest makes them tick.

Soul noir is about life as one's own shadow, never really touching another human being, wanting no obligations, and interacting with others strictly on the basis of expedient transactions. Soul noir is not evil by definition, but it can be cynical and indifferent to human suffering. People with soul noir might believe in God and admire humanism a great deal, but struggle to connect with others. Connecting is a dirty, risky business. Sticking your neck out to bring the love of God to bear in the world can get your heart broken. It can be exhausting and painful when people abuse good will and become dependent on you for unconditional support. The soul noir might live in people who truly believe they have been redeemed, and who are empowered by their intelligence, talent, and resources. Rather than use their own empowerment to leaven the love of God into society, however, they opt for isolation. They might resent the weak, the poor, and the criminal because, no matter the measure of charity and second chances, the weak, poor, and criminal never go away and the world is never fixed.

CONSCIENCE

Some people justify extreme individualism with the assertion that they are rightfully exercising their conscience. What can that mean? Conscience as a moral compass is often misunderstood. Gandhi once recalled an incident in which he was chided for arousing public conflict and contempt because he encouraged people to exercise their conscience. There were many, his critics complained, who used the term "conscience" as rationalizations for exerting one's will or ego. Gandhi recognized that not everyone received his spiritual teachings in the way he had intended, and that many did not understand that right exercise of conscience required special discipline. "Willfulness is not conscience," he penned; "Conscience is the ripe fruit of strictest discipline."[21] He asserted that right exercise of conscience requires meditation on one's own thinking, and assessments of one's thinking that applied the highest standard of regard for human dignity and the well-being of all, including one's adversaries.

The term "conscience" originates in Latin, and refers to a shared knowledge, especially a joint knowledge of right and wrong.[22] It is a curious word

20. *The Maltese Falcon*, directed by John Huston (1941; Burbank, CA: Warner Brothers, 2000). DVD.

21. Iyer, p. 210.

22. Online Etymology, "Conscience," para. 1–2.

that points to something internal—a phenomenon whereby individuals negotiate meaning and discern right action with something inside themselves. A Freudian might say that this other "something" is the superego, or the stock of norms and socially acceptable attitudes and behaviors that members of a society assimilate in order to get along. Religious traditions, however, posit that this "something" is larger than self, and larger than the collective wisdom and morality of a given society. In religious traditions, this "something" is transcendent of all manmade manners and rules, and essentially divine in origin and substance. Hence, for the faithful, entering into dialogue with one's conscience is to enter into dialogue with something sacred and eternal, such as God, a higher power, a great spirit.

Extreme individualism sometimes crowds God and spirituality out of our inner dialogue about right and wrong. As Gandhi noted, the exercise of conscience requires strict discipline. It requires mediation, cross examination of one's motives and intentions, and a thorough exploration of the implications of one's choices for others. It requires, for example, an approach to decision-making that does not begin with the question, "How can I get what I think is best," and instead, begins with the question of, "How can I use this moment of decision to improve everybody's circumstances?" The educator might begin with the question of, "In what ways are people ignorant, and what can I do to help them overcome ignorance?" The journalist might begin with the question, "What is the truth about what is happening, and how can I bring this truth to the community?" The senator might ponder, "Where is the well-being of the public at great risk, and how might legislation help to eliminate that risk?"

This discipline of conscience, or "co-reasoning with God," (as the faithful see it) is difficult for human beings under any circumstances. It is especially difficult for people raised in a world where the spiritual self and inner voice are constantly muzzled by political and commercial rhetoric. One of the greatest gifts we can give each other as we build and refine our rhetorical capital, is the encouragement to listen to one's inner voice. The special gifts of slowness to judgment and unconditional love nourish our ability to form a personal narrative that is, in turn, non-judgmental and loving. Our inner voices and scenarios are shaped in part by what others think of us, and many of us are convinced that unless we live by society's prevailing narratives, we are not worthy of respect, protection, and love. There is no way to truly know how much of our dastardly and destructive discourse is the result of the simple act of denying somebody an alternative to toxic narratives when they needed them the most.

DADDY LET'S ME SAY THAT

Rhetorical empowerment and control over our own narratives begin at birth. Before we attend our first kindergarten class, we already learned lots about the relationship between words and power. As toddlers, we learned not only about words, but tone, and how to proceed after hearing something that is cooing and cheerful, and how to respond when hearing something that is loud and commanding. We learned that sounds and expressions can manipulate others. By watching and listening to adults, we knew something about who had the power in the family and who did not, and whose feelings counted and whose did not. We probably learned some rules about gossip, lying, and secrets. No doubt some readers got into trouble as children by saying something vulgar, only to be confused by the double standards whereby daddy can say naughty things, but the kids cannot.

Some of us got a head start on building rhetorical capital, because our parents took us to the library and taught us to read before we were five years-old. Some got to hear grandparents and baby-sitters read stories and pause during dramatic moments to get us to think about what was happening to the characters and why. Some got to draw pictures of the stories and then tell a new story based on the old. Some learned how to speak and write in more than one language before they went to high school. Others never learned to read before they entered the first grade, and grew up in front of a screen filled with cartoons, video games, and commercials.

Parents are not the only ones who are empowering children and teaching them about communication and the narratives we ought to live. On average, children ages two to five years-old spend 32 hours a week in front of a TV, and children ages six to eleven years-old spend about 28 hours in front of the TV. These kids are watching television programs and DVDs and playing video games, and about three fourths of them have TVs in their own bedrooms.[23] Over the last several years, television content, video games, and music have all become more violent in content. By the time a child is 18 years old, he or she has witnessed about 200,000 acts of violence on television alone.[24] Handheld devices are also popular with children. Children under the age of eight spend over two hours a day on these devices, while kids between the ages of eight and eleven spend about

23. Boyse, "Television and Children," para 3.
24. American Academy of Family Physicians, "Violence in the Media," para. 12.

four and a half hours on them.[25] Nearly one half of children under the age of eight have their own tablet device.[26]

Social media is also very popular across all ages. In one study, 45 percent teens reported that they are online line on a "constant basis," and just 31 percent said that this level of consumption has a positive effective on their lives, because it keeps teens connected and enables them to share opinions. The 24 percent who indicated that social media has a negative impact on them cited their difficulties with face-to-face interactions, the distractiveness of the devices, and their feelings that people are sharing fake images of who they really are.[27] The fact that people are sensitive to fake images reminds us that people still care about truth, and still yearn for relationships that are built on an authenticity of personhood.

Whether or not the consumption of violent content has any impact on TV viewers and video game players has been debated for decades. There are studies that "prove" violence in media does not cause people to be violent.[28] There are studies that "prove" it does.[29] It is very difficult to prove that violent images causes violent actions because violence is a complex behavior that is impact by several variables, including parenting, experience, socialization in schools and churches, and neurological factors. Research tells us, however, that we are influenced by what we see, and often imitate what we see without even thinking about it.[30]

In a study of eight to twelve-year olds, one group of children was shown a film in which people used guns to shoot others, and the second group was shown a film without guns and shooting. Both groups were placed in spaces where they could play with anything in the room, including a disabled gun that had been "hidden" in a drawer. About 83 percent of the children found the gun. None of those who viewed the film *without* the gun played with it. Half of those who found the gun and saw the film *with* the gun, not only played with it, but 20 percent pulled the trigger multiple times, as they pretended to shoot playmates at close range.[31] Many assert that repeated exposure to violent images decreases empathy and increases one's appetite

25. Bhattacharjee, "How Does Your Child," para. 5–7.

26. Kamenetz, "Young Children," para 6.

27. Anderson and Jiang, "Teens, Social Media," para. 2, 3, 12–17.

28. Bushman and Anderson, "Understanding Causality," pp. 1816–18.

29. Huesmann, et al., "Early Exposure," pp. 208–19. Also see Savage and Yancy, Effects" for a meta-analysis.

30. Bargh's "Our Unconscious Mind" is a fascinating look at our unconscious minds and the science of behavior.

31. Lo Bue, "Violent Media," para. 4–9.

for instant gratification.[32] Other charge that since human beings are violent by nature, television, video games, and social media will forever reflect that nature.[33]

The way we are oriented to the world determines our conceptualization of empowerment and its right use. An orientation that envisions the individual as an organic part of a living and dynamic community is different from an orientation that envisions the individual as an entity that is existentially disconnected to others. In the first orientation, individuals learn that they are obligated to serve the ecological needs of community, be it local or global. In the second orientation, individuals learn that their obligations revolve around oneself. The American narrative embraces both orientations. Our public discourse often seems like that of a madman as we alternate between rhetoric filled with love of community and the desire to wisely steward creation, and rhetoric filled with narcissism and the desire to control and deplete all creation.

Our rhetorical capital and public discourse are in trouble partially because our narratives are often hypocritical and oppositional. Pulled in multiple directions by commercial propaganda, political diatribes, peer pressure, family dynamics, religious pontification, and social media, the first order of business in the restoration and refinement of our rhetorical capital is to study our own narratives, and to determine whether they are confederates, or ones that are truly authentic and aligned with our deepest sense of self and our highest sense of purpose.

32. See Gentile, *Media Violence and Children* and Withey and Abeles, *Television and Social Behavior.*

33. See Trend, *Myths about Media Violence*, pp. 31–36.

Chapter 11

A Rhetorical Conclusion

CONCEALING FROM OURSELVES

Rhetoric is the brick and mortar of our culture, as what comes out of our mouths builds the secular world and the spiritual spaces of our lives. The previous chapters have explored the ways in which we have and have not honored the gift of communication. Sometimes we have used our public discourse to unite, heal, and inspire each other to do our best. Sometimes we have used our words to create myths about each other, ruin reputations, and create obstacles to well-being. Sometimes we are very prophetic, and use our public platforms to alert us to certain threats to our civility and faith. Sometimes we use our public platforms to threaten public safety and people's lives. Sometimes we think about how well we have integrated our personal narratives, spirituality, and rhetorical capital. Sometimes we do not think about these things at all, and move mindlessly through our world and relationships.

This discussion has presented a case for why we cannot depend too much on certain institutions and entities to restore, build, and refine our rhetorical capital. While there are many people working in education, media, government, and religious ministries who are working very hard to improve the integrity and benevolence of our communication, they are typically not the one's dominating the conversation and policy-making in society or their own institutions. Given the intensity of partisan animosity in our public discourse, and given America's struggle to be humble and dispassionate about world domination, I believe that it is fair to make the following claims:

1. We cannot expect that every college and university will build and refine rhetorical capital in a systematic and thorough way because they
   often have agendas that do not well support curriculum and instruction that consistently, explicitly, and substantially fosters growth in
   students' epistemological beliefs, understanding and use of rhetoric,
   critical thinking, and critical reading as a developmental phenomenon. We can, however, expect that some instructors will improve their
   own instruction relative to enriching rhetorical capital, because they
   are personally motivated to do so and are supported by others.

2. We cannot depend on the media to build and refine rhetorical capital
   because the majority of mainstream media is controlled by people who
   want to maximize profits, even if it means catering to the masses who
   want spectacles and entertainment, not hard news and erudite analysis. Further, because media is largely owned by private corporations, it
   has an incentive to maximize the positive spin that news and editorials
   put on corporate capitalism, even when it is used in deadly ways. We
   can, however, expect that once in a while a dissenter or prophetic voice
   will stand up inside the news industry and call for his or her peers to
   be more honest and less biased in their reporting, because there are
   many journalists who still believe that they have a duty to protect and
   enlighten the public.

3. We cannot wholly rely on government leaders to build and refine
   rhetorical capital because too many elected officials and their staff
   members believe that aggressive rhetoric and dastardly discourse is a
   sign of power, and the thing that gets them elected. There will always
   be people who will vote for strongmen. There will always be people
   who will live by a dualistic and simplistic view of the world and its
   problems, who hate those who ask them to look too deeply at their
   values and challenge them to change. We can expect that on occasion
   a dissenter in high office will condemn dastardly discourse, because
   there have always been people in our government with courage and vision who speak truth to power—even if it means getting fired or forced
   to resign.

4. We dare not assume that all religious discourse is aimed at improving
   rhetorical capital, because it is often tainted by political and material
   ambitions, cultural biases, bigotry, and toxic theology. It often glori-
   fies manmade institutions, materialism, militancy, and the elevation of
   the individual at the expense of the masses. We can expect that some
   ministers and religious laypersons will contest the materialistic and
   tribalistic approach to God, because the legacy of such leaders is rich

and dynamic in the American experience, and because many people understand the relationship between the prophetic voice and society's finest examples of self-improvement and growth.

5. It is in our best interest to join the right bandwagon, and repair our public discourse, because a nation that cannot tell the truth, welcome diverse opinions, and think through propaganda, will collapse in its own decadence. Many of our narratives and myths are hurting us. Children who reflexively defend the existence Santa Claus when they are three years old are cute, but adults who reflexively defend the existence of God as Santa Claus, or the market as Santa Claus, or the government as Santa Claus are dangerous. They are dangerous because they reinforce the ideas that our "ultimate concern" is material, and that we are entitled to prosperity on our terms, even when those terms exploit workers, deprive the poor of basic needs, foster indifference to suffering and bigotry, and destroy the natural environment.

In March, 1968, about 13 weeks before he was assassinated, Robert Kennedy spoke before a university community about the war in Vietnam and making peace. He said, "I urge you to learn the harsh facts that lurk behind the mask of official illusion with which we have concealed our true circumstances, even from ourselves."[1] At the time Kennedy uttered those words, Americans were fighting a war in Vietnam under the illusion that the U.S. was winning, and under the illusion that our leaders had given us the full truth about U.S. motives to fight.

Fifty years later, Kennedy's words remind us that our true circumstance may not be as we may think. Our schools, colleges, and universities may not be doing their best to educate future scholars, professionals, and voters. Our news media may not be giving us the whole picture, nor reporting objectively. Our government officials may not care as much about the common citizen as they say they do. Our religious leaders may not be able to bear the weight of the cross, as they love the celebrity and wealth that comes of feeding us a steady diet theological happy meals that promise prosperity and world dominance. In addition, we may not be as helpless or as doomed as we sometimes feel, and we probably possess more talent and capacity to improve our lives that what we ever thought we had. In other words, the truth of circumstances cuts two ways; things may be more dismal than we have been led to believe, and at the same time, things may be brighter than what we have assumed.

---

1. Kennedy, R. F. "Conflict in Vietnam," para. 43.

Our true circumstance is similar to the true circumstances of all who have gone before us. Yes, we are struggling with our "ultimate concern." Yes, we are struggling with how to communicate with people who are ethnically, religiously, politically, economically, sexually, and educationally different from ourselves. Yes, we are finding it difficult to feel secure with opening our nation to our neighbors in need, and we are finding ourselves full of fears and insecurities that we do not even want to admit. Yes, as people who believe in a higher power, God, spirituality, and/or humanism, we are struggling with how to translate our beliefs into actions that mean something. Finally, like many who have gone before us, are we not struggling so feverishly because we have not yet learned to treasure that which cannot be taken or destroyed?

The good news is that there is much that we can do as individuals to increase our rhetorical capital and improve the quality of discourse in our own circles of influence. All of us have the potential to shift the narratives that drive our lives. An acquaintance, Steve, who owns a local tobacco shop, tells me it's a tough world, but believes it can change. He said candidly, "It's all about the man in the mirror. . .Lots of people look in the mirror and don't know how to fix things."[2] Sometimes the man in the mirror does not want to see what is there, or wants to deny what he sees. Steve noted that many people do not tell the truth because they are afraid people will get angry. He scoffs, "It's better to tell the truth and have people be mad for a little while, because in the long run it's better to have life based on reality."

IMPECCABLE

In his book about Toltec wisdom and how to free ourselves from self-destruction and enslavement to our own egos, Don Miguel Ruiz wrote in *The Four Agreements* that, "Your word is the power you have to create. Your word is the gift that comes directly from God. . .Regardless of what language you speak, your intent manifests through word. . ."[3] Ruiz invites us to be "impeccable" with our word, which means far more than saying what we mean, and meaning what we say.

2. "The Man in the Mirror" is a term used by Michael Jackson in his song (Epic Records, 1987) about homelessness and making social changes that begin with improving oneself. The phrase is also the title of a book written by Patrick Morley (Grand Rapids, MI: Zondervan, 1989) that explores how men can get out of the macho, super hero, rat-race, and into a more spiritually satisfying life.

3. Ruiz, *Four Agreements*, pp. 26–27.

The word impeccable comes from the Latin word "pecatus" which refers to sin. To be impeccable, therefore is to be without sin. Impeccable speech is abundant in gratitude, tenderness, charity, mercy, patience, respect, and affirmation of human dignity. Ruiz argues that words become sinful when we use them to shame, blame, ruin reputations, provoke violence, encourage hate, and spread false information.[4] Societies that glorify competition, dominance, and brute strength have little use for impeccable speech. The attributes of impeccable speech are often perceived as cowardly or effeminate. In society's that are very aggressive and competitive, impeccable speech is often counter cultural.

Impeccable speech is restorative and life-giving in at least three distinct ways. First, it offers adversaries an honorable way out of conflict. It offers reconciliation without imposing vengeful and crushing retaliations. It explores adversarial relationships with an open mind to the possibility that adversarial dynamics were created by oneself and not the other.

Second, impeccable speech has the potential to liberate us from the pain and anger. We often bring anguish upon ourselves when we verbally abuse others. Words often drive wedges between ourselves and those we love, because we are using them for the purposes of waxing our egos and not for the purpose of true communication. This is sometimes revealed when our words caused others to cry or shut down, and our reflexive response is to accuse others of being "too sensitive," or "always taking things the wrong way." What is "too sensitive?" "Too sensitive for who?" Sometimes the anger we feel when people get upset about the things we say is an invitation to think about our intentions for having a conversation in the first place.

Third, impeccable speech can be restorative and life-giving because impeccable speech is not infallible speech. It is possible to speak without sin and speak in error. With innocence and good intentions, we sometimes say things we believe are true and they are not. With good intentions, we sometimes chose indelicate words and accidentally hurt someone's feelings. Impeccable speech is not perfect speech. The impeccable listener allows for people to recover from words uttered in error, fear, and frustration. The impeccable speaker is humble enough to apologize and adjust his or her discourse.

OUR STORIES, OUR GLORIES

We all know what we are supposed to say when somebody asks us about who we are and what is the driving narrative of our life, right? The answer

4. Ibid, pp. 27–37.

depends on who is asking. If we are responding to a potential employer, we have a "you need to hire me right now" narrative; if we are courting a special someone, we have the "I will love and honor you forever" narrative; and, if we are speaking with a priest or minister, we get holy really fast. We have many narratives about who we are, and some may be fantasies, and some may be diametrically opposed to each other. The ones that can be the most problematic are the ones of which we are unaware. These can be problematic because we are typically not in control of them. They are frequently the ones that we activate without really thinking about what we are doing or saying, and *why* we are saying and doing these things; they are automatic, and sometimes reactionary.

A good place to begin the task of building and refining our own rhetorical capital and public discourse might be to identify our narratives. By placing our narratives under a microscope, we undertake a process that may be a first step in assessing our own authenticity, and answering the questions of whether we are who we think we are, and whether we are the person we want to be. The key elements of our narratives include:

- **A description of our origins**. This identifies our heritage in the historical sense, and identifies what we believe about our spiritual or existential origins. These things often reveal our attitude towards life and whether we see it as inherently sacred, or are ambivalent about any spiritual implications. We may consider how we situate ourselves among others, and whether cosmic or Earthly hierarchies and status are meaningful to our sense of self. This description also commonly references family and its unique culture.

- **An explanation of our purpose**. Again, this may speak to material considerations and address a sense of sacred purpose in life. The sacred purpose may be concerned with spiritual lessons, redemption, and one's evolution as a human being. In exploring our purpose, we might discover that we have material and spiritual purposes that are at odds with each other. Our sense of purpose reveals much about how we perceive our obligations to others. We may wrestle with purpose. Some posit that it exists at birth, while others hold that it is shaped over time by experience. Our sense of purpose might also illuminate the expectations and assumptions we have about the world. It also may reveal the distribution of realism and idealism in our world views.

- **A list of our values and why we hold these values above others**. Like the other items on this list, our values tell us something about how we see ourselves in relation to all others, including the natural environment. Like other items on the list, responses might vary depending on our moods and recent experiences. The listing of values is challenging because we often do not want to reveal what we treasure. It may be embarrassing to disclose our values. Full disclosure to others is not the point of the inventory. The objective of the exercise is to be honest with ourselves, and to thoroughly consider why we value as we do, and the implications of what we covet and hold dear.

- **A description of our adversaries and barriers**. This list revels obstacles—real or perceived—that we face as we make our way towards our goals and purposes. These may include external variables such as discrimination, cultural taboos, or bullies at work, and also include internal variables, such as lack of confidence, laziness, or cynicism. The description may lead us to consider how we face our adversaries, and how we rationalize our treatment of those who frustrate our ambitions or insult our identities and sense of purpose. Descriptions of adversaries and barriers may also lead us to think about our sense of entitlement and need to control things, and whether entitlement and control are doing us any good.

AUTHENTICITY AND DISSENT

Some people are in trouble because they have never thought about their narrative. Some are in trouble because they have competing narratives and they do not see that that the narratives are often irreconcilable. Some are in trouble because they are living somebody else's narrative, and they are sick from the inside out with an inauthenticity that leaves them dissatisfied with life for reasons they do not understand. Some avoid trouble by being mindful of the narratives they embrace, and by deliberately cultivating only those thoughts and actions that are aligned with their "ultimate concerns."

The minute we are born—and sometimes even before we are born—others begin to construct our narrative. As mysterious facets of our personhood that were woven into our chemistry while in the womb emerge in our youth, we begin to sense "ultimate purpose" and feel ourselves drawn to certain experiences and commitments. If we are awake, we become acutely aware of the difference between the thing inside of us that makes us feel alive, purposeful, authentic, and whole, and the thing outside of us that makes us feel desperate for air, lost, phony, and incomplete. If we are asleep, we may dream that we are alive, purposeful, authentic, and whole, only to awaken to a great deal of unhappiness and beliefs that make no sense.

The authenticity of our narratives and the decency of our discourse sometimes depends on our willingness to dissent from popular opinion and prevailing norms. Without dissent, discourse readily becomes an echo chamber. True discourse welcomes dissent, because diversity of experience and opinion are organic features in the human experience, and with an understanding of diverse experience comes the wisdom that truth itself is sometimes paradoxical in its complexity. True discourse is motivated by the desire to learn from others and is made possible by our willingness to put the ego on simmer and be humbled by our own ignorance.

Educators, journalists, government officials, and religious clerics are in a good position to see where and how discourse gets dastardly. Their professions deeply immerse them in exchanges of ideas and persuasive rhetoric, and so they learn to detect important differences in the quality of communication, hidden intentions, and the effects of word choice, tone, accuracy, and thoroughness. Their dissent—their courageous refusal to go along with crowd on mediocre education, verbally bullying in the press, tolerance of bi-partisan political tribalism, and toxic theology—has a special potency because they are experts and authorities in their fields, and thus enjoy a larger measure of credibility than the average American. They are not very helpful in the cause of rescuing discourse from indecency and incivility, however, when they refuse to speak publicly to correct erroneous assertions, and confront abusive rhetoric in their professional domain.

A democratic society does not merely tolerate dissent, it creates space for it. It respects the dissenter's capacity to bring to the discussion things that might otherwise have been ignored. Dissenters cause us to pause the conversation and think about what has and has not been said. Think, for instance, about a conversation in which you, the reader, disciplined yourself to remain silent when somebody was saying things that were untrue or deeply offense, and you willed yourself to hear what that person said, and considered it from their point of view. Think about what happened to your word choice, the volume of your voice, and the pause between statements. In this instance, was there more room for compassion, more patience with ambiguity, and more humility in your approach to truth?

Silence can be a form of dissent. In a culture that daily tells us to be combative, aggressive, and reactionary when people lie to us, insult us, or say things that are offensive, those who do not comply are dissenters. They have dissented from the normal practice of verbal confrontation, and created space to listen, be thoughtful, and respond with care and respect. The heat in an argument often cools when people say, "I am listening; I see what you are saying; and, I need some time to think about it." Doing this habitually may help us overcome the compulsion to constantly assert or defend our egos.

FACING DEMONS

Those who like power appreciate the capacity of echo chambers to mesmerize and tranquilize audiences. Being able to convince others that society is living out one narrative that is benevolent and fair to all when in fact it is living out a narrative that is malevolent and unjust is quite a feat, but people around the world do it every day. The unawareness and denial of our circumstances makes it easy for us to go on with life focused on the mundane, and not know how much the mundane diverts attention away from our "ultimate concerns."

We may better understand our narratives and "ultimate concerns" by which we live by listening to what is inside us. Our bodies and our minds are always talking to us, so listening to "the within" is important. The irritation we feel when people are talking for the sake of talking tells us that we are not spiritually, emotionally, or intellectually nourished by the discourse. The fatigue and irritation we feel when people lie to us and chronically make excuses for bad behavior suggests that we may need to set boundaries around who we let into our lives. The anger we feel when others assault our reputations or misrepresent us warns us not to take our egos too seriously, so that anger and retaliation do not consume charity and reason. The confusion we experience as our leaders take us down the rabbit holes of deceit, duplicity, and denial tells us that we need to work harder on getting the facts, and that we need to teach our children how to find truth in a world where people lie a lot.

Every day, we experience bodily and psychological cues that we are hungry for rhetoric that refreshes our humanity and fills us with truth and hope. Many of us were never taught how to pay attention to such cues. Instead we were taught how to ignore and suppress our feelings, and to displace our discomforts, anger, sadness, and fear into compulsive behaviors that soothed us. We learned to misread feelings and not trust our guts when people spit in our faces and told us it was snowing.

Some of us learned to feel guilty and inferior because our narrative did not match everyone else's narrative. We kept our selves in psychological hell for years because we internalized someone else's agenda for our lives that was oppositional to the one we felt was our own. Some of us were so obsessed with pleasing others that we embraced political correctness even when we knew it was madness. Some of us were destroyed by demons who told us that our prophetic voices were stupid, arrogant, and impractical when they were not. Despite our faith that God endowed us with dignity and sacred purpose, some of us allowed others to intimidate us. Some confused piety with acquiescence and did not speak up when we should have.

The fact that many of us were never taught how to read physical and psychological cues is tragic, because it leaves us so very vulnerable to soul noir and the abuses of others. In our world, people make fortunes by studying our behavior, attitudes, and values, and then using the data to modify and control our political, social, and consumer behavior. This is no myth. Psychologists learned in the 1940s and 1950s that people's habits and beliefs are not always rational, and that we often chase things because they sparkle and shine.[5] Subsequent to the digital revolution, the game of making rhetoric and propaganda sparkle and shine has gotten more sophisticated. Most of us are not well prepared to distinguish silver from silicate.

The digital age has profoundly comprised, if not eradicated the private life. We leave trails of ourselves when we surf the Internet, and so should not be surprised to find that the ads that appear as we read seem to have read our minds and know exactly what we want. In a world where predatory capitalism is afoot, new entrepreneurs are licking their chops. Eliot Shefler is a co-founder of The Spinner, a website that sells digital manipulation services. For a fee, The Spinner will deliver articles to people as they view their social media. The articles are presented as random pop-ups, except there is nothing random about it.[6] The articles are based on the purchaser's targeted behavior modification. The most popular topic for the article blitz is sex, as customers want to fire up someone else's libido.

Every time we use the Internet, hundreds of digital trackers are stalking our moves. Every search phrase, every click, and every minute we linger on a particular site tells those who use the data something about who we are, what captures our interest, and how we are willing to spend our money. Tracking is an easy way for companies to identify potential customers, but it is also a means of prying into our private lives.[7] Our Internet use is raw data, and when we generate raw data, we do not always know where it is going, who pays for it, and how it will be used. The global nature of the Internet avails our data to people in foreign nations, friend and foe alike.

In closing, this part of the book is supposed to be where authors tell readers how they can save the world, or live happily ever after. My apologies,

---

5. See Packard's *Hidden Persuaders* and Issenberg's *Victory Lab*, an exploration of how academics, political advisors and ad executives use data to package and promote political campaigns and candidates.

6. Olsen, "For $29 Dollars," para. 1–3.

7. See Angwin's *Dragnet Nation* and Zuboff's *Age of Surveillance Capitalism*. Both raise profound questions about what it means to be human in the digital age dominated by private interests. Brittany Kaiser's *Targeted* documents Cambridge Analytica's success with harvesting personal digital data and how Facebook and other entities used the data to manipulate voter outcomes in the U.S. and abroad.

as this is not an authentic or honest way to end the discussion. Whether human beings will prevail despite global warming, religious and ethnic bigotry, epidemics, famine, and men's endless lust for wars that impoverish their nations and their souls is beyond my knowledge. History teaches us that great catastrophes have left remnants to begin anew. Maybe that is our future. At present, no critical mass is in place to bring partisan lawmakers together to set aside egos and special interests, and to collaborate with empathy and good will with global leaders to avert disasters on the horizon. There exists no critical mass to revise and rejuvenate higher education and mass media, and rescue them from mediocrity and corruption. There are only individuals who may or may not be willing or able to create a critical mass.

Whether we will be part of a critical mass that beats drums for tribal wars and material empires, or be part of a critical mass for peace, compassion, and modesty of want depends on our narrative. It is important to know who we are, and to distinguish our voice from the dazzling but deadly confederates. Exploring the narratives that drive our lives will probably not radically change the direction of global economics and political agendas, but it might change the way we, as individuals, think about and participate in these things. It is also possible that in owning one's narrative, one achieves a spiritual and psychological freedom and solace not formerly known.

To jump start an inquiry into our own narratives and approach to public discourse, chapter twelves offers inventories that may be used for private personal reflection, and for personal reflection coupled with discussion in clinical or study group sessions. The inventories focus on our narratives, values, perceptions, and behavior. It may be helpful to keep a journal that documents conversations and reactions to rhetoric and public discourse, so that when one completes the inventories, one has points of reference. Responses to the inventory are useful only to the extent that they are honest. Our responses might indicate we need to learn more about the world, or that we might benefit from tempering our egos.

The next chapter will also provide a template for *Across the Aisle*, an activity that can be used in classrooms and religious retreats. *Across the Aisle* is an exercise designed to identify the stereotypes and assumptions that we make about our "adversaries," and to explore how those stereotypes and assumptions impact our sense of reality and communication with others. *Across the Aisle* is different from the inventories, as it will initiate and facilitate not only personal reflection, but dialogue between diverse groups. In addition, whereas the inventories invite participants to select options in a "forced-response" format (in this case a Likert scale), *Across the Aisle* invites open-ended responses. *Across the Aisle* requires many hours to complete and is intended for in depth discussions with others that is guided by a moderator who keeps track of time, and intervenes when participants stray from the topic or rules. As a classroom experience, *Across the Aisle* could take two or three days. As a retreat, it could take a whole day, or be facilitated over two days and supplemented by speakers, films and religious ceremonies.

On some level, we all know that we can change the channel, but that does not change the truth. In looking at our rhetorical capital and public discourse from the perspective of the individual and the institution, it is apparent that we have many, many opportunities to improve the quality of our lives by improving the way we speak and listen to each other. We have the occasion, here and now, to think about our rhetoric and discourse, and whether it is hurting or helping us. We have the occasion to face our myths, fears, mistrust, and hate, and to be inspired by our spiritual and personal gifts. We have always had these occasions. On some level, I believe we know that we will not die not from our fear, mistrust, hatred, and ignorance of the world, but from the excuses we made to do nothing about them.

Chapter 12

Inventories and Across the Aisles

PURPOSE AND DIRECTIONS

The purpose of this inventory is to assist individuals with understanding the narratives by which they live, and to help them reconcile their beliefs, habits, and attitudes with the values they espouse. The inventory will help people explore stereotypes and assumptions about others, determine whether they are fair, and explore their psychological sources and functions. This inventory may illuminate the source of personal confusion or conflict, and may help people think about alternatives to the way they consume information and communicate with others. By comparing one's self-rating with ratings others give them on the same items, individuals may gain insights to what may be at the root of difficulties they have with communication and relationships.

The ultimate purpose of these tools is to create interest in routine introspection. Without deep meditations on what lies within us , the inventories may be little more than mechanical devices that fine-tune personal management. Ideally, we want more than self-management. Ideally, we want to be transformed so that we always listen to the thing inside of us that tugs us away from our egos. Ideally, we want to attend the wonder and urging beyond the senses, where with new eyes we may see the sacred waiting to be acknowledged in people and all creation.

The *Narrative Inventory* is focused on only our narratives. The *Rhetorical Capital Inventory* is organized into five parts, each with a single focal point: Beliefs; Knowing; Listening; Skills; and, Habits. Each category has eight items or statements. Participants are to select a number one through five that best represents their response to the item or statement. The rating scale is the same for both inventories and all categories. Each part of the inventory is followed by reflection questions aimed at helping participants explore tangents or to dig deeper into the nuance of one's response.

RATING SCALE

1. Strongly Disagree
2. Mildly Disagree
3. Equally Agree and Disagree
4. Mildly Agree
5. Strongly Agree

THE NARRATIVE INVENTORY

1. In my narrative, I see my origins primarily as spiritual
2. In my narrative, I see my origins as primarily material and historical
3. In my narrative, I see my purposes as primarily spiritual
4. In my narrative, I see my purpose as primarily physical and material
5. In my narrative, people must always come before things
6. In my narrative, I answer only to God for my conduct and speech
7. In my narrative, I answer only to society's laws for my conduct and speech
8. In my narrative, it is my responsibility to see that truth prevails in society
9. In my narrative, it is acceptable to impose conditions on my caring for others
10. In my narrative, spiritual ideals must be subordinate to practical needs for survival
11. In my narrative, people who do not have faith in God are a problem
12. In my narrative, people who are not patriotic are a problem

Follow-Up Questions for World View

a. What do your responses suggest about your connection to the material world?

b. What was your comfort level in responding to the questions, and does that reveal anything about your level of confidence, self-understanding, or fear of judgment?

c. What do your responses suggest about the conditions you impose on relationships?

d. When you think about your origins and purpose, do you feel these are tentative and uncertain, or absolute and certain?

THE RHETORICAL CAPITAL INVENTORY

Beliefs

1. I believe leaders have a moral obligation to tell the truth

2. I believe that leaders have a special obligation to speak diplomatically and respectfully

3. I believe that corporations should be held to high standards of transparency in business

4. I believe that government should be held to high standards of transparency

5. I believe that it is important to hold people accountable for political correctness

6. I believe people generally tell the truth

7. I believe that democracy is affected by the quality of our public discourse

8. I believe that people have enough common sense to figure out when someone is lying or manipulating them with propaganda, and do not need much education to effectively think critically

Follow-Up Questions for Beliefs

a. Do you use communication skills to determine whether someone is fit to be a leader, and if so what skills are important, and if not, why?

b. What were your visceral reactions to the statements about transparency, what do you think fuels these reactions, and what are your reactions to people who do not share your beliefs about transparency?

c. What do your responses reveal about your ability to trust that others are committed to society's well-being, and how does that trust level affect you and the way you relate to others?

d. What do your responses imply about your confidence in a democratic way of life, and does your confidence level impact the way you participate in civic activities, such as voting and volunteering?

Knowing

1. I know a lot about the world's people, history, cultures, and current events

2. I know when people are lying to me

3. When see or hear something I do not know about, I research it

4. I know the difference between superficial reporting and scholarly research

5. I can easily spot gaps in information in news reports and why it matters

6. I know what research tells us about the effects of social media

7. I know how reading and rhetoric are taught at all levels from K-12 and in post-secondary education, and I believe these are well-taught at present

8. I know how to assess whether a website is credible

Follow-Up Questions for Knowing

a. When responding to these questions, did you ever question your honesty or accuracy, and if so what do you think that indicates?

b. When responding to these questions, did you experience any feelings about your level of education, and if so, do those feelings impact the way you relate to others who have less education than you, and others who have more education you?

c. What do your responses indicate about the depth of information you seek about the world?

d. What do your responses suggest about your level of vulnerability to propaganda?

Listening

1. I give equal respect to those who share my opinions and to those who have opinions different from my own

2. I listen extra carefully when speakers are discussing complex ideas and things that are outside my areas of expertise

3. When people start arguing in my presence, I try to make peace and encourage others to listen respectfully to each other

4. I am sensitive to my own biases when I listen or I read something

5. Most people would say that I am a very good listener

6. I consciously tell myself to be tolerant and patient so I can listen respectfully to people who are verbally abusive and vulgar

7. I am very sensitive to the unspoken values that are embedded in advertising and entertainment

8. I believe there is a time and place for vulgarity and aggressive language, so people should get used to hearing it

Follow-Up Questions for Listening

a. When you responded to these questions, were you aware of an "inner dialogue" with yourself, and if so, what does that reveal about how you listen?

b. What do your responses reveal about the conditions you apply to the quality of your listening and attention?

c. What do your responses suggest about how you might improve the quality of your listening?

d. What do your responses suggest about the strengths you bring to listening?

Skills

1. I am very good at judging the intentions of those who speak in all formats and venues

2. I can easily differentiate between relevant and irrelevant rhetoric

3. I can easily differentiate between biased and objective discourse

4. I can easily differentiate between strong and weak evidence offered for assertions

5. I can easily differentiate between fair and unfair assertions

6. I am very proficient with identifying implications and making inferences

7. I can easily detect the meaning and significance of assertions

8. I can easily tell when a person's response to a question really does not answer the question

Follow-Up Questions for Skills

a. When responding to these items, did you think about examples that might represent evidence for your response, and if so, what did you discover?

b. What do your responses suggest about the strengths and limitations of your skills?

c. Do you think you have a moral obligation to refine and cultivate these skills; if so why; if not, why?

d. When responding to these items, did you wish that you were better at some skills, and if so, do you know how you might improve the skills you want to improve and/or get assistance in doing so?

Habits

1. Every day, I reserve at least 30 minutes for quite time alone

2. I consistently seek the company of people who help me make sense of news and rhetoric

3. I am comfortable with dissent, and consistently and openly challenge people when they spread false information, engage in hate speech, or abuse others with words

4. I am always aware of how my choices in words, tone, and body language impact my conversations with others

5. Each month, I read at least one book that teaches me about how the world works and/or how I can be a better person in difficult times

6. I consistently regard my communication as an expression of my spirituality and/or humanity

7. I refrain from taking differences in opinion personally

8. I frequently reflect on the alignment between my values, my "ultimate concern" and how I communicate with others

Follow-Up Questions for Habits

a. What do your responses indicate about the quality of your reflective or contemplative life?

b. What do your responses suggest about your efforts to learn about the world?

c. How does your comfort level with dissent impact your relationships and sense of integrity?

d. Given your habits, would you say that you regard communication as a ministry and why?

General Reflection

a. What do the responses to these 40 questions suggest about the strengths and limitations that you bring to communication with others?

b. What do the responses to these 40 questions reveal about how you select and digest information in news and social media, and what do they suggest about your knowledge of the world?

c. What do the responses to these 40 questions suggest about where you place responsibility for miscommunication or difficult discourse with others?

d. What do the responses to these 40 questions reveal about your "inner dialogue," personal narrative, and willingness to correct the dastardliness within yourself?

e. Have your responses to these 40 questions impacted your thoughts and opinions about the needs of the common citizen relative to rhetorical knowledge and skill, or your thoughts and opinions about the obligations of secular officials, journalists, educators, and religious leaders relative to their use of rhetoric and engagement in public discourse?

ACROSS THE AISLE

Across the Aisle blends cognitive and humanist theories of behavior and intervention. The cognitive theory of behavior offered an alternative to the psychodynamic theories of behavior, which postulated that behaviors and dysfunctions in personality were the product of the subconscious, the id, ego, and superego. The cognitive theory asserts that a person's thoughts and beliefs are at the root of pathological behavior and psychological distress, and at the foundation of change and wellness.

Pioneers of the cognitive approach to behavior and therapy argued that once individuals interrogated their own belief and thoughts, they were able to access the accuracy and utility of their beliefs and thoughts.[1] By changing beliefs and thoughts that were inaccurate and dysfunctional, individuals also changed the behaviors linked to the beliefs and thoughts. The cognitive approach differs from a behavioral management approach. The cognitive approach to reducing and controlling anger, for example focus on discerning the "why" of anger and violence, and helps individuals change thinking that is erroneous, destructive and self-defeating.[2] Anger management, the behavioral approach, focuses on identifying triggers of anger and violence, coping mechanisms, and relaxation techniques.

The humanistic theory posits that all people are concerned with existential questions concerning the purpose of their lives, the autonomous

1. Beck, "Cognitive Therapy," pp. 368–71.
2. Walker and Bright, "Cognitive Therapy for Violence," pp. 174–81.

construction of identity or self-actualization, and transpersonal experiences, which concern spirituality and religion.[3] Humanistic therapy helps individuals explore their sense of self, and the integrity of their own their beliefs and actions relative to their existential and spiritual convictions. In *Across the Aisle*, reflections on the moral consequences of one's thinking is essential to understanding the extent to which individuals' approach to public discourse and communication are fair, and are aligned with one's beliefs about one's role in the wellness of others. The wellness of others and the fairness of one's treatment of others are two core values represented in humanistic theories of psychology.[4]

The purpose of *Across the Aisle* is to identify our stereotypes of and assumptions about others, and to explore how they impact our communication and public discourse. The aim is also to have participants examine how their beliefs and concerns are very close to, or identical to the beliefs and concerns of their "adversaries." At the end of this exercise, individuals will be able to make summative observations about their beliefs, attitudes, openness, fairness, and effectiveness as listeners and communicators. In addition, they will be able to identify some strategies for improving their communication and regard for others.

As the goal of the activity is to improve communication between "adversaries," it is expected that participants in *Across the Aisle* will be individuals who have diverse and/or polarizing beliefs and attitudes. In this example, the Blue Group represents Liberals and Progressives on the political spectrum, while the Red Group Represents Conservatives. Having a relatively equal number of people in each group is helpful, and limiting the number in groups to five or six participants is ideal as it gives individuals adequate time to speak. It is possible to facilitate larger numbers of participants by subdividing Groups Blue and Red for the break-out sessions. All groups and subgroups must, however, be part of the all-participant discussion that concludes the exercise.

Across the Aisle requires the moderation of someone who is professionally trained in facilitating intensive group work and discussion. This could be a religious cleric, teacher, therapist, consultant, or social worker. As *Across the Aisle* is an intense encounter with oneself and others, it has the potential to spark arguments. It is recommended that participants and facilitators make a commitment to the following four rules before undertaking the activity:

3. Schneider and Leitner, "Humanistic Psychotherapy," pp. 949–57.
4. Duff, Rubenstein, and Prilleltensky, "Wellness and Fairness," pp. 128–36.

- Participants must make a commitment to devote the full amount of time required for the activity. Participating for only a part of the exercise is disrupting to others, and does not give participants the full measure of what can be learned and experienced in the exercise.

- Participants must help others to generate fair and thorough rules for listening and speaking, and follow those rules once consensus has been reached.

- Participants must commitment to keeping an open mind throughout the exercise.

- Participants must honor confidentiality about what happens and what is said during the activity, keeping in mind the importance of respecting others' reputations.

MAPPING THE ACTIVITY

The preliminary step in *Across the Aisle* is to plan the event, and determine whether there are enough professional facilitators to keep people comfortable and focused. If this activity is offered as a religious retreat or organizational event, it may be wise to announce it many weeks in advance, and have descriptions of the event available so potential participants can determine their level of interest and commitment to the event. Chose an appropriate space for the event. Ideally, the space has quite breakout rooms for small groups, a large room for assemblies, a place to prepare and serve snacks and meals, adequate rest room facilities, and a place where people are not likely to become distracted by phone calls, traffic, or other events in shared spaces. It may also be wise to offer separate events for different age groups. Children may be able to complete the tasks in *Across the Aisle*, but their concerns may radically differ from adults and older teens.

The first step of the event concerns introductions and logistics. Begin the day by gathering all participants together for an introduction to the activity. This introduction may offer a few words about who is sponsoring the event and why. Next, each person in the large assembly may be invited to introduce himself or herself, and to briefly report why they decided to enroll in this activity. After that, individuals will be organized into break out groups. In this example, individuals are called to self-identify as "Blue" or "Red" depending on their perceptions of their own political philosophy and convictions. The process of self-selection for groups may be facilitated with a guide for people's decisions. The guide might present two columns of traditional characteristics and beliefs, one that represents liberal traditions, the other that represents conservative traditions. For example, the liberal (Blue) column might list the following:

- Supports multi-culturalism in public education

- Supports woman's right to terminate pregnancy

- Supports tuition-free college

- Advocates expansion of public services such as health and child care

- Supports tax increases for the wealthiest 10 percent

- Supports a ban on semi-automatic rifles

- Opposes idea that corporations are entitled to same rights as individuals (such as free speech though campaign donations)

- Wants amnesty for all undocumented emigrants to U.S.

Naturally, the conservative column (Red) may have statements that are the opposite of the statements in the liberal column. The self-selection process must be void of judgment, and it is not a time for debating what it means to be liberal or conservative. There may be several people who find themselves torn between the groups, as they are liberal on some issues and conservative on others. Individuals should be encouraged to select the group with which they generally identify. They may also be encouraged to consider who they voted for in the last election to get some sense of their preferences.

Before individuals break out into their groups for group activities, the facilitators may review the day's schedule and general rules of the facility. The introduction should alert participants to the fixed rules regarding group sharing time in the large group assembly, and allow for participants to add rules if they want to add them. In addition to the four rules earlier mentioned, rules may address how much time individual get to speak, whether group members may ask questions in breakout sessions, what it means to listen with respect, whether electronic devices should be permitted, and what the secretaries and reporters should do. Rules should be posted either on poster paper or on a screen in the general assembly room.

The second step in *Across the Aisle* is Session One. Here, individuals gather with their group (Blue or Red) for the first break-out session. Each group must select a secretary who will keep notes for the whole group. This person may or may not also be the reporter who will present group findings during the large assembly. In Session One, small groups will generate a list of all the stereotypes that they believe people associate with *their group*, and will also offer some insights as to where those stereotypes come from. They may make notes on why the stereotypes are fair or unfair, and how they think the stereotypes impact communication between their group and the group's adversaries. This session may be followed by a brief refreshment break.

The third step in *Across the Aisle* is to continue the small group activity, and complete Session Two. In this next round, participants will identify stereotypes that they have of *their adversaries*, or the other group. They will make note of why these stereotypes exist, whether they are fair or unfair, and how these stereotypes might impact communication between the two groups. Again, the secretary keeps notes on findings and thoughts.

The fourth step in *Across the Aisle* is time for each person in each group to quietly reflect on what they have learned so far, and perhaps to make notes on things they would like to learn more about. This silent time is for thinking about which stereotypes are unique to groups and which they have in common. This is a time also to meditate on what has been easy and what has been difficult to think and talk about and why. This reflection will help participants complete the last exercise of the whole event, and so they are encouraged to take notes on their thoughts.

The fifth step is for each group to finalize the list of stereotypes as generated in Session One and Two, and be sure that the list is manageable. For example, if there were dozens of stereotypes and assumptions that surfaced, perhaps it would be helpful to list only the top four or five items. Notes that speculate on what motivates the presumed beliefs and attitudes of each group should be recorded, as these may represent assumptions that need to be discussed when both groups gather to share their findings. Each group should select a reporter. A luncheon may fit neatly into the day after this step.

The six step is to gather all groups together for a presentation of findings. The moderator calls upon one group at a time to present their list of stereotypes of *the other group*. Each group gets equal time. No one is permitted at this time to speak except the reporter, so responses and questions will have to wait until a later step. The participants are encouraged to take notes as the reporters are presenting their findings. They may or may not offer much explanation for why the stereotypes exist, but they are allowed to report questions that their groups raised. Each group presents their findings without interruption, and the moderator may determine (for the sake of time management), to limit reports to four or five key findings.

The seventh step in *Across the Aisle* is for all participants to gather for a short structured personal reflection guided by reflection questions to be discussed. This is a quiet exercise and time for introspection, and may be followed by a short break. The prompts for reflection may be written or posted and may include:

1. What, if anything, did the stereotypes of each of these groups have in common in terms of content and rationale for the stereotype?

2. What, if anything, does each group have in common relative to concerns about society, the future, and their personal well-being?

3. What did you learn today about stereotypes, trust, fear, assumptions, and truth?

4. What would you like to change about yourself, so that you are more approachable to others, or so that you improve your communication skills?

The eighth step in *Across the Aisle* is the actual all-participant discussion based on the reflection questions. The moderator will take responses for one prompt/question at a time, and then allow for others to ask questions or add a comment. The moderator is responsible for keeping people focused, so that all questions in the reflection may be addressed adequately. The participants may raise their hands to make a contribution, so group reporters need not speak for others in this step. It is very important to have enough time for the last two questions, as these are central to the purpose of the activity as a whole. It is essential to manage time well, so that all participants feel like their voice was respected. A sample schedule for the one-day event is as follows:

- 8:00–9:00 AM: Welcome and Introduction (Step 1)

- 9:00–9:15 AM: Break to break out spaces

- 9:15–10:00 AM: Breakout Session I "Identify the Stereotypes of My Group" (Step 2)

- 10:00–10:45 AM: Breakout Session II "Identify Stereotypes of Other Group" (Step 3)

- 10:45–11:00 AM: Refreshment Break

- 11:00–11:30 AM: Reflection on Findings "What Do We See Here?" (Step 4)

- 11:30–12:00 Noon: Group Finalizes List of Stereotypes for Both Groups (Step 5)

- 12:00–1:00 PM: Lunch

- 1:00- 2:30 PM: All Assembly Discussion. First group reporter presents group findings without interruption, the second group reporter presents group findings without interruption (Step 6)

- 2:30–2:45 PM: All assembly reflection (pair-shares may be allowed) "What do these groups have in common relative to values, attitudes, concerns and needs?" (Step 7)

- 2:45–3:00 PM: Refreshment Break

- 3:00–4:00 or 4:30 PM: All assembly share thoughts on common ground, what they learned, and what changes people would like to make in their own attitudes and behavior (Step 8)

It is possible to condense this activity into a half-day event, but in doing so, the quality of the reflection and group discussion might be compromised. It is also possible to extend this activity into more than one day. An overnight retreat, for example, might allow time for a prayer service, a reconciliation ritual, recreation, or a film and subsequent discussion. An overnight might also permit individuals to engage in private intensive conversations with peers, pastors, or counselors. Local community members, professors, pastors, business leaders, and journalists might also participate as guest speakers to address special concerns, especially if recent events, such as killings, vandalism, or verbal confrontations have recently occurred locally.

The inventories and exercises offered in this text are not intended to be a substitute for professional therapy, or for post-secondary course work in critical thinking, media and ethics, or other social and critical studies. They may, however, be useful in helping individuals see the value of therapy or spiritual advising, and they may be helpful in personal meditations and prayer.

It takes more than will power to rescue dignity, decency, and civility from dastardly discourse. It takes a transformation of one's personal narrative, whereby one's ego is subordinate to causes that are greater than ourselves, and whereby our material wants are minimal and our spiritual wants are great. The transformation ideally leaves us humbled by our ignorance, more empathetic towards our adversaries, and more willing to contest the use of public platforms and venues to disseminate lies, hatred, and mindless materialism. Where transformations are sincere and greater causes occupy the whole of our hearts, we ourselves would not permit dastardly discourse to soil the tongue.

Bibliography

Abrams, Floyd. *Friend of the Court: On the Front Lines of the First Amendment.* New Haven, CT: Yale University Press, 2013.

Adams, James. "For Harold Morris, Its Lies, Damned Lies, and Photography." *The Globe and Mail*, May 8, 2018. https://www.theglobeandmail.com/arts/for-errol-morris-its-lies-damned-lies-and-photography/article4200452/.

Ahmad, Mahmood. "U.S. Think Tanks and the Politics of Expertise: Role, Value, and Impact." *The Political Quarterly* 79, No. 4 (2008) 529–555.

Aiello, Thomas. "Constructing 'Godless Communism': Religion, Politics, and Popular Culture, 1954–1960." *Americana: The Journal of American Popular Culture (1900-present)* 4, no. 1 (2005). http://www.americanpopularculture.com/journal/articles/spring_2005/aiello.htm.

Aikman, David. *A Man of Faith: The Spiritual Journey of George W. Bush.* Nashville, TN: W. Publishing Group, 2004.

Alexander, Patricia A. The Path to Competence: A lifespan Development Perspective on Reading. *Journal of Literacy Research* 37, no. 4 (2005) 413–36.

Alger, Dean E. *The Media and Politics.* Belmont, CA: Wadsworth, 1996.

Ali, Lorraine. "At the Democratic Debates, CNN Set the Trap. But Blame the Candidates for Taking the Bait." *Los Angeles Times*, August 1, 2019. https://www.latimes.com/entertainment-arts/tv/story/2019-08-01/democratic-debates-cnn-detroit-trap-bait.

Alterman, Eric. *What Liberal Media?* New York, NY: Basic, 2003.

———. *When Presidents Lie: A History of Official Deception and its Consequences.* New York, NY: Viking, 2004.

American Academy of Arts and Sciences. "National Endowment for the Humanities (NEH) Funding Levels." Cambridge, MA: American Academy of Arts and Sciences, Funding Indicators, (2018). https://www.humanitiesindicators.org/content/indicatorDoc.aspx?i=75.

American Civil Liberties Union. "Separation of Families by the Numbers." (2019). https://www.aclu.org/issues/immigrants-rights/immigrants-rights-and-detention/family-separation.

American Council of Trustees and Alumni. *A Crisis in Civics Education.* American Council of Trustees and Alumni, Washington, D.C., 2016. https://www.nationalreview.com/2017/03/americans-history-civics-knowledge-education-federal-government/.

———. *What Will They Learn? A Survey of Core Requirements of our Nation's Colleges and Universities, 2018–2019*. Washington, D. C. (2019). https://www.goacta.org/publications/what-will-they-learn-2018–19-survey-on-core-requirements.

Anderson, Lorin W. and David R. Krathwohl, eds. *A Taxonomy for Teaching, Learning and Assessing*. London: Pearson, 2000.

Anderson, Matthew. "Evangelical and Catholics after Trump." *America* 219, no. 10 (2018)18–23.

Anderson, Monica and Jingjing Jiang. "Teens, Social Media & Technology, 2018." Pew Research Center. (May 31, 2018). https://www.pewinternet.org/2018/05/31/teens-social-media-technology-2018/.

Angwin, Julie. *Dragnet Nation: A Quest for Privacy, Security, and Freedom in a World of Relentless Surveillance*. New York, NY: Times, 2014.

Applebaum, Yoni. "'I Alone Can Fix it." *The Atlantic*. (July 21, 2016). https://www.theatlantic.com/politics/archive/2016/07/trump-rnc-speech-alone-fix-it/492557/.

Arum, Richard and Josipa Roska. *Academically Adrift: Limited Learning on College Campuses*. Chicago, IL: University of Chicago Press, 2011.

Assembly Bill 705, Sess. 2017, (Cal. 2017). https://leginfo.legislature.ca.gov/faces/billNavClient.xhtml?bill_id=201720180AB705.

Associated Press. "Protests at UC Davis Lead to Cancelling of Speech by Breitbart's Milo Yinnopoulos, Who Slams University." *Los Angeles Times*. (January 14, 2017). https://www.latimes.com/local/lanow/la-me-uc-davis-protest-20170113-story.html.

Association of American Colleges and Universities. "Statement on Liberal Education" Washington, D.C.: Association of American Colleges and Universities. (1998). https://www.aacu.org/about/statements/liberal-education.

———. "VALUE Rubric: Reading." Association of American Colleges and Universities. (2017). https://www.aacu.org/value/rubrics/reading.

Astin, Alexander W. "Making Sense out of Degree Completion Rates." *Journal of College Student Retention: Research, Theory & Practice* 7, no. 1 (2005) 5–17.

Attewell, Paul, David Lavin, Thurston Domina, and Tania Levey. "New Evidence on College Remediation." *The Journal of Higher Education* 77, no. 5 (2006) 886–924.

Attkisson, Sharyl. *The Smear: How Shady Political Operatives and Fake News Control What You See, Think, and How You Vote*. New York, NY: HarperCollins, 2017.

Axelrod, Alan and Charles Phillips, eds. "Religious Wars." *Encyclopedia of Wars Vol.3* (2004)1484–85.

Axtell, James. "The Death of the Liberal Arts College." *History of Education Quarterly* 11, no. 4 (1971) 339–52.

Bacevich, Andrew J. *American Empire. The Realities and Consequences of U.S. Diplomacy*. Cambridge, MA: Harvard University Press, 2002.

Baer, Justin D., Andrea L. Cook, and Stéphane Baldi. *The Literacy of America's College Students*. Washington, D.C.: American Institutes for Research, 2006. https://www.air.org/sites/default/files/downloads/report/The20Literacy20of 20Americas20College20Students_final20report_0.pdf.

Bagdkian, Ben. *The New Media Monopoly*. Boston, MA: Beacon, 2004.

Bailard, Catie Snow. "Corporate Ownership and News Bias Revisited: Newspaper Coverage of the Supreme Court's *Citizen's United* Ruling." *Political Communication* 33, (2016): 583–604.

Baker, Vicky. "The Preachers Getting Rich from Poor Americans. *BBC News*. (May 29, 2019). https://www.bbc.com/news/stories-47675301.

Baldi, Stéphane. *New Study of the Literacy of College Students Finds Some are Graduating with Only Basic Skills*. American Institutes for Research, 2006. http://www.air.org/news/documents/Release200601pew.htm.

Banks, James A. "Multicultural Education: Development, Dimensions, and Challenges." *Phi Delta Kappan* 75, no. 1 (1993) 22–28.

Banks, Adelle. "All the President's Clergymen: The Issues." *National Catholic Reporter*, (September 5, 2017). https://www.ncronline.org/news/politics/all-presidents-clergymen-issues.

Banks, Adelle. "Key Evangelical Players on Trump's Advisory Board." *National Catholic Reporter*. (September 5, 2017). https://www.ncronline.org/news/politics/key-evangelical-players-trumps-advisory-board.

Bardacke, Frank. *Trampling Out the Vintage: Cesar Chavez and the Two Souls of the United Farm Workers*. New York, NY: Verso, 2012.

Bargh, John A. "Our Unconscious Mind." *Scientific American* 310, no. 1 (2014) 30–37.

Barnes, Luke. "President Praises Conservative Radio Host Who called him the 'Second Coming of God,' 'King of Israel.'" *Think Progress*. (August 23, 2019) https://thinkprogress.org/president-praises-conservative-radio-host-wayne-allyn-root-jews-love-trump-2afde41f9a17/.

Barry, Arlene L. "The Evolution of Reading Tests and Other Forms of Education Assessment. *The Clearing House* 71, no. 4 (1998) 231–35.

Barzun, Jacques. *House of Intellect*. New York, NY: Harper & Brothers, 1959.

Bass, Harold F., Mark J. Rozell, and Gleaves Whitney. "Introduction." In *Religion and the American Presidency*, 3rd edition, edited by Mark J. Rozell and Gleaves Whitney, 1–12. New York, NY: Palgrave, 2018.

Bauer-Wolf, Jeremy. "Another Speaker Shut Down." Inside Higher Education. (March 29, 2019). https://www.insidehighered.com/news/2019/03/29/beloit-cancels-erik-prince-talk-after-student-protests.

———. "Free Speech Laws Mushroom in the Wake of Campus Protests." *Inside Higher Education* (September 16, 2019). https://www.insidehighered.com/news/2019/09/16/states-passing-laws-protect-college-students-free-speech.

Beard, Charles A. *An Economic Interpretation of the Constitution of the United States*. Mineoloa, NY: Dover, 2012.

Beck, Aaron T. "Cognitive Therapy: A 30-Year Retrospective." *American Psychologist* 46, No. 4 (1991) 368–75.

Bellah, Robert N. "Civil Religion in America." *Daedalus* 96, no. 1 (1967) 1–26.

Bernays, Edward. *Propaganda*. New York, NY: Liveright Publishing Corporation, 1928.

Bhattacharjee, Puja. "How does Your Child's Screen Time Measure Up?" CNN Health (November 15, 2017). https://www.cnn.com/2017/11/15/health/screen-time-averages-parenting/index.html.

Bin Laden, Osama. "Letter to America." *The Guardian* (November 24, 2002). https://www.theguardian.com/world/2002/nov/24/theobserver.

Bloom, Allen. *The Closing of the American Mind: How Higher Education has Failed Democracy and Impoverished the Souls of Today's Students*. New York, NY: Simon & Schuster, 2012.

Boatman, Angela, and Bridget Terry Long. "Does Remediation Work for All Students? How the effects of Postsecondary Remedial and Developmental Courses Vary by Level of Academic Preparation." *Educational Evaluation and Policy Analysis* 40, no. 1 (2018) 29–58.

Boeri, Tito, Gordon Hanson, and Barry McCormick, eds. *Immigration Policy and the Welfare System: A Report for the Fondazione Rodolfo Debendetti in Association with the William Davidson Institute.* Oxford, UK: Oxford University Press, 2002.

Bosley, Lisa. "I Don't Teach Reading: Critical Reading Instruction in Composition Courses. *Literacy Research and Instruction* 47, no. 4 (2008) 285–308.

Botstein, Leon. "Redeeming the Liberal Arts." *Liberal Education* 104, no. 4 (2018). https://www.aacu.org/liberaleducation/2018/fall/botstein.

Bouchard, Gérard. "National Myths: An Overview." In *National Myths, Constructed Pasts, Contested Presents,* edited by G. Bouchard, 278–97. New York, NY: Routledge, 2013.

Boylan, Hunter R. "Exploring Alternatives to Remediation." *Journal of Developmental Education* 22, no. 3 (1999) 2–11.

Boyse, Kyla. "Television and Children." Michigan Medicine. University of Michigan. (August, 2010). http://www.med.umich.edu/yourchild/topics/tv.

Brandes, Stuart. *Warhogs: A History of War profits in America.* Lexington, KY: University Press of Kentucky, 1997.

Brost, Brian D. and Karen A. Bradley. Student Compliance with Assigned Reading: A Case Study. *Journal of Scholarship of Teaching and Learning* 6, No. 2 (2006)101–11.

Browder, Jenna. "Robert Jeffress' Mega-Churched Forced to Remove 'America is Christian Nation' Billboards." CBN News. (June 18, 2018). https://www.firstdallas. org/news/dr-robert-jeffress-the-founders-of-our-nation-encouraged-public-displays-of-faith-and-we-should-too/.

Buchbinder, Howard. The Market Oriented University and the Changing Role of Knowledge. *Higher Education* 26, no. 3 (1993) 331–47.

Buckley, Thomas E. "Thomas Jefferson and the Myth of Separation." In *Religion and the American Presidency,* 3rd edition, edited by Mark J. Rozell and Gleaves Whitney, 45–58. New York, NY: Palgrave, 2018.

Bullock, Alan. *Hitler: A Study in Tyranny.* New York, NY: Harper Perennial, 1971.

Bunzel, John H. *The New Force on the Left: Tom Hayden and the Campaign against Corporate America.* Stanford, CA: Stanford University Press, 1983.

Burke, Edmund III. Frantz Fanon's "The Wretched of the Earth." *Daedalus* 105, no. 1 (1976)127–35.

Bush, George W. "Address to Joint Session of Congress following 9/11 Attacks." (September 20, 2001). American Rhetoric. https://americanrhetoric.com/speeches/gwbush911jointsessionspeech.htm.

———. "Graduation Speech at West Point." (June 1, 2002). The White House. https://georgewbush-whitehouse.archives.gov/news/releases/2002/06/20020601-3.html.

———. "Operation Iraqi Freedom Address to the Nation." (March 19, 2003). American Rhetoric. https://americanrhetoric.com/speeches/wariniraq/gwbushiraq31903. htm.

———. "President Bush calls for Renewing the U.S. Patriot Act." The White House (April 19, 2004). https://georgewbush-whitehouse.archives.gov/news/releases/2004/04/20040419-4.html.

———. "Press Conference" (December 20, 2006). White House Archives. https://georgewbush-whitehouse.archives.gov/news/releases/2006/12/20061220-1.html.

———. "Ultimatum to Saddam Hussein Address to the Nation." (March 17, 2003). American Rhetoric. https://americanrhetoric.com/speeches/wariniraq/gwbushiraq31703.htm.

Bushman, Brad J., and Craig A. Anderson. "Understanding Causality in the Effects of Media Violence." *American Behavioral Scientist* 59, no. 14 (2015) 807—21.

Calamur, Krishnadev. "A Short History of 'America First.'" *The Atlantic*. (January 21, 2017). https://www.theatlantic.com/politics/archive/2017/01/trump-america-first/514037/.

Campbell, David E. "The 2004 Election: A Matter of Faith." In *A Matter of Faith: Religion in the 2004 Presidential Election*, edited by David E. Campbell, 1–12. Washington, D.C.: Brookings Institution, 2007.

Campbell, Edward, D. C. Jr. *The Celluloid South*. Knoxville, TN: University of Tennessee, 1981.

Campbell, Horace. *Barack Obama and Twenty-Fist Century Politics*. New York, NY: Pluto, 2010.

Campisi, Jessica. "Trump on 'Chosen One' Remark: I Didn't Realize Media Would Claim I Had a 'Messiah Complex.'" *The Hill* (August 24, 2019). https://thehill.com/homenews/administration/458670-trump-doubles-down-on-chosen-one-remarks-being-sarcasm-says-media.

Carter, Jimmy. "Inaugural Address," January 20, 1977. The American Presidency Project. https://www.presidency.ucsb.edu/documents/inaugural-address-0.

Cassino, Dan. *Fox News and American Politics: How One Channel Shapes American Politics and Society*. New York, NY: Routledge, 2016.

Chapman, Peter. *Bananas. How United Fruit Company Shaped the World*. New York, NY: Canongate, 2007.

Chappel, James. *Modern Catholic: The Challenge of Totalitarianism and the Remaking of the Church*. Cambridge, MA: President and Fellows of Harvard College, 2018.

Chen, Grace. "The Catch 22 of Community College Graduation Rates." *Community College Review*. (July 7, 2018). https://www.communitycollegereview.com/blog/the-catch-22-of-community-college-graduation-rates.

Cherif, Abour, H., Gerald. E. Adams, Farahnaz Movahedzadeh, and Margaret. A. Martyn. *Why Do Students Fail? Faculty Perspective*. Higher Learning Commission, 2014. http://cop.hlcommission.org/Learning-Environments/cherif.html.

Chickering, Arthur W. and Zelda F. Gamson. "Development and Adaptations of the Seven Principles for Good Practice in Undergraduate Education." *New Directions for Teaching and Learning* 1999, no. 80 (1999) 75–81.

Choi, David. "Hate Crimes Increase 226% in Places Trump Held a Campaign Rally in 2016, Study Claims." *Business Insider*. (March 23, 2019). https://www.businessinsider.com/trump-campaign-rally-hate-crimes-study-maga-2019-3.

Chomsky, Noam. *Language and Politics*, 2nd ed. Edited by C. P. Otero. Oakland, CA: AK, 1988.

Christie, Les. "Foreclosures up a Record 81% in 2008." CNN Money. January 15, 2009. https://money.cnn.com/2009/01/15/real_estate/millions_in_foreclosure/.

Christopher, Warren. "America's Leadership, America's Opportunity." *Foreign Policy* 98 (Spring, 1995) 6–27.

Chua, Amy. *World on Fire: How Exporting Free Market Democracy and Breeds Ethnic Hatred and Global Instability*. New York, NY: Anchor, 2003.

Cimino, Richard. "'No God in Common:' American Evangelical Discourse on Islam after 9/11." *Review of Religious Research* 47, no. 2 (2005)162–74.

Clayson, Dennis. E. "Student Evaluations of Teaching: Are They Related to What Students Learn? A Meta-Analysis and Review of the Literature." *Journal of Marketing Education* 31, no. 1 (2009)16–30.

Clinton, William J. "Address before a Joint Session of Congress on Administration Goals." (February 17, 1993). *Public Papers of the Presidents of the United States, William J. Clinton, 1993 Book I, January 20-July 31, 1993* 113–122. Washington, D.C.: United States Government Printing Office, 1994.

———. "Inaugural Address," (January 30, 1993). The American Presidency Project. https://www.presidency.ucsb.edu/documents/inaugural-address-51.

Clump, Michael A., Heather Bauer, and Catherine Bradley. The Extent to Which Psychology Students Read Textbooks: A Multiple Class Analysis of Reading across the Psychology Curriculum. *Journal of Instructional Psychology* 31, no. 3 (2004): 227–32.

Coffey, Thomas M. *Iron Eagle: The Turbulent Life of General Curtis Lemay.* New York, NY: Random House, 1987.

Cohen, Emily. "Gandhi's Concept of Nonviolence in International Relations." *Glendon Journal of International Studies/Revue d'études Internationales de Glendon* 2 (2002): 33–41.

Cohen, Phillip J. *Serbia's Secret War: Propaganda and the Deceit of History.* College Station, TX: Texas A & M University, 1996.

Cohen, Robert. *Freedom' Orator: Mario Savio and the Racial Legacy of the 1960s.* New York, NY: Oxford University Press, 2009.

———. "The New Left's Love-Hate Relationship with the University." In R. Flacks & N. Lichtenstein, *The Port Huron Statement* edited by R. Flacks and N. Lichtenstein, 107–24. Philadelphia, PA: The University of Pennsylvania Press, 2015.

Cole, Brendon. "Pastor Robert Jeffress says Trump is Christian 'Warrior' and Democrats Worship Pagan God Moloch, 'Who Allowed for Child Sacrifice.'" *Newsweek.* (October 2, 2019). https://www.newsweek.com/robert-jeffress-donald-trump-defends-christians-todd-starnes-show-1462525.

Cole, Devan. "Trump Tweets Racist Attacks at Progressive Democratic Women." CNN. (July 14, 2019). https://www.cnn.com/2019/07/14/politics/donald-trump-tweets-democratic-congresswomen-race-nationalities/index.html.

Cole, Matthew, Brian Ross, Angela M. Hill, and Lee Ferran. "'Repugnant' Photos Emerge of U.S. Soldiers Accused of Sport Killing." ABC News (March 21, 2011). https://abcnews.go.com/Blotter/repugnant-pictures-emerge-us-soldiers-accused-sport-killings/story?id=13183933.

College Board. "SAT Suite Results." College Board SAT Program. Miami, FL. (2018). https://reports.collegeboard.org/sat-suite-program-results/class-2018-results.

———. "Understanding Scores." College Board SAT Program. Miami, FL. (2018). https://collegereadiness.collegeboard.org/pdf/understanding-sat-scores.pdf.

Complete College America. *Remediation: Higher Education's Bridge to Nowhere.* Complete College America, 2012. https://www.insidehighered.com/sites/default/server_files/files/CCA%20Remediation%20ES%20FINAL.pdf.

Connolly, Griffin. "House to Probe Rise in the Crimes since Trump was Elected." *Roll Call* (April 4, 2019). https://www.rollcall.com/news/congress/lawmakers-to-probe-rise-of-hate-crimes-and-white-nationalism-in-u-s.

Costin, Frank, William. T. Greenough, and Robert Menges. "Student Ratings of College Teaching: Reliability, Validity, and Usefulness." *Review of Educational Research* 41, no. 5 (1971) 511–35.

Cox, Steven. R., Daniel L. Friesner, D. L., and Mohammed Khayum. Do Reading Skills Courses Help Underprepared Readers Achieve Academic Success in College? *Journal of College Reading and Learning* 33, no. 2 (2003)170–96.

Cray, Charlie. "Greenpeace Analyzes the Lewis Powell Memo: Corporate Blueprint to Dominate Democracy." Greenpeace (September 21, 2011). https://www. greenpeace.org/usa/greenpeace-analyzes-the-lewis-powell-memo-corporate-blueprint-to-dominate-democracy/.

Crawford, Robert. *What is Religion?* New York, NY: Routledge, 2002.

Crime Data Explorer. "United States." Federal Bureau of Investigation. (September, 2018). https://crime-data-explorer.fr.cloud.gov/explorer/national/united-states/crime.

Crockett, Clayton. "On the Disorientation of the Study of Religion." In *What is Religion? Origins, Definitions, Explanations*, edited by T. A. Indinopulos, & B. C. Wilson, 1–14. Leiden, The Netherlands: Brill, 1998.

Cunningham, Annie. E. and Keith E. Stanovich. "What Reading Does for the Mind." *American Educator* 22 (1998) 8–17.

Dale Daniel. "Donald Trump Has Said _____ False Things as U.S. President." *Toronto Star*, October 28, 2019. https://projects.thestar.com/donald-trump-fact-check/.

Daniels, Mitch. *Keeping the Republic*. New York, NY: Sentinel, 2011.

Darder, Antonia, Marta Baltodano, and Rodolfo D. Torres, Rodolfo D. "Critical Pedagogy: An Introduction." In *The Critical Pedagogy Reader* edited by A. Darder, M. Baltado and R. D. Torres, 1–21. New York, NY: Routledge Falmer, 2003.

D'Agostino, Susan and Jay Kosegarten, Jay. "Reevaluating Teaching Evaluations." *Liberal Education* 101, no. 3 (2015). https://www.aacu.org/liberaleducation/2015/summer/agostino.

Dale, Daniel and Tanya Talaga. "Donald Trump: The Unauthorized Database of False Things." *Toronto Star*, November 4, 2016. https://www.thestar.com/news/word/useelection/2016/11/04/donald-trump-the-unauthorized-database-of-false-things.

Dayen, David. *Chain of Title: How Three Ordinary Americans Uncovered Wall Street's Great Foreclosure Fraud*. New York, NY: New Press, 2016.

Dean, John. *The Nixon Defense: What He Knew and When He Knew It*. New York, NY: Penguin, 2014.

DeBenedetti, Charles. *An American Ordeal: The Anti-War movement of the Vietnam Era*. Syracuse, NY: Syracuse University Press, 1990.

Dehaene, Stanislaus. *Reading in the Brain: The New Science of How We Read*. New York, NY: Penguin Group, 2009.

Del Rosso, Jared. *Talking about Torture: How Political Discourse Shapes the Debate*. New York, NY: Columbia, 2015.

Delucchi, Michael. "'Liberal Arts' College and the Myth of Uniqueness." *Journal of Higher Education* 68, no. 4 (1997) 414–426.

Democracy Now. "We Made a 'Devil's Bargain': Former President Bill Clinton Apologizes for Trade Policies that Destroyed Haitian Rice Farming." April 1, 2010. https://www.democracynow.org/2010/4/1/clinton_rice.

Desilver, Drew. "A Majority of U.S. Colleges Admit Students Who Apply." Pew Research Center, April 9, 2019. https://www.pewresearch.org/fact-tank/.

Diamond, Jeremy and Kristen Appleton. "Paula White: Trump's Televangelist in the White House." CNN News, November 8, 2019. https://www.cnn.com/2019/11/07/politics/paula-white-televangelist-white-house/index.html.

Diamond, Sara. *Spiritual Warfare: The Politics of the Christian Right*. Boston, MA: South End, 1989.

Donia, Robert J. *Radovan Karadzic: Architect of the Bosnian Genocide*. New York, NY: Cambridge University Press, 2015.

Douglass, James. *JFK and the Unspeakable: Why He Died and Why it Matters*. New York, NY: Touchstone, 2008.

Draper, Robert. *Dead Certain: The Presidency of George W. Bush*. New York, NY: Free Press, 2007.

Draper, Roni. J. "Every Teacher a Literacy Teacher? An Analysis of the Literacy-Related Messages in Secondary Methods Textbooks." *Journal of Literacy Research* 34, no. 3, (2002) 357–84.

Duff, Johnathan, Carolyn Rubenstein, and Isaac Prilleltensky. "Wellness and Fairness: Two Core Values for Humanistic Psychology." *The Humanistic Psychologist* 44, no. 2 (2016) 127–141.

Dulles, John Foster. "Challenge and Response in United States Policy." *Foreign Affairs* 36, no. 11 (1957) 25–43.

Dumbrell, John. *American Foreign Policy: Carter to Clinton*. New York, NY: Palgrave, 1997.

Dunbar, Norah E., Matthew L. Jensen, Elena Bessarabova, Judee K. Burgoon, Daniel Rex Bernard, Kylie J. Harrison, Katherine M. Kelley, Bradley J. Adame, and Jacqueline M. Eckstein. "Empowered by Persuasive Deception: The Effects of Power and Deception on Dominance, Credibility, and Decision Making." *Communication Research* 41, no. 6 (2014) 852–76.

Durkheim, Emile. *The Elementary Forms of Religious Life*. Translated by Karen E. Fields. New York, NY: Free Press, 1995.

Education Funding Partners. http://www.edufundingpartners.com/.

Edwards, Chris. "Agricultural Subsidies." Downsizing the Federal Government, April 16, 2018. https://www.downsizinggovernment.org/agriculture/subsidies.

Ehrenreich, Barbara. *Bright-Sided: How Positive Thinking is Undermining America*. New York, NY: Metropolitan, 2009.

Eisenhower, Dwight. "Atoms for Peace," (Speech, United Nations, New York, December 8, 1953). *American Rhetoric*. https://www.americanrhetoric.com/speeches/dwightdeisenhoweratomsforpeace.html.

———. "Farewell Speech," (Speech, Washington, DC, January 17, 1961), *American Rhetoric*. https://www.americanrhetoric.com/speeches/dwightdeisenhowerfarewell.html.

———. "The Chance for Peace," (Speech, Washington, DC, April 16, 1953), Ike Eisenhower Foundation. https://www.dwightdeisenhower.com/DocumentCenter/View/135/Chance-For-Peace-Address-PDF.

———. "Transcript of Eisenhower's Speech at G.O.P. Convention, July 15, 1964." New York Times Archive. https://www.nytimes.com/1964/07/15/archives/transcript-of-eisenhowers-speech-to-the-gop-convention.html.

Entman, Robert M. "Cascading Activation: Contesting the White House's frame after 9/11." *Political Communication* 20, no. 4 (2003) 415–32.

Erickson, Betty. L., Calvin B. and Diane W. Strommer. *Teaching First-Year College Students.* San Francisco, CA: Jossey-Bass, 2006

FAIR. "Interlocking Directorates." Fairness and Accuracy in Reporting, 2019. https://fair.org/interlocking-directorates/.

Fahri, Paul. "On NBC, the Missing Story about Parent Company General Electric." *The Washington Post*, March 29, 2010. https://www.washingtonpost.com/lifestyle/style/on-nbc-the-missing-story-about-parent-company-general-electric/2011/03/29/AFpRYJyB_story.html.

Feldstein, Richard. *Political Correctness: A Response from the Cultural Left.* Minneapolis, MN: University of Minnesota Press, 1997.

Ferrall, Victor E. Jr. *Liberal Arts at the Brink.* Cambridge, MA: Harvard University Press, 2011.

Finnegan, Lisa. *No Questions Asked: News Coverage Since 9–11.* Westport, CT: Praeger, 2007.

First Baptist Dallas. "Dr. Robert Jeffress: The Founders of Our Nation Encouraged Public Displays of Faith and We Should Too." First Baptist Dallas, December 18, 2018. https://www.firstdallas.org/news/dr-robert-jeffress-the-founders-of-our-nation-encouraged-public-displays-of-faith-and-we-should-too/.

Fisch, William B. "Hate Speech in the Constitutional Law of the United States." *University of Missouri School of Law Scholarship Repository*, 2002. https://scholarship.law.missouri.edu/cgi/viewcontent.cgi?article=1413&context=facpubs.

Fishetti, John C. "W.E.B. DuBois: The Roots of Critical Race Theory." In *A Critical Pedagogy of Resistance: 34 Pedagogues We Need to Know*, edited by J.D. Kirylo, 33–36. Rotterdam: Sense, 2013.

Flecha, Ramón, Jésus Gómez, and Lidia Puigvert. "The Theory of Communicative Action." *Counterpoints* 250, (2001): 109–127.

Flower, Linda, and John R. Hayes. "A Cognitive Process of Writing." *College Composition and Communication* 34, no. 4 (1981) 365–87.

Fogelsong, David S. *America's Secret War against Bolshevism: U.S. Intervention in the Russian Civil War, 1917–1920.* Chapel Hill, NC: University of North Carolina, 1995.

Foley, Edward B. "Is it Ever OK for a President to ask a Foreign Country to Investigate a Political Rival?" *Politico Magazine*, October 6, 2019. https://www.politico.com/magazine/story/2019/10/06/trump-ukraine-investigate-rival-229341.

Follman, Mark, Gavin Aronsen, and Deanna Pan. "A Guide to Mass Shootings in America." *Mother Jones*, August 31, 2019. https://www.motherjones.com/politics/2012/07/mass-shootings-map/

Forrest-Pressley, Donna Lynn and Gary T. Waller. *Cognition, Metacognition, and Reading.* New York, NY: Springer-Verlag, 1984.

Francis, Michelle Andersen and Michelle Simpson. Vocabulary Development," in *Handbook of College Reading and Study Strategy Research*, 2nd Ed., edited by R. F. Flippo and D.C. Caverly, 97–120. New York, NY: Routledge, 2009.

Frank, Justin A. *Trump on the Couch: Inside the Mind of a President.* New York, NY: Penguin, 2018.

Freire, Paulo. "From Pedagogy of the Oppressed." In *The Critical Pedagogy Reader* edited by A. Darder, M. Baltodano, Marta, and R. D. Torres, 57–68. New York, NY: Routledge Falmer, 2003.

———. *Pedagogy of the Oppressed*. Trans. By Myra Bergman Ramos. New York, NY: Bloomsbury Academic, 2018.

French, David. "Evangelicals are Supporting Trump out of Fear, not Faith." *Time*, June 27, 2019. https://time.com/5615617/why-evangelicals-support-trump/.

Fritz, Ben, Keefer, Bryan, and Nyhan, Brendan. *All the President's Spin: George Bush, the Media, and the Truth*. New York, NY: Touchstone, 2004.

Friedrichs, David O. *Trusted Criminal: White Collar Crime in Contemporary Society*. Belmont, CA: Wadsworth, 2010.

Froman, Michael B. *Development of the Idea of Détente: Coming to Terms*. London, Macmillan, 1991.

Fulbright, J. William. "The Clear and Present Danger," November 2, 1974. Speech Vault. http://www.speeches-usa.com/Transcripts/jw_fulbright.html.

Funt, Danny. "The Transformation of David Brooks." *Columbia Journalism Review*, Oct. 27, 2015. https://www.cjr.org/the_profile/the_transformation_of_david_brooks. php.

Gaddis, John Lewis. "The Unexpected John Foster Dulles: Nuclear Weapons, Communism, and the Russians." *John Foster Dulles and the Diplomacy of the Cold War*, edited by Richard H. Immerman, 47–78. Princeton, NJ: Princeton University Press, 1990.

Gamble, Richard M. "Savior Nation: Woodrow Wilson and the Gospel of Service." *Humanitas* 14, no. 1 (2001) 4–22.

Gandhi, Mahatma. *The Essential Gandhi* edited by Louis Fischer. New York, NY: Vintage Spiritual Classics, 1962.

Garner, Ruth. *Metacognition and Reading Comprehension*. Westport, CT: Ablex, 1987.

Gates, Jimmie. "More than 200 Applied for Chicken Plant Jobs at Job Fair after MS ICE Raids" *Mississippi Clarion Leger*, August 14, 2019. https://www.clarionledger.com/story/news/politics/2019/08/14/ms-ice-raid-job-fair-numbers-applicants-koch-foods-chicken-plant-forest-morton-deboners/2010080001/.

Gates, John M. "War-related Deaths in the Philippines, 1898–1902." *Pacific Historical Review* 53, no. 3 (1984) 367–78.

Gelber, Kathrine and Luke McNamara. "Evidencing the Harms of Hate Speech. *Social Identities* 22 no. 3 (2016) 324–41.

Gentile, Douglas A. ed. *Media Violence and Children: A Complete Guide for Parents and Professionals*. Westport, CT: Praeger, 2003.

Gerard, Emmanuel. *Death in the Congo. Murdering Patrice Lumumba*. Cambridge, MA: Harvard University Press, 2015.

Gerstle, Gary. "Theodore Roosevelt and the Divided Character of American Nationalism." *The Journal of American History* 86, no. 3 (1999) 1280–1307.

Gerstenfeld, Phyllis. B., Diane R. Grant, D. R., and Chau-Pu Chiang. "Hate Online: A Content Analysis of Extremist Internet Sites. *Analyses of Social Issues and Public Policy* 3, no.1 (2003) 9–44.

Gilens, Martin and Craig Herman. "Corporate Ownership and news Bias: Newspaper Coverage of the 1996 Telecommunications Act." *Journal of Politics* 62, no. 2 (2000) 369–86.

Glass, Andrew. "Bush Sends Marines to Somalia, December 4, 1992." *Politico,* December 4, 2018. https://www.politico.com/story/2018/12/04/this-day-in-politics-dec-4-1992-1037009.

Gleckman, Howard. "Who is Middle Class Anyway?" *Forbes,* December 10, 2018. https://www.forbes.com/sites/howardgleckman/2018/12/10/who-is-middle-class-anyway/#6de5fd2313f2.

Glenza, Jessica. "Paula White: The Pastor Who Helps Trump Hear what God has to Say." *The Guardian,* March 27, 2019. https://www.theguardian.com/us-news/2019/mar/27/paula-white-donald-trump-pastor-evangelicals.

Goodstein, Laurie. "All the President's Clergy: Obama Looks to Five Religious Leaders for Council." Americans United for Separation of Church and State, March 16, 2009. https://www.au.org/blogs/wall-of-separation/all-the-presidents-clergy-obama-looks-to-five-religious-leaders-for-counsel.

Gorzycki, Meg, Geoffrey Desa, Pamela Howard, and Diane Allen. "Reading is Important, but I Don't Read: Undergraduates' Experiences with Academic Reading." *Journal of Adolescent and Adult Literacy* 64, no. 4 (2020).

Gottschalk, Petter. "Gender and White Collar Crime: Only Four Percent Female Criminals." *Journal of Money Laundering Control* 15, no. 3 (2012) 262–73.

Graber, Doris A and Joanna Dunaway, Joanna. *Mass Media and American Politics.* Thousand Oaks, CA: Sage, 2018

Graff, Gerald. *Professing Literature: An Institutional History.* Chicago, IL: University of Chicago Press, 1987.

"Grassley Withers under Religious Right Heat." *Church and State Magazine,* February, 2011. https://www.au.org/church-state/february-2011-church-state/featured/grassley-withers-under-religious-right-heat.

Green, Emma. "On Praying for the President." *The Atlantic,* June 3, 2019. https://www.theatlantic.com/politics/archive/2019/06/trump-prayer-mass-shooting/590920/.

———. "One Way We Push Back against Evil is through the Leaders We Elect." *The Atlantic,* October 28, 2017. https://www.theatlantic.com/politics/archive/2017/10/robert-jeffress-trump/544196/.

———. "Why Some Christians Love the Meanest Parts of Trump." *The Atlantic,* August, 18, 2019. https://www.theatlantic.com/politics/archive/2019/08/ben-howe-evangelical-christians-support-trump/596308/.

Grumbach, Gary and Elisha Fieldstadt. "Former Blackwater Contractor Found Guilty of Murder in Iraq Massacre." NBC News, December 19, 2018. https://www.nbcnews.com/news/us-news/former-blackwater-contractor-accused-firing-first-shots-iraq-massacre-found-n949966.

Guerrero, Aldo. "National Plutocrat Radio." FAIR, July 15, 2015. https://fair.org/home/national-plutocrat-radio/.

Gunn, T. Jeremy, and Mounia Slighoua. "The Spiritual Factor: Eisenhower, Religion, and Foreign Policy." *The Review of Faith & International Affairs* 9, no. 4 (2011) 39–49.

Gustainis, Justin. J., and Dan. F. Hahn. "While the Whole World Watched: Rhetorical Failures of Anti-war Protest. *Communication Quarterly* 36, no. 3 (1988) 203–16.

Guthrie, Stewart Elliott. "Religion: What is it?" *Journal for the Scientific Study of Religion* 35, no. 4 (1996) 412–19.

Haas, Michael. *George W. Bush, War Criminal? The Bush Administration's Liability for 269 War Crimes.* Westport, CT: Praeger, 2009.

Haas, Christina and Linda Flower. "Rhetorical Reading Strategies and the Construction of Meaning." *College Composition and Communication* 39, no. 2 (1988) 167–83.

Habermas, Jürgen. *Theory of Communicative Action, Vol 1: Reason and the Rationalization of Society.* Trans. By Thomas McCarthy. Boston, MA: Beacon Press. 1984.

Haberski, Raymond. *God and War: American Civil Religion since 1945.* New Brunswick, NJ: Rutgers University Press, 2012.

Halpern, Sue. "Facebook's False Standards for not Removing a False Nancy Pelosi Video." *The New Yorker*, May 28, 2019. https://www.newyorker.com/tech/annals-of-technology/facebooks-false-standards-for-not-removing-a-fake-nancy-pelosi-video.

Halpern, Diane. F. and Milton D. Hakel. "Applying the Science of Learning to the University and Beyond: Teaching for Long-term Retention and Transfer." *Change* 35, no. 4 (2003) 36–41.

Hamilton, James T. *All the News That's Fit to Sell: How the Market Transforms Information into News.* Princeton, NJ: Princeton University Press, 2004.

Harbert, Tam. "Here's How Much the 2008 Bailouts Really Cost." MIT Sloan School, February 21, 2019. https://mitsloan.mit.edu/ideas-made-to-matter/heres-how-much-2008-bailouts-really-cost.

Harris, Adam. "The Liberal Arts May not Survive the 21st Century." *The Atlantic*, Dec. 13, 2018. https://www.theatlantic.com/education/archive/2018/12/the-liberal-arts-may-not-survive-the-21st-century/577876/.

Hart Research Associates. *Fulfilling the American Dream: Liberal Education and the Future of Work.* Washington, D.C.: Hart Research Associates, 2018. https://www.aacu.org/sites/default/files/files/LEAP/2018EmployerResearchReport.pdf.

Hartman, Andrew. *A War for the Soul of America: A history of Culture Wars.* Chicago, IL: University of Chicago Press, 2015.

Hauptman, Laurence M. "Mythologizing Westward Expansion: Schoolbooks and the Image of the American Frontier before Turner." *The Western Historical Quarterly* 8, no. 3 (1977) 269 –282.

Hauser, Robert M., Christopher. F. Edley, Judith. A. Koening, and Elliot Stuart, eds. *Measuring Literacy: Performance Levels for Adults, Interim Report.* Washington, D.C.: National Academies Press, 2005.

Hawdon, James, Atte Oksanen, and Pekka Räsänen. "Exposure to Online Hate in Four Nations: A Cross-National Consideration." *Deviant Behavior* 38, no. 3 (2017) 254–66.

Hawley, Joshua David. *Theodore Roosevelt: Preacher of Righteousness.* New Haven, CT: Yale University Press, 2008.

Hayden, Tom. "Crafting the Port Huron Statement: Measuring its Impact in the 1960s and After." In *Sources and Legacies of the New Left's Founding Manifesto*, edited by In Richard Flacks and Nelson Lichtenstein, 16–35. Philadelphia, PA; University of Pennsylvania Press, 2015.

———. *The Port Huron Statement. The Visionary Call of the 1960s Revolution.* New York, NY: Thunder's Mouth, 2005.

Hayes, Matthew. "RFK's Secret Role in the Cuban Missile Crisis." *Scientific American*, August 6, 2019. https://blogs.scientificamerican.com/observations/rfks-secret-role-in-the-cuban-missile-crisis/.

Hendershot, Heather. *Open to Debate: How William F. Buckley put Liberal America on the Firing Line*. New York, NY: HarperCollins, 2016.

Herbst, Jurgen. The Yale Report of 1828. *International Journal of the Classical Tradition* 11, no. 2 (9187) 213–31.

Hook, Richard. J. "Students' Anti-Intellectual Attitudes and Adjustment to College." *Psychological Reports* 94, no. 3 (2004) 909–14.

Herman, Edward S. and Noam Chomsky. *Manufacturing Consent: The Political Economy of Mass Media*. New York, NY: Pantheon, 2002.

Hermida, Julian. "The Importance of Teaching Academic Reading Skills in First-year University Courses." *The International Journal of Research and Review* 3, (2009) 20–30.

Hertweck, Kate. "Zombie Apocalypse: Biology of Disease, Biology 1320." University of Texas at Tyler, 2019. https://www.uttyler.edu/biology/files/biology1320.pdf.

Hertzog, Jonathan P. "From Sermon to Strategy: Religious Influence on the Foundations and Implementation of U.S. Foreign Policy in the Early Cold War." In *Religion and the Cold War: A Global Perspective*, edited by Philip E. Muehlenbeck, 44–64. Nashville, TN: Vanderbilt University Press, 2012.

Heschel, Abraham J. *Who is Man?* Stanford, CA: Stanford University Press, 1965.

Higgins, Michael W. *Heretic Blood: The Spiritual Geography of Thomas Merton*. Eugene, OR: Wipf and Stock, 1998.

Hilkey, Judy. *Character is Capital: Success Manuals and Manhood in Gilded Age America*. Chapel Hill, NC: University of North Carolina Press, 1997.

Hitchens, Christopher. *No One Left to Lie To: The Triangulations for William Jefferson Clinton*. New York, NY: Verso, 1999.

Hitler, Adolph. *Mein Kampf*. Trans. By James Murphy, 1939. London: Hurst & Blackett, 1924. http://www.greatwar.nl/books/meinkampf/meinkampf.pdf.

Hoeffel, Joseph M. *The Iraq Lie: How the White House sold the War*. San Diego, CA; Progressive Press, 2014.

Hoeft, Mary. E. "Why University Students Don't Read: What Professors Can Do to Increase Compliance." *International Journal for the Scholarship of Teaching and Learning* 6, no. 2 (2012)1–14.

Holschuh, Jodi Patrick and Aultman, Lori Price. (2009). "Comprehension Development." In *Handbook of College Reading and Study Strategy Research*, 2nd edition, edited by Rona. F. Flippo and David C. Caverly, 121–44. New York, NY: Routledge, 2009.
———. and Eric. J. Paulson. *The Terrain of College Developmental Reading. Executive Summary and Paper Commissioned by the College Reading & Learning Association*, 1–18. College Station, TX: Texas State University, 2013.

Holycross, Jordan and Olivia Riggio. "Morning Edition's Think Tank Sources Lean to the Right." FAIR, September 18, 2018. https://fair.org/home/morning-editions-think-tank-sources-lean-to-the-right/.

Hoopes, Townsend. "God and John Foster Dulles." *Foreign Policy* 13 (1973)154–77.

Houston, Susan. M., Catherine Lebel, Tami Katzir, F. R. Manis, E. Kan, G. R. Rodriguez, and E. Sowell. "Reading Skill and Structural Brain Development." *Neuroreport* 25, no. 5 (2014) 347.

Howard, Pamela. J., Meg Gorzycki, Geoffrey Desa, and Diane D. Allen, D. "Academic Reading: Comparing Students' and Faculty Perceptions of Its Value, Practice, and Pedagogy." *Journal of College Reading and Learning* 48 no. 3 (2018)189–209.

Hoxby, Caroline, M. "The Changing Selectivity of American Colleges." *Journal of Economic Perspectives* 23, no. 4 (2009) 95–118.

Huber, Mary Taylor. "Disciplines, Pedagogy, and Inquiry-Based Learning about Teaching." *New Directions for Teaching and Learning* 107, (2006) 69–77.

Huesmann, L. Rowell, Jessica Moise-Titus, Cheryl-Lynn Podolski, and Leonard D. Eron. "Longitudinal Relations between Children's Exposure to TV Violence and Their Aggressive and Violent Behavior in Young Adulthood: 1977–1992." *Developmental Psychology* 39, no. 2 (2003) 201–21.

Hughes, Geoffrey. *Political Correctness: A History of Semantics and Culture.* West Essex, UK: John Wiley & Sons, Ltd, 2010.

Hughes-Wilson, John. *JFK: An American Coup D'etat: The Truth Behind the Kennedy Assassination.* London: John Blake, 2016.

Ihara, Rachel and Annie Del Principe. "'I Bought the Book and I Didn't Need It': What Reading Looks Like at an Urban Community College." *Teaching English at the Two-year College* 43, no. 3 (2016) 229–44.

Immerman, Richard H. "Confessions of an Eisenhower Revisionist: An Agonizing Reappraisal." *Diplomatic History* 14, no. 3 (1990) 319–42.

———. *John Foster Dulles: Piety, Pragmatism and Power in U.S. Foreign Policy.* Biographies in American Foreign Policy, Joseph A Frey, Series Editor. Wilmington, DE: Scholarly Resources, 1999.

Independent Lens. "Who Owns the Media?" PBS, KQED. (2017). https://www.pbs.org/independentlens/democracyondeadline/mediaownership.html.

Intersegmental Committee of the Academic Senates of the California Community Colleges, the California State University, and the University of California. *Academic Literacy: A Statement of Competencies of Students Entering California's Public Colleges and Universities.* Sacramento, CA: Academic Senate for California Community Colleges, 2002. http://icas-ca.org/Websites/icasca/images/Competency/AcademicLiteracy2002.pdf.

Isakson, Richard L., and Marne B. Isakson. "Preparing College Students to Learn More from Academic Texts through Metacognitive Awareness of Reading Strategies." In *Improving Reading Comprehension through Metacognitive Reading Strategies Instruction* edited by K. Mokhtari, 155–76. Lanham, Maryland: Rowman & Littlefield, 2016.

Ish-Shalom, Piki. "The Rhetorical Capital of Theories: The Democratic Peace and the Road to the Roadmap." *International Political Science Review* 29, no. 3 (2008) 281–301.

Issenberg, Sasha. *The Victory Lab: The Secret Science of Winning Campaigns.* New York, NY: Broadway Books, 2013.

Ivie, Robert L. "Diffusing Cold War Demagoguery: Murrow vs. McCarthy on 'See it Now.'" In *Cold War Rhetoric: Strategy, Metaphor and Ideology*, edited by Martin Medhurst, Robert L. Ivie, Phillip Wander, and Robert L. Scott, 81–102. East Lansing, MI: Michigan State University Press, 1997.

Iyer, Raghavan, ed. *The Essential Writings of Mahatma Gandhi.* Oxford, UK: Oxford University Press, 1991.

Jackson, David. "Donald Trump Accepts GOP Nomination, says 'I Alone Can fix' System." *USA Today*, July 21, 2016. https://www.usatoday.com/story/news/politics/elections/2016/07/21/donald-trump-republican-convention-acceptance-speech/87385658/.

Jackson, Jacob. "CSU Ends Remedial Courses." Public Policy Institute of California. (August 10, 2017). https://www.ppic.org/blog/csu-ends-remedial-courses/.

Jacobson, Annie. *Surprise, Kill, Vanish: The Secret History of CIA Paramilitary Armies, Operatives, and Assassins.* New York, NY: Little, Brown, 2019.

Janney, Peter. *Mary's Mosaic: The CIA Conspiracy to Murder John F. Kennedy, Mary Pinchot Meyer, and their Vision for World Peace.* New York, NY: Skyhorse. 2016.

Jaschik, Scott. "Shouting Down a Lecture." *Inside Higher Education,* March 3, 2017. https://www.insidehighered.com/news/2017/03/03/middlebury-students-shout-down-lecture-charles-murray.

Jefferson, Thomas. *The Jefferson Bible: The Life and Morals of Jesus of Nazareth.* Mineoloa, NY: Dover, 2006.

Jenkins, Jack. "Trump is Dismantling Obama's Religion Initiatives." Think Progress, October 19, 2017. https://thinkprogress.org/trump-dismantling-obamas-religion-initiatives-49d89df9b0e4/.

John XXIII. *Pacem in Terris.* [Peace on Earth] Encyclical of Pope John XXIII on Establishing Universal Peace in Truth, Justice, Charity, and Liberty, April 11, 1963. Vatican Library. http://w2.vatican.va/content/john-xxiii/en/encyclicals/documents/hf_j-xxiii_enc_11041963_pacem.html.

Johnson, Eric A. and Karl-Heinz Reuband. *What we Knew: Terror, Mass Murder, and Everyday Life in Nazi Germany.* New York, NY: Basic Books, 2005.

Johnson, Syd. "Zombie Ethics, Humanities 2702." Michigan Tech University, 2015. http://hdmzweb.hu.mtu.edu/husyllabi/2014_2015/2015_Summer/HU2702%20Thical%20Theory%20&%20Moral%20Problems%20-%20S.%20Johnson.pdf.

Jones, Jeffrey. "U.S. Media Trust Continues to Recover from 2016 Low." Gallup, October 12, 2018. https://news.gallup.com/poll/243665/media-trust-continues-recover-2016-low.aspx.

Jordan, Barbara. "1976 Democratic National Convention Keynote Address," (Speech, New York, NY, July 12, 1976), American Rhetoric. https://www.americanrhetoric.com/speeches/barbarajordan1976dnc.html.

Joseph, Sister Miriam. *The Trivium: The Liberal Arts of Logic, Grammar, and Rhetoric.* Philadelphia, PA: Paul Dry Books, 2002.

Kaiser, Brittany. Targeted: The Cambridge Analytica Whistleblower's Story of How Big Data, Trump, and Facebook Broke Democracy and How it Can Happen Again. New York, NY: HarperCollins, 2019.

Kamarck, Elaine. "The Fragile Legacy of Barack Obama." Brookings, April 6, 2018. https://www.brookings.edu/blog/fixgov/2018/04/06/the-fragile-legacy-of-barack-obama/.

Kamenetz, Anya. "Young Children are Spending Much More Time in Front of Small Screens." NPR Ed. (October 29, 2017). https://www.npr.org/sections/ed/2017/10/19/558178851/young-children-are-spending-much-more-time-in-front-of-small-screens.

Kane, Ruth, Susan Sandretto, and Chris Heath. "Telling Half the Story: A Critical Review of Research on Teaching Beliefs and Practices of University Academics." *Review of Educational Research* 72, no. 2, (2002)177–228.

Karabel, Jerome. "Open Admissions." In *American Higher Education Transformed, 1940–2005: Documenting the National Discourse,* edited by W. Smith and T. Bender, 148–51. Baltimore, MD: Johns Hopkins University Press, 2009.

Keller, Timothy A., and Marcel A. Just. "Altering Cortical Connectivity: Remediation-Induced Changes in the White Matter of Poor Readers." *Neuron* 64, no. 5 (2009) 624–31.

Kelly, Travis. "Mayday, 1960." *Counter Punch*, November 27, 2009. https://www.counterpunch.org/2009/11/27/mayday-1960/.

Kennedy, John F. "Civil Rights Address," (Speech, Washington, DC, June 11, 1963), American Rhetoric. https://americanrhetoric.com/speeches/jfkcivilrights.htm.

———. "Commencement Speech at American University," (Speech, Washington, DC, June 10, 1963), John F. Kennedy Library and Museum. https://www.jfklibrary.org/archives/other-resources/john-f-kennedy-speeches/american-university-19630610.

———. "Inaugural Address," (Speech, Washington, DC, January 20, 1961), John F. Kennedy Presidential Library and Museum. https://www.jfklibrary.org/learn/about-jfk/historic-speeches/inaugural-address.

Kennedy, Robert F. "Conflict in Vietnam," (Lecture, Manhattan, KS, March 18, 1968), Landon Lecture Series on Public Issues. https://www.k-state.edu/landon/speakers/robert-kennedy/transcript.html.

Kincheloe, Joe. "The Foundations of Critical Pedagogy." In *Critical Pedagogy Primer* edited by J. L. Kincheloe, 45–106. New York, NY: Peter Lang, 2008.

King, Martin Luther, Jr. *All Labor has Dignity*. Edited by Michael K. Honey. Boston, MA: Beacon, 1963.

———. "Beyond Vietnam," (Speech, New York, NY, April 4, 1967), The Martin Luther King, Jr. Research and Education Center. Stanford University. https://kinginstitute.stanford.edu/king-papers/documents/beyond-vietnam.

———. "Letter from a Birmingham Jail," (Letter, Birmingham, AL, August, 1963), University of North Carolina, Greensboro. https://www.uncg.edu/hhs/docs/MLKLetter1963.pdf.

Kinzer, Stephen. *Overthrow: America's Century of Regime Change from Hawaii to Iraq*. New York, NY: Times, 2006.

———. *The Brothers: John Foster Dulles, Allen Dulles, and Their Secret World War*. New York, NY: Times, 2013.

Kitchener, Karen. S., and Patricia M. King. "The Reflective Judgment Model: Ten Years of Research." In *Adult Development, Vol. 2. Models and Methods in the Study of Adolescent and Adult Thought* edited by M. L. Commons, C. Armon, L. Kohlberg, F. A. Richards, T. A. Grotzer, and J. D. Sinnott, 63–78. New York, NY, England: Praeger, 1990.

Klinenberg, Eric. "Beyond 'Fair and Balanced'," *Rolling Stone*, February 24, 2005. https://www.rollingstone.com/politics/politics-news/beyond-fair-and-balanced-233659/.

Kolhatkar, Sheelah. "The Growth of Sinclair's Conservative Media Empire," *The New Yorker*, October 28, 2018. https://www.newyorker.com/magazine/2018/10/22/the-growth-of-sinclairs-conservative-media-empire.

Kramer, Paul A. "Race-making and Colonial Violence in the US Empire: The Philippine-American War as Race War." *Diplomatic History* 30, no. 2 (2006) 169–10.

Krieg, Gregory. "Its Official: Clinton Swamps Trump in Popular Votes." *CNN News*, December 22, 2016. https://www.cnn.com/2016/12/21/politics/donald-trump-hillary-clinton-popular-vote-final-count/index.html.

Kuhlenbeck, Mike. "Theocratic Mercenary Erik Prince and the Christian Right." *The Humanist*, June 19, 2018. https://thehumanist.com/magazine/july-august-2018/features/theocratic-mercenary-erik-prince-christian-right.

Kuh, George. *High-Impact Practices: What They Are, Who Has Access to Them, and Why They Matter.* Washington, D.C. Association of American Colleges and Universities, 2008. https://www.aacu.org/leap/hips.

———. "What We're Learning about Student Engagement from NSSE." *Change.* (March/April, 2003) 24–32.

Kulik, James. A. "Student Ratings: Validity, Utility, and Controversy." *New Directions for Institutional Research* 109, (*2001*) 9–25.

Kurt, Daniel. "Are You In the Top One Percent of the World?" *Investopedia.* (September 25, 2019). https://www.investopedia.com/articles/personal-finance/050615/are-you-top-one-percent-world.asp.

LaBelle, Thomas J. and Christopher Ward. *Ethnic Studies and Multiculturalism.* New York, NY: State University of New York Press, 1996.

Lacy, Tim. *The Dream of a Democratic Culture: Mortimer J. Adler and the Great Books Idea.* Palgrave Studies in Cultural Intellectual History. New York, NY: Palgrave Macmillan, 2013.

Lane, Jack. C. "The Yale Report of 1828 and Liberal Education: A Neo-Republican Manifesto." *History of Education Quarterly* 27, no. 3 (1987) 325–38.

Latham, Michael E. *The Right Kind of Revolution. Modernization, Development, and U.S. foreign Policy from the Cold War to the Present.* Ithaca, NY: Cornell University Press, 2011.

Lauro, Sarah Juliet. "Introduction." In *Zombie Theory: A Reader* edited by S. J. Lauro and K. Embry, vii–xxiv. Minneapolis, MN: University of Minnesota Press, 2017.

Lauro, Sarah. J., and Karen Embry. "A Zombie Manifesto: The Nonhuman Condition in the Era of Advanced Capitalism." *Boundary 2*, 35, no 1 (2008) 851–98.

Lavin, David E. and David Hyllegard, David. *Against the Odds: Open Admissions and the Life Chances of the Disadvantaged.* New Haven, CT: Yale University Press, 1996.

Lavin, David E. and Jacobson, Barbara. *Open Admissions at the City University of New York: Description of Academic Outcomes after Three Semesters.* New York, NY: City University of New York, 1973. https://files.eric.ed.gov/fulltext/ED078808.pdf.

Lazer, David. M., Matthew A. Baum, Yochai Benkler, Adam J. Berinsky, Kelly M. Greenhill, Filippo Menczer, . . . and Jonathan L. Zittrain. "The Science of Fake News." *Science*, 359, no. 6380. (2018)1094–1096.

Lee, Martin A. and Norman Solomon. *Unreliable Sources: A Guide to Detecting Bias in News Media.* New York, NY: Lyle Stuart, 1992.

Lee, Shane and Phillip Sinitiere. *Holy Mavericks. Evangelical Innovators and the Spiritual Market Place.* New York, NY: New York University Press, 2009.

Lei, Simon. A., Kerry A. Bartlett, K. A., Suzanne E. Gorney, and Tamra R. Herschbach. "Resistance to Reading Compliance among College Students: Instructors' Perspectives." *College Student Journal* 44, no. 2 (2010) 219–29.

Leo XIII. *Rerum Novarum* [On Capital and Labor], (1891). Papal Encyclicals Online. https://www.papalencyclicals.net/leo13/l13rerum.htm.

Lipstadt, Deborah E. *Antisemitism Here and Now.* New York: Schocken, 2019.

Lo Bue, Vanessa. "Violent Media and Aggressive Behavior in Children." *Psychology Today.* (January 8, 2018). https://www.psychologytoday.com/us/blog/the-baby-scientist/201801/violent-m%C3%A9dia-and-aggressive-behavior-in-children.

Lowe, Patty, ed. *Seventh Generation Earth Ethics: Native Voices of Wisconsin*. Madison, WI: Wisconsin Historical Society, 2014.

Lydston, George Frank. *Diseases of Society*. Philadelphia, PA: J. P. Lippincott, 1904.

Macmillan, Margaret. *Paris 1919. Six Months that Changed the World*. New York, NY: Random House, 2003.

MacPhee, William. *Structured to Fail: Implosion of the Global Economy*. Victoria, BC: Friesen, 2014.

Makdisi, Ussama. *Faith Misplaced: The Broken Promise of U.S.-Arab Relations, 1820–2001*.New York, NY: Public Affairs, 2001.

Malkin, Craig. "Pathological Narcissism and Politics: A Lethal Mix." In *The Dangerous Case of Donald Trump* edited by B. Lee, 51–68. New York: St. Martin's. 2017.

Manarin, Karen. "Reading Value: Student Choice in Reading Strategies." *Pedagogy* 12, no. 2 (2012) 281–97.

Mann, James, *Rise of the Vulcans: The History of Bush's War Cabinet*. New York, NY: Penguin, 2004.

Martin, William. "The Christian Right and American Foreign Policy." *Foreign Policy*, 144, (Spring 1999) 66–80.

Masci, David. "Almost All U.S. Presidents, Including Trump, Have Been Christians." Pew Research Center, January 20, 2019. https://www.pewresearch.org/fact-tank/2017/01/20/almost-all-presidents-have-been-christians/.

Masta, Katerina Eva and Elisa Shearer. "News Use across Social Media Platforms 2018." Pew Research Center, September 10, 2018. https://www.journalism.org/2018/09/10/news-use-across-social-media-platforms-2018/.

Mattox, John Mark. *St. Augustine and the Theory of Just War*. New York, NY: Continuum, 2006.

May, Ernest R. *Imperial Democracy: The Emergence of America as a Great Power*. New York, NY: Harcourt, Brace, & World, 1961.

Mayer, Jane, *Dark Money. The Hidden History of the Billionaires Behind the Rise of the Radical Right*. New York, NY: Anchor, 2017.

Maza, Christina. "Trump will start the End of the World, Claim Evangelicals Who Support Him." *Newsweek*, January 12, 2018. https://www.newsweek.com/trump-will-bring-about-end-worldevangelicals-end-times-779643.

McCarthy, Charles. *The Wisconsin Idea*. New York, NY: Macmillan, 1912.

McCarthy, Eugene. "Denouncing the Vietnam War." (Speech, Chicago, IL, December 2, 1967), Speech Vault. http://www.speeches-usa.com/Transcripts/eugene_mccarthy-vietnam.html.

McCartney, Paul T. Power and Progress: *Identity, the War of 1898, and the Rise of American Imperialism*. Baton Rouge, LA: Louisiana State University, 2006.

McGranahan, Carole. An Anthropology of Lying: Trump and the Political Sociality of Moral Outrage. *American Ethnologist* 44, no. 2 (2017) 243–48.

McGregor, Sarah. "Foreign Holdings of U.S. Securities Rise to Record $18 Trillion." *Bloomberg*, February 2, 2018. https://www.bloomberg.com/news/articles/2018-02-28/foreign-holdings-of-u-s-securities-rise-to-record-18-trillion.

McLaughlin, Kenneth. *Empowerment: A Critique*. New York, NY: Routledge, 2016.

McMaster, H. R. *Dereliction of Duty: Lyndon Johnson, Robert McNamara, the Joint Chiefs of Staff, and the Lies that Led to Vietnam*. New York, NY: HarperCollins, 1997.

McNair, Brian. *Fake News: Falsehood, Fabrication and Fantasy in Journalism*. New York, NY: Routledge, 2018.

Melendez, Lynn. "Mayor of Jerusalem Accused SFSU of Trying to Silence Jim." ABC News, April 6, 2017. https://abc7news.com/news/mayor-of-jerusalem-accused-sfsu-of-trying-to-silence-him/1843900/.

Mercieca, Jennifer R. and Justin Vaughn. "Barack Obama and the Rhetoric of Heroic Expectations." In *The Rhetoric of Heroic Expectations*, 24 edited by J. S. Vaughn and J. R. Mercieca, 1–20. College Station, TX: Texas A & M, 2004.

Merisotis, Jamie. P. and Ronald A. Phipps. "Remedial Education in Colleges and Universities: What's Really Going On?" *The Review of Higher Education* 24, no. 1 (2000) 67–85.

Merrell, James. H. "Second Thoughts on Colonial Historians and American Indians." *The William and Mary Quarterly* 69, no. 3 (2012) 451–512.

Merton, Thomas. *Cold War Letters*. Maryknoll, NY: Orbis, 2006.

Meyer, Michael. *What is Rhetoric?* Oxford, UK: Oxford University Press, 2017.

Michael, Robert. *A Concise History of American Antisemitism*. Lanham, MD: Rowman & Littlefield, 2005.

Miller, Michael. *Fake News: Separating Truth from Fiction*. Minneapolis, MN: Twenty-First Century, 2019.

Mishel, Lawrence and Julia Wolfe, Julia. "CEO Compensation has Grown 940% Since 1978." *Economic Policy Institute*, August 14, 2019. https://www.epi.org/publication/ceo-compensation-2018/.

Mitchell, Stacy. "The Rise and Fall of the Word 'Monopoly' in American Life." *The Atlantic*, June 20, 2017. Retrieved from https://www.theatlantic.com/business/archive/2017/06/word-monopoly-antitrust/530169/.

Moody, Josh. "A Guide to the Changing Number of U.S. Universities." *U.S. News & World Report*, February 15, 2019. https://www.usnews.com/education/best-colleges/articles/2019-02-15/how-many-universities-are-in-the-us-and-why-that-number-is-changing.

Mooney, Michael. "Trump's Apostle." *Texas Monthly*, August, 2019. https://www.texasmonthly.com/articles/donald-trump-defender-dallas-pastor-robert-jeffress/.

Morel, Lucas F. "Lincoln's Political and Religious Politics." In *Religion and the American Presidency*, 3rd ed. edited by Mark Rozell and Gleaves Whitney, Gleaves 83–116. New York, NY: Palgrave, 2018.

Morgan, J. Graham. "The Development of Sociology and the Social Gospel in America." *Sociological Analysis* 30, no. 1 (1969) 42–53.

Morning Edition. "Restaurant Owners Grapple with Hiring Undocumented Immigrants." National Public Radio. (August 16, 2019). https://www.npr.org/2019/08/16/751672791/restaurant-owners-grapple-with-hiring-undocumented-immigrants.

Morrison, Larry R. "The Religious Defense of American Slavery before 1830." *The Journal of Religious Thought* 37, no. 2 (1980) 16–29.

Moyers, Bill. *Secret Government: The Constitution in Crisis*. Newport Beach, CA: Seven Locks, 1988.

Mulcahy-Ernt, Patricia I., and David C. Caverly. "Strategic Study-Reading." *Handbook of College Reading and Study Strategy Research* 2 (2009) 177–98.

Murray, Jeffrey. W. "Constructing the Ordinary: The Dialectical Development of Nazi Ideology." *Communication Quarterly* 46, no. 1 (1998) 41–59.

Muttitt, Greg. *Fuel on the Fire: Oil and Politics in Occupied Iraq.* New York, NY: New Press, 2012.

National Center for Education Statistics. "Basic Reading Skills and the Literacy of America's Least Literate Adults." Washington, D. C.: U.S. Department of Education, 2009. https://nces.ed.gov/pubs2009/2009481.pdf.

———. "Fall Enrollment and Number of Degree-Granting Postsecondary Institutions, by Control and Religious Affiliation of Institution: Selected Years, 1980 through 2015." U.S. Department of Education. Washington, D. C.: U.S. Department of Education, 2015. https://nces.ed.gov/programs/digest/d16/tables/dt16_303.90.asp.

———. "National Assessment of Adult Literacy." National Center for Education Statistics. Washington D.C., 2019. https://nces.ed.gov/naal/perf_levels.asp.

———. "Undergraduate Retention and Graduation Rates." National Center for Educational Statistics, Washington, D. C.: U.S. Department of Education, 2019. https://nces.ed.gov/programs/coe/indicator_ctr.asp.

National Commission on Excellence in Education. *A Nation at Risk.* Washington, D.C.: U.S. Department of Education, 1983. https://www.edreform.com/wp-content/uploads/2013/02/A_Nation_At_Risk_1983.pdf.

National Conference of Catholic Bishops. "The Challenge of Peace: God's Promise and Our Response." (May 3, 1983). Washington, D.C.: National Conference of Catholic Bishops. http://www.usccb.org/upload/challenge-peace-gods-promise-our-response-1983.pdf.

National Council on Aging. "Elder Abuse Facts." National Council on Aging, 2019. https://www.ncoa.org/public-policy-action/elder-justice/elder-abuse-facts/.

National Priorities Project. "Federal Spending: Where does the Money go?" Institute for Policy Studies, 2019. https://www.nationalpriorities.org/budget-basics/federal-budget-101/spending/.

National Science Foundation. "Federal Funds for Research and Development: Fiscal Years, 2016–17." Washington, D.C.: National Science Foundation, 2019. https://ncsesdata.nsf.gov/fedfunds/2016/html/ffs2016_dst_004.html.

NBC News. "Read Greta Thunberg's Full Speech at the United Nations Climate Action Summit." NBC News, September 23, 2019. https://www.nbcnews.com/news/world/read-greta-thunberg-s-full-speech-united-nations-climate-action-n1057861.

Noam, Eli M. and The International Media Concentration Collaboration. *Who Owns the World's Media? Media Concentration and Ownership around the World.* New York: Oxford University Press. 2017.

Norris, Robert S. "The Cuban Missile Crisis: A Nuclear Order of Battle, October/November, 1962." The Wilson Center, October 24, 2012. https://www.wilsoncenter.org/sites/default/files/2012_10_24_Norris_Cuban_Missile_Crisis_Nuclear_Order_of_Battle.pdf.

———. and Hans M. Kristensen. "Global Nuclear Weapons Inventories, 1945–2010." *Bulletin of Atomic Scientists* 66, no 4 (2010) 77–83. https://www.tandfonline.com/doi/pdf/10.2968/066004008.

Nussbaum, E. Michael, Carol Anne M. Kardash, and Steve Ed Graham. "The Effects of Goal Instructions and Text on the Generation of Counterarguments during Writing." *Journal of Educational Psychology* 97, no. 2 (2005) 157.

Obama, Barack. "Executive Order 13491—Ensuring Lawful Interrogations," January 20, 2009. The White House. https://obamawhitehouse.archives.gov/the-press-office/ensuring-lawful-interrogations.

———. "Inaugural Address" (Speech, Washington, DC, January 20, 2009), The American Presidency Project. https://www.presidency.ucsb.edu/documents/inaugural-address-5.

———. "Remarks by the President at the National Prayer Breakfast." (Speech, Washington, D.C., February 5, 2015). The White House https://obamawhitehouse.archives.gov/the-press-office/2015/02/05/remarks-president-national-prayer-breakfast.

———"Remarks by the President and Vice President at Easter Prayer Breakfast," (Speech, Washington, DC, March 30, 2016), The White House. https://obamawhitehouse.archives.gov/the-press-office/2016/03/30/remarks-president-and-vice-president-easter-prayer-breakfast.

Oh, Inae. "Trump Who Once Said He Liked to Grab Women 'by the Pussy' Mocks Biden for Recent Allegations." *Mother Jones*, April 3, 2019. https://www.motherjones.com/politics/2019/04/trump-biden-allegations/.

Olmstead, Katherine S. *Challenging the Secret Government: The Post-Watergate Investigations of the Secret Government*. Chapel Hill, NC: University of North Carolina Press. 1996.

Olmstead, Wendy. *Rhetoric: A Historical Perspective*. Malden, MA: Blackwell, 2006.

Olsen, Parmy. "For $29 Dollars this Man Will Help Manipulate Loved Ones with Targeted Facebook and Browser Links. *Forbes*, January 15, 2019. https://www.forbes.com/sites/parmyolson/2019/01/15/a-shadowy-entrepreneur-claims-his-online-manipulation-business-is-thriving/#63f2ef3d72a9.

Online Etymology. "Conscience." https://www.etymonline.com/search?q=conscience.

Ortega, Oliver. "Greta Thunberg Leads the Climate Change Revolution." *The Observer*, September 24, 2019. https://ndsmcobserver.com/2019/09/greta-thunberg-leads-the-climate-change-revolution/.

Osteen, Joel. *Think Better Live Better. A Victorious Life begins in Your Mind*. New York, NY: Hatchette, 2016.

Osteen, Mark. *Nightmare Alley: Film Noir and the American Dream*. Baltimore, MD: Johns Hopkins University Press, 2013.

Packard, Vance. *The Hidden Persuaders*. New York, NY: Random House, 1957.

Parke, Caleb. "Obama's Former Faith Advisor Blasts Dem Resolution on Non-Believers as 'Politically Stupid.'" Fox News, August 30, 2019. https://www.foxnews.com/politics/democrats-religious-obama-adviser.

Paul VI. *Popularorum Progressio* [On the Development of Peoples]. (1967). Papal Encyclicals Online. https://www.papalencyclicals.net/paul06/p6develo.htm.

Paul, Richard and Linda Elder. *How to Read a Paragraph: The Art of Close Reading*. Tomales, CA: Foundation for Critical Thinking, 2008.

Pearse, Redmond. "The Historical Roots of CIA-Hollywood Propaganda." *American Journal of Economics and Sociology* 76, no 2 (2017) 280–310.

Pecorari, Diane, Phillip Shaw, Aileen Irvine, Hans Malmström, and Špela Mežek. "Reading in Tertiary Education: Undergraduate Student Practices and Attitudes." *Quality in Higher Education* 18, no. 2 (2012) 235–56.

Perez, Christina. "Different Tests, Same Flaws: Examining the SATI, SATII, and ACT." *Journal of College Admissions* 177, (Fall, 2002). https://files.eric.ed.gov/fulltext/EJ787985.pdf.

Perry, Michael. *Labor Rights in the Jewish Tradition.* New York, NY: Jewish Labor Commission, 1993. http://www.jewishlaborcommittee.org/LaborRightsInTheJewishTradition.pdf.

Perry, Suzanne. "Senator's Investigation into Ministries Leads to Tax Review." *The Chronicle of Philanthropy*, January 7, 2011. https://www.philanthropy.com/article/Senators-Investigation-Into/159231.

Perry, William G. *Forms of Intellectual and Ethical Development in the College Years. A Scheme.* New York, NY: Holt, Rinehart and Winston, 1970.

Pew Charitable Trusts. "Federal and State Funding of Higher Education: A Chartbook." Pew Charitable Trusts, 2015. https://www.pewtrusts.org/~/media/assets/2015/06/federal_state_funding_higher_education_final.pdf.

Pew Research Center. "Religious Landscape Study," Pew Research Center, 2019. https://www.pewforum.org/religious-landscape-study/.

———. "When Americans Say they Believe in God, What Do They Mean?" Pew Research Center, April 25, 2018. https://www.pewforum.org/2018/04/25/when-americans-say-they-believe-in-god-what-do-they-mean/.

———. "Worldwide, Many See Belief in God as Essential to Morality." Pew Research Center, March 13, 2014. https://www.pewresearch.org/global/2014/03/13/worldwide-many-see-belief-in-god-as-essential-to-morality/.

Phillips, Jonathan. *The Fourth Crusade and the Sack of Constantinople.* New York: Viking, 2004.

Phillips, Peter. "Beyond the new American Censorship." In *News Incorporated: Media Ownership and its Threat to Democracy* edited by E. D. Cohen, 35–52. Amherst, NY: Prometheus, 2005.

Porter, Heather D. "Constructing an Understanding of Undergraduate Disciplinary Reading: An Analysis of Contemporary Scholarship." *Journal of College Reading and Learning* 48, no. 1 (2018) 25–46.

Poulakos, John. "Toward a Sophistic Definition of Rhetoric." *Philosophy and Rhetoric* 16, no 1 (1983) 35–48.

Poverty U.S.A. "Poverty Population in the U.S.A." Washington, D.C.: United States Conference of Catholic Bishops, 2019. https://www.povertyusa.org/facts.

Preble, Christopher A. "Whoever Believed in the Missile Gap? John F. Kennedy and the Politics of National Security." *Presidential Studies Quarterly* 33, no. 4 (2003) 801–26.

President's Council of Advisors on Science and Technology. *Engaged to Excel: Producing an Additional One Million College Graduates with Degrees in Science, Technology, Engineering and Mathematics.* Washington, D.C.: Office of the President, 2012. https://obamawhitehouse.archives.gov/sites/default/files/microsites/ostp/pcast-engage-to-excel-final_2-25-12.pdf.

Preston, Andrew. "Peripheral Visions: American Mainline Protestants and the Global Cold War." *Cold War History* 13, no. 1 (2013): 109–130.

Prouty, L. Fletcher. *JFK, the CIA, Vietnam, and the Plot to Assassinate John F. Kennedy.* New York, NY: Skyhorse, 2011.

Purkiss, Jessica and Jack Serle. "Obama's Covert Drone War in Numbers: Ten times More Strikes than Bush." The Bureau of Investigative Journalism, January 17,

2017. https://www.thebureauinvestigates.com/stories/2017-01-17/obamas-covert-drone-war-in-numbers-ten-times-more-strikes-than-bush.

Reagan, Ronald. "National Affairs Campaign Address on Religious Liberty," (Speech, Dallas, TX, August 22, 1980), American Rhetoric. https://www.americanrhetoric.com/speeches/ronaldreaganreligiousliberty.htm.

———. "State of the Union Address," (Speech, Washington, DC, January 25, 1988), Miller Center. https://millercenter.org/the-presidency/presidential-speeches/january-25-1988-state-union-address.

Reed, Eric. "What is the National Debt Year by Year from 1790 to 2018?" *The Street*, February 26, 2019. https://www.thestreet.com/politics/national-debt-year-by-year-14876008.

Reeves, Richard. *President Kennedy: Profile of Power*. New York, NY Touchstone, 1993.

Reich, Robert, B. *Beyond Outrage: What has Gone Wrong with Our Economy and Our Democracy, and How to Fix It*. New York, NY: Random House, 2012.

———. *Economics in Wonderland. A Cartoon Guide to a Political World Gone Mad and Mean*. Seattle, WA: Fantagraphics, 2017.

———. *The System: Who Rigged It, How We Fix It*. New York, NY: Knopf, 2020.

Remnick, David. "Nancy Pelosi on Impeachment, and Ronan Farrow on Campaign Silence." Podcast: "Nancy Pelosi: 'Timing is Everything.'" The New Yorker Hour. (October 18, 2019). https://www.newyorker.com/podcast/the-new-yorker-radio-hour/nancy-pelosi-on-impeachment-and-ronan-farrow-on-a-campaign-of-silence.

Rent Jungle. "Rent Trend Data in San Francisco, California." https://www.rentjungle.com/average-rent-in-san-francisco-rent-trends/.

Reuters Video. "Trump Calls Migrant Caravan 'Invasion' at Campaign Rally." Reuters. May 9, 2019. https://www.reuters.com/video/2019/05/09/trump-calls-migrant-caravans-invasion-at?videoId=547721354.

Roberts, Peter. "Paulo Freire and Political Correctness." *Educational Philosophy and Theory* 29, no. 2 (1997) 83–101.

Rochester, Martin. "Critical Demagogues." *Education Next* 3, no. 4 (Fall, 2003). https://www.educationnext.org/criticaldemagogues/.

Rojstaczer, Stuart and Christopher Healy, Christopher. "Where A is Ordinary: The Evolution of American College Grading, 1940–2009." *Teachers College Record* 114, no. 7 (2012) 1–23.

Roosevelt, Theodore. *Fear God and Take Your Own Part*. New York, NY: George H. Doran, 1926.

Root, Danielle. "Voter Suppression during the 2018 Midterm Elections." Center for American Progress, November 20, 2018. https://www.americanprogress.org/issues/democracy/reports/2018/11/20/461296/voter-suppression-2018-midterm-elections/.

Rose, Joel and Bobby Allyn. "Scenes of Tearful, Flu-Stricken and Underfed Migrant Kids Emerge in New Accounts." NPR, January 27, 2019. https://www.npr.org/2019/06/27/736781192/scenes-of-tearful-flu-stricken-and-underfed-migrant-kids-emerge-in-new-accounts.

Rosenfeld, Seth. "Mario Savio's FBI Odyssey: How the Man Who Challenged the Machine Got Caught in the Gears and the Wheels of J. Edgar Hoover's Bureau." *SF Gate*, Oct. 10. 2004. https://www.sfgate.com/bayarea/article/Mario-Savio-s-FBI-Odyssey-How-the-man-who-2718306.php.

Rosenthal, Alan. *The Third House: Lobbyists and Lobbying in the States*. 2nd Ed. Washington, D.C.: Congressional Quarterly, 2001.

Ruiz, Don Miguel. *The Four Agreements. A Toltec Wisdom Book*. San Rafael, CA: Amber-Allen, 1997.

Ryan, Tracey E. "Motivating Novice Students to Read Their Textbooks." *Journal of Instructional Psychology* 33, no. 2 (2006)135–40.

Saha, Koustuv, Eshwar Chandrasekharan, and Munmun De Choudhury. "Prevalence and Psychological Effects of Hateful Speech in Online College Communities." In *Proceedings of the 11th ACM Conference on Web Science*, June, 26–30, 2019, Boston, MA. https://dl.acm.org/citation.cfm?id=3326032.

Salazar, James B. *Bodies of Reform: The Rhetoric of Character in Gilded Age America*. New York, NY: New York University Press, 2010.

Samuelson, Robert. "Robert Samuelson: David Brooks, Let Me Respectfully Suggest: Lighten Up." *US Post*, April 19, 2019. https://www.usposts.net/2019/04/robert-samuelson-david-brooks-let-me-respectfully-suggest-lighten-up/.

Sappington, John, Kimberly Kinsey, and Kirk Munsayac. "Two Studies of Reading Compliance among College Students." *Teaching of Psychology* 29, no. 4 (2002) 272–74.

Savage, Joanne, and Christina Yancey. "The Effects of Media Violence Exposure on Criminal Aggression: A Meta-Analysis." *Criminal Justice and Behavior* 35, no. 6 (2008) 772–91.

Savio, Mario. "Sit-in Address on the Steps of Sproul Hall" (Speech, Berkeley, CA, December 2, 1964), American Rhetoric. https://americanrhetoric.com/speeches/mariosaviosproulhallsitin.htm.

Scahill, Jeremy. *Blackwater: The Rise of the World's Most Powerful Mercenary Army*. New York, NY: Nation, 2008.

Schabas, William A. "Hate Speech in Rwanda: Road to Genocide." In *Genocide and Human Rights* edited by Mark Lattimer, 231–61. New York, NY: Routledge, 2017.

Schieman, Scott, and Jong Hyun Jung. "'Practical Divine Influence:' Socioeconomic Status and Belief in the Prosperity Gospel." *Journal for the Scientific Study of Religion* 51, no. 4 (2012) 738–56.

Schiffer, Kathy. "Donald Trump Names 34 Members to Council of Catholic Advisors." *National Catholic Register*, September 22, 2016. http://www.ncregister.com/blog/kschiffer/donald-trump-names-33-members-to-council-of-catholic-advisers.

Schlesinger, Stephen and Stephen Kinzer, Stephen. *Bitter Fruit: The Story of the American Coup in Guatemala*. 2nd Ed. New York, NY: David Rockefeller Center for Latin American Studies, 2005.

Schneider, Kirk J., and Larry M. Leitner. "Humanistic Psychotherapy." In *Encyclopedia of Psychotherapy* Vol. 1, (2002) 949–957.

Schrader, Dawn. E. "Intellectual Safety, Moral Atmosphere, and Epistemology in College Classrooms." *Journal of Adult Development* 11, no. 2 (2004) 87–101.

Schrader-Frechette, Kristin. *Taking Action, Saving Lives: Our Duties to Protect the Environmental and Public Safety*. New York, NY: Oxford University Press, 2007.

Schrecker, Ellen. *No Ivory Tower: McCarty & the University*. New York, NY: Oxford University Press, 1986.

———. *The Age of McCarthyism: A Brief History with Documents*, 2nd edition. New York, NY: Palgrave, 1994.

Schwartz, Herman. "The Bork Legacy." *The Nation*, December 20, 2012. https://www. thenation.com/article/bork-legacy/.

Schweizer, Peter. *Secret Empires. How the American Political Class Hides Corruption and Enriches Family and Friends*. New York: HarperCollins, 2019.

Scott, Peter Dale. *The Road to 9–11*. Berkeley, CA: University of California Press, 2007.

Seldes, George. *Facts and Fascism*. New York, NY: In Fact, 1943.

Shanahan, Timothy and Cynthia Shanahan. "What is Disciplinary Literacy and Why Does it Matter?" *Topics in Language Disorders* 32, no. 1 (2012) 7–18.

Shearer, Elisa and Katrina Masta. "News across Social Media Platforms, 2018." Pew Research Center, September 10, 2018. https://www.journalism.org/2018/09/10/news-use-across-social-media-platforms-2018/.

Silva, Christiana. "Trump's Full List of 'Racist' Comments about Immigrants, Muslims, and Others." *Newsweek*, January 11, 2018. https://www.newsweek.com/trumps-full-list-racist-comments-about-immigrants-muslims-and-others-779061.

Sinclair Broadcast Group. "Former CNN Staffer Claims Ratings, Bias Driving 2020 Coverage ahead of Dem Debate." Local 12, October 15, 2019. https://local12.com/news/nation-world/former-cnn-staffer-claims-ratings-bias-driving-2020-coverage-ahead-of-dem-debate.

Singer, Peter. *The President of Good and Evil. Questioning the Ethics of George W. Bush*. New York, NY: Plume, 2004.

Singer, Peter Warren. *Corporate Warriors: The Rise of the Privatized Military Industry*. Ithaca, NY: Cornell University, 2003.

Skeide, Michael. A., Uttam Kumar, Ramesh K. Mishra, Viveka N. Tripathi, Anupam Guleria, Jay P. Singh. . . and Falk Huettig. "Learning to Read Alters Cortico-Subcortical Cross-Talk in the Visual System of Illiterates." *Science Advances* 3, no. 5 (2017) e1602612.

Skidmore, Max J. "Theodore Roosevelt on Race and Gender." *The Journal of American Culture* 21, no. 2 (1998) 35.

Smietana, Bab. "Most Churchgoers say God Wants Them to Prosper Financially." LifeWay Research, July 31, 2018. https://nonprofitquarterly.org/senator-grassley-and-the-televangelists/.

Smith, Alan, Alex Moe, Kasie Hunt and Leigh Ann Cadwell. "House Votes to Condemn Trump's Racist Comment With Only Four Republicans Backing the Measure." NNBC News, July 16, 2019. https://www.nbcnews.com/politics/donald-trump/house-vote-resolution-condemning-trump-s-racist-comments-n1030266.

Snyder, Thomas D. *120 Years of American Education: A Statistical Portrait*. Washington, D.C.: U.S. Department of Education, 1993. https://nces.ed.gov/pubs93/93442.pdf.

Solotaroff, Paul. "In the Belly of the Beast." *Rolling Stone*, December 10, 2013. https://www.rollingstone.com/interactive/feature-belly-beast-meat-factory-farms-animal-activists/.

Sonner, Brenda S. "A is for 'Adjunct': Examining Grade Inflation in Higher Education." *Journal of Education for Business* 76, no. 1 (2000) 5–8.

Soral, Wiktor, Michał Bilewicz, and Mikołaj Winiewski. "Exposure to Hate Speech Increases Prejudice through Desensitization." *Aggressive Behavior* 44, no. 2 (2018) 136–46.

Statistia. "College Enrollment in the United States from 1965 to 2017 with Projections up to 2028 for Pubic and Private Colleges (in Millions)." Statistia, 2019. https://

www.statista.com/statistics/183995/us-college-enrollment-and-projections-in-public-and-private-institutions/.

Statistics Times. "List of Countries by GDP (Nominal)." International Monetary Fund, 2019. http://statisticstimes.com/economy/countries-by-gdp.php.

Statistia Research Team. "Do You Approve or Disapprove of the Way Donald Trump is Handling His Job as President?" Statistia, September 30, 2019. https://www.statista.com/statistics/666113/approval-rate-of-donald-trump-for-the-presidential-job/.

Steel, Ronald. *Pax Americana*. New York, NY: Viking, 1967.

Steeves, Kathleen Anderson, Philip Evan Bernhardt, James P. Burns, and Michele K. Lombard. "Transforming American Educational Identity after Sputnik." *American Educational History Journal* 36, no. 1/2 (2009) 71–87.

Stephens-Davidowitz, Seth. *"Everybody Lies: Big Data, Little Data, and What the Internet Can Tell Us about Who We Really Are."* New York, NY: HarperCollins, 2017.

Stern, Jessica. "Obama and Terrorism." *Foreign Affairs* 94, no. 5 (September/October, 2015). https://www.foreignaffairs.com/articles/obama-and-terrorism.

Stern, Sol. "The Propaganda in Our Ed Schools." *Minding the Campus*, October 26, 2010. https://www.mindingthecampus.org/2010/10/26/the_propaganda_in_our_ed_schoo/.

Stevens, Ann. H. "The Philosophy of General Education and its Contradictions: The Influence of Hutchins." *The Journal of General Education* 50, no. 3 (2001) 165–91.

Stewart, Sheilynda, Doo Hun Lim, and JoHyun Kim. "Factors Influencing College Persistence for First-Time Students." *Journal of Developmental Education* 38, no. 3 (2015) 12–20.

Sundar, S. Shyam. "The MAIN Model: A Heuristic Approach to Understanding Technology Effect on Credibility." In *Digital Media, Youth, and Credibility*, edited by M. J. Metzger and A. J. Flannigan, 73–100. Cambridge, MA: MIT Press, 2008.

Shearer, Gottfried, E. "News Use across Social Media Platforms 2017." Pew Research Center, September 7, 2017. www.journalism.org/2017/09/07/news-use-across-social-media-platforms-2017.

St. Clair-Thompson, Helen, Alison Graham, and Sara Marsham, Sara. "Exploring the Reading Practices of Undergraduate Students." *Education Inquiry* 9, no. 3 (2018) 284–97.

Stover, Justin. "There is No Place for the Humanities." *The Chronicle of Higher Education*, March 4, 2018. https://www.chronicle.com/article/There-Is-No-Case-for-the/242724.

Tagg, John. "Teachers as students: Changing the Cognitive Economy through Professional Development." *Journal on Centers for Teaching and Learning*, 2, (2010) 7–35.

Talbot, David. *The Devil's Chessboard: Allen Dulles, the CIA, and America's Secret Government*. New York, NY: Harper Perennial, 2015.

Tandoc Edson Jr, Zhen W. Lim, and Richard Ling. "Defining "Fake News: A Typology of Scholarly Definitions." *Digital Journalism* 6, no. 2 (2018) 137–53.

Taubman, Philip. *Secret Empire: Eisenhower, the CIA, and the Hidden Story of America's Space Espionage*. New York, NY: Simon & Shuster, 2003.

Taubman, William. *Khrushchev: The Man and His Era*. New York, NY: W. W. Norton, 2003.

The Kill Team. Directed by Dan Krauss. Brooklyn, New York: Motto Pictures, 2013.

"The Lewis Powell Memo: A Corporate Blueprint to Dominate Democracy." Greenpeace, 2019. https://www.greenpeace.org/usa/democracy/the-lewis-powell-memo-a-corporate-blueprint-to-dominate-democracy/.

Therriault, Susan Bowles and Ariel Krivoshey. *College Persistence Indicators Review Research*. Washington, D.C.: American Institutes for Research, 2014.

Thomas, Evan. "Governing with a Hidden Hand." *The Daily Beast*, July 14, 2017. https://www.thedailybeast.com/governing-with-a-hidden-hand.

————. *Ike's Bluff: President Eisenhower's Secret Battle to Save the World*. New York, NY: Little, Brown, 2012.

Thompson, Jason. "Magic for a People Trained in Pragmatism: Kenneth Burke, *Mein Kampf*, and the Early 9/11 Oratory of George W. Bush. *Rhetorical Review* 30, no. 4 (2011) 350–71.

Thorndike, Edward L. "Reading as Reasoning: A Study of Mistakes in Paragraph Reading." *Journal of Educational Psychology* 8, no. 6 (1917) 323–32.

Thorsen, Niels Aage. *The Political Thought of Woodrow Wilson, 1875–1910*. Princeton, NJ: Princeton University Press, 2014.

Tillich, Paul. *The Dynamics of Faith*. (Originally published Harper & Row, 1957). New York, NY: Perennial Classics, 2001.

Tinker, George E. *Missionary Conquest: The Gospel and Native American Cultural Genocide*. Minneapolis, MN: Fortress, 1993.

Tinto, Vincent. *Leaving College: Rethinking the Causes and Cures of Student Retention*. Chicago, IL: University of Chicago, 1987.

————. "Reflections on Student Persistence." *Student Success* 8, no. 2 (2017) 1–8.

Todd, Chuck. "It's Time for the Press to Stop Complaining—And to Start Fighting Back." *The Atlantic*, September 3, 2019. https://www.theatlantic.com/ideas/archive/2018/09/its-time-for-the-press-to-stop-complainingand-to-start-fighting-back/569224/.

Toros, Harmonie. "We Don't Negotiate with Terrorists!': Legitimacy and Complexity in Terrorist Conflicts." *Security Dialogue* 39, no. 4 (2008) 407–26.

Torres, Ella and Kelsey Walsh. "Elizabeth Warren gets Most Speaking Time at Democratic Debate." ABC News, October 15, 2019. https://abcnews.go.com/Politics/elizabeth-warren-dominates-speaking-time-democratic-debate/story?id=66305385.

Toye, Richard. *Rhetoric: A Very Short Introduction*. Oxford: Oxford University Press, 2013.

Trend, David. *The Myth of Media Violence: A Critical Introduction*. Victoria, Australia, 2007.

Trump, Donald. "President Trump Address on Mass Shootings." (Transcript), CSPAN, August 5, 2019). https://www.c-span.org/video/?463254-1/president-trump-calls-nation-condemn-racism-bigotry-white-supremacy-mass-shootings.

Tsai, Wan-Hsiu Sunny. "Patriotic Advertising and the Creation of the Citizen-Consumer." *Journal of Media and Communication Studies* 2, no. 3 (2010) 076–84.

Tuchman, Barbara. *The March of Folly*. New York, NY: Alfred A. Knopf, 1984.

Tye, Larry. *The Father of Spin. Edward Bernays and the Birth of Public Relations*. New York, NY: Henry Holt, 1998.

Unger, Craig. *House of Bush, House of Saud. The Secret Relationship between the World's Two Most Powerful Dynasties*. New York, NY: Scribner, 2004.

United Nations. *Universal Declaration of Human Rights*. United Nations. https://www.
un.org/en/universal-declaration-human-rights/.

United States Catholic Bishops. *Economic Justice for All: Pastoral Letter on Catholic Social
Teaching and the U.S. Economy*. Washington, D. C.: United States Conference of
Catholic Bishops, 1986. http://www.usccb.org/upload/economic_justice_for_all.
pdf.

University of California, Los Angeles. *General Catalogue* 1, no. 9. Los Angeles, CA:
UCLA, 1961. https://www.registrar.ucla.edu/Portals/50/Documents/catalog-
archive/1950–1999/61–62catalog.pdf.

University of California, Los Angeles. *General Catalogue, 2018–2019*. Los Angeles, CA:
UCLA, 2019. Retrieved from: http://catalog.registrar.ucla.edu/.

U.S. Department of Education. *A Test of Leadership: Charting the Future of U.S. higher
Education*. Washington, D. C., 2006. https://www2.ed.gov/about/bdscomm/list/
hiedfuture/reports/pre-pub-report.pdf.

Vafeas, Mario. "Attitudes Toward, and Use of, Textbooks among Undergraduates: An
Exploratory Study." *Journal of Marketing Education*. 35, no. 3 (2013) 245–58.

Van Dijk, Teun A. "Principles of Critical Discourse Analysis." *Discourse & Society* 4, no.
2 (1993) 249–83.

Van Ells, Mark D. "Assuming the White Man's Burden: The Seizure of the Philippines,
1898–1902." *Philippine Studies* 43, no. 4 (1995) 607–22.

Vasquez, Megan. "Trump Threatens to 'Obliterate' Turkey's Economy if They Do
Anything 'Off Limits' with ISIS." CNN News, October 7, 2019. https://www.cnn.
com/2019/10/07/politics/donald-trump-syria-obliterate-turkey-isis/index.html.

Vicory, Justin. "Job Fair after ICE Raids: Here's Who Showed Up for Koch Food Plant
Jobs." *Clarion Ledger*, August 12, 2019. https://www.clarionledger.com/story/
news/2019/08/12/ms-ice-raids-koch-foods-job-fair-forest-who-how-many-
applied/1976033001/.

Vrz, Lana. "Joel Osteen Net Worth 2019." *The Washington Note*, October 4, 2019.
https://thewashingtonnote.com/joel-osteen-net-worth-2019/.

Wagner, John. "'Crazed Lunatics:' Trump Again Attacks the News Media as 'Enemies of
the People.'" *The Washington Post*, January 7, 2019. https://www.washingtonpost.
com/.

Walker, Julian. S., and Jennifer A. Bright. "Cognitive Therapy for Violence: Reaching the
Parts that Anger Management Doesn't Reach." *The Journal of Forensic Psychiatry
& Psychology* 20, no. 2 (2009) 174–201.

Wallace, George. "Segregation Now, Segregation Forever." (Speech, Montgomery,
AL, January 14, 1963), Blackpast. https://www.blackpast.org/african-american-
history/speeches-african-american-history/1963-george-wallace-segregation-
now-segregation-forever/.

Wallis, Jim. "Dangerous Religion: George Bush's Theology of Empire." In *Evangelicals
and Empire: Christian Alternatives to the Status Quo* edited by B. E. Benson and P.
G. Helzel, 25–32. Grand Rapids, MI: Brazos, 2008.

Walstad, William B. and Ken Rebeck. "The Status of Economics in the High School
Curriculum." *The Journal of Economic Education* 31, no. 1 (2000) 95–101.

Wardy, Robert. *The Birth of Rhetoric: Gorgias, Plato and Their Successors*. New York,
NY: Routledge, 2005.

Warner, Darrell B., and Katie Koeppel. "General Education Requirements: A
Comparative Analysis." *The Journal of General Education* 58, no. 4 (2009) 241–58.

Watson Institute International Affairs. *Cost of War. Iraqi Civilians*. Brown University, November 2018. https://watson.brown.edu/costsofwar/costs/human/civilians/iraqi.

Watts, Linda S. "Democratizing Higher Education in the United States." In *Democratizing Higher Education: International Comparative Perspective* edited by P. Blessinger and J. P. Anchan, 15–29. New York, NY: Routledge, 2015

Weikart, Richard. *Hitler's Religion: The Twisted Beliefs That Drove the Third Reich.* Washington, D. C.: Regnery, 2016.

Weimer, Maryellen. *Learner-Centered Teaching. Five Key Changes to Practice*, 2nd Ed. San Francisco, CA: Jossey-Bass, 2013.

Weinberg, Arthur, and Lila Weinberg, eds. *The Muckrakers*. Urbana, IL: University of Illinois Press. 2001.

Weiner, Tim. *Legacy of Ashes. The History of the CIA*. New York, NY: Anchor, 2007.

Weiss, Michael J., Mary G. Visher, and Heather Wathington. "Learning Communities for Students in Developmental Reading: An Impact Study at Hillsborough Community College." New York, NY: National Center for Postsecondary Research, 2010.

Wheeler, Stanton, David Weisburd, Elin Waring, and Nancy Bode. "White Collar Crimes and Criminals." *American Criminal Law Review* 25 (1987) 331–57.

Whelan, Andrew, Ruth Walker, and Christopher Moore, eds. *Zombies in the Academy.* Chicago: University of Chicago Press, 2013.

White, John. *Intelligence, Destiny, and Education. The Ideological Roots of Intelligence Testing.* New York, NY: Routledge, 2006.

Wissing, Douglas A. *Funding the Enemy. How U.S. Taxpayers Bankroll the Taliban*. New York, NY: Prometheus, 2012.

Withey, Stephen and Ronald P. Abeles, (Eds.). *Television and Social Behavior. Beyond Violence and Children*. New York, NY: Routledge, 2013.

Willis, Oliver. "Jon Stewart on Crossfire: 'Stop, Stop, Stop, Stop Hurting America.'" *Media Matters*, October 15, 2004. https://www.mediamatters.org/jon-stewart-crossfire-stop-stop-stop-stop-hurting-america.

Wilson, John K. "Academic Freedom in America after 9/11." *Thought & Action: The NEA Higher Education Journal* 21, (Fall, 2005) 119–31.

Wilson, Peter, H. *The Thirty-Years War: Europe's Tragedy*. Cambridge, MA: Belknap, 2011.

Wilson, Woodrow. "Address to the Senate on the Versailles Peace Treaty." (Speech, Washington, DC, July 10, 1919). The American Presidency Project. https://www.presidency.ucsb.edu/documents/address-the-senate-the-versailles-peace-treaty.

———. "League of Nations." (Speech, Pueblo, Colorado, September 25, 1919), U.S. Embassy. https://usa.usembassy.de/etexts/speeches/rhetoric/wwleague.htm.

Wolf, Maryanne. *Reader Some Home. The Brain in a Digital World*. New York, NY: HarperCollins, 2018.

Woodward, Bob. *Bush at War*. New York, NY: Simon & Schuster, 2002.

Worldwatch Institute. "State of Consumption Today." Worldwatch Institute, September 12, 2019. http://www.worldwatch.org/node/810.

Wright, Douglas. "Many College Freshmen take Remedial Courses." Washington, D. C.: National Center for Education Statistics, 1985. https://files.eric.ed.gov/fulltext/ED262742.pdf.

Wright, Lawrence. *The Looming Tower: Al Qaeda and the Road to* 9–11. New York, NY: Vintage, 2007.

Youn, Ted I. K. "Introduction." In *Paradoxes of the Democratization of Higher Education*, edited by T. I. K. Youn, ix–xxi. *Research in Social Problems and Public Policy* 22. Bingley, UK: Emerald Group, 2017.

Zhou, Christina. "Christians who Support Trump are Morally and Spiritually Superior than Other Devotees, Pastor Robert Jeffress tells Fox News." *Newsweek*, March 24, 2019. https://www.newsweek.com/christians-who-support-trump-are-morally-and-spiritually-superior-other-13733933.

Zibel, Alan. "Revolving Congress: The Revolving Congress Class of 2019 Flocks to K Street." Public Citizen, May 30, 2019. https://www.citizen.org/article/revolving-congress/.

Zimmerman, Marc. "Empowerment Theory." In *Handbook of Community Psychology* edited by J. Rappaport and J., Seidman, 43–64. Boston, MA: Springer, 2006.

———, Barbara Israel, Amy Schultz, and Barry Checkoway. "Further Explorations in Empowerment Theory: An Empirical Analysis of Psychological Empowerment." *Journal of Community Psychology* 20, no. 6 (1992) 707–27.

Zuboff, Shoshana. *The Age of Surveillance Capitalism: The Fight for a Human Future at the New Frontier of Power.* New York, NY: Public Affairs, 2019.

Index

www.ingramcontent.com/pod-product-compliance
Lightning Source LLC
Chambersburg PA
CBHW061726270326
41928CB00011B/2128